D0753783

THE REAL
ENIGMA HEROES

The author presents Prince Charles and the Duchess of Cornwall with a copy of *The Real Enigma Heroes* during a royal visit to Bletchley Park.

THE REAL
ENIGMA HEROES

PHIL SHANAHAN

The
History
Press

The cover painting of the *Petard*'s boarding party arriving at the U-559 is courtesy of the artist, Michael Roffe. The sale of the picture in 2001 raised money for the campaign to honour the three men.

Phil Shanahan's book will be a great source of pride, not only to the families of the men and the communities they came from, but to all those who revere the Royal Navy and its role in preserving our democracy against the evils of Nazism.
– Julian Lewis MP, Shadow Defence Minister

An excellent book, written with pace and clarity ... it deserves the widest possible audience.
– The Bath Chronicle

The Real Enigma Heroes *corrects the historical record.*
– Hayden B. Peake (writing on the official CIA website)

So much of the subject matter of The Real Enigma Heroes *reads like a well-plotted thriller that is hard to know whether to learn from it as a historical book or just enjoy it as a cracking good story ... the two main strands of the book – the story of the heroes and Shanahan's initiative to make them household names – are expertly intertwined and genuinely tweak the emotions.*
– The Navy News

This paperback version of *The Real Enigma Heroes* is dedicated to the memory of my father, Jim Shanahan, and also to my great friend, Steve Leighton, who died far too young.

It is also written in remembrance of Able Seaman Colin Grazier GC, Lt Tony Fasson GC and NAAFI assistant Tommy Brown GM – the real Enigma heroes whose stories inspired me to give so much of myself in their honour.

Finally, I dedicate the book to the people who continue to enrich my life and who I am so proud to call my family: my wife Claire, who has shared in everything I've done since we first met in 1984, my daughter Bryony whose birth was the most meaningful moment of my life, my mother Thelma, sister Libby, brother-in-law Neville, niece Sally, nephew James and my in-laws, Ann and Richard Goosey.

First published 2008

Reprinted 2008
This paperback edition 2010
The History Press Ltd
The Mill, Brimscombe Port
Stroud, Gloucestershire, GL5 2QG
www.thehistorypress.co.uk

© Phil Shanahan, 2008

The right of Phil Shanahan to be identified as the Author
of this work has been asserted in accordance with the
Copyrights, Designs and Patents Act 1988.

All rights reserved. No part of this book may be reprinted
or reproduced or utilised in any form or by any electronic,
mechanical or other means, now known or hereafter invented,
including photocopying and recording, or in any information
storage or retrieval system, without the permission in writing
from the Publishers.

British Library Cataloguing in Publication Data.
A catalogue record for this book is available from the British Library.

ISBN 978 0 7524 5785 7

Typesetting and origination by The History Press
Printed in Great Britain
Manufacturing managed by Jellyfish Print Solutions Ltd

CONTENTS

ABOUT THE AUTHOR

Phil Shanahan has been a journalist for more than twenty years and was awarded the Freedom of Bletchley Park for his efforts in gaining Grazier, Fasson and Brown public recognition. The campaign he led to honour the Enigma heroes won three of the biggest awards for campaigning regional journalism in the UK.

In 2008 he was invited to officially open Hut 8 at Bletchley Park to the public – the very hut where the German Enigma codes were cracked. Phil Shanahan now runs his own writing/media consultancy business, Enigma Communications.

For more information on *The Real Enigma Heroes* and to see a video of the author talking about the story, visit: **www.enigmacommunications.co.uk** and follow the links to the book. The video can also be viewed on YouTube.

ACKNOWLEDGEMENTS

I am grateful to so many people for their help with this book, and with the campaign to honour the men celebrated in these pages. I just hope that anybody who has been excluded will have the grace to forgive me and remember that the most important thing is what we achieved together for three great but unsung British heroes.

Firstly, I must thank my fellow members of the Colin Grazier Memorial Committee for their sustained efforts over a number of years. I am proud to have worked with Jim Welland, Mary Edwards, Arthur Shakespeare, Joe Bates, Ray Jennings and the late Bill Wilson. I would like to give a particular mention to my right-hand man on the committee, John Harper, former assistant editor of the *Tamworth Herald*.

I would also like to thank the previous group editor of *Central Independent Newspapers*, Sam Holliday, for his support during the campaign, and the current group editor, Gary Phelps, for continuing to back my efforts to keep this important story alive – particularly its connections with Tamworth and Staffordshire. From the outset I enjoyed the full backing of Northcliffe Media.

I received much support from Tamworth Borough Council during the campaign and hope that its staff continue to recognise and capitalise on the significance of this story to the town they serve. I hope the council will ensure the monument is maintained to the highest standards, and I hope that one day weather-proof information boards will be placed next to it. In the future I would also love to see the town house a permanent exhibition on its links with this incredible chapter in history.

I am extremely grateful to Dr Mark Baldwin MA MSc PhD, a specialist in Second World War intelligence and codebreaking, for his thorough checking of my manuscript. I am similarly indebted to Bletchley Park guide and archivist John Gallehawk. Both men are experts on the Enigma story and have an infectious enthusiasm for the subject.

My wife Claire acted as a quality controller and soundboard and spent many hours going through my early proofs. My friend and former colleague, John Bennett, also trawled through my copy. Thanks also to the *Herald*'s 'image wizard', Emmerson Todd.

Robert de Pass, former first lieutenant on HMS *Petard*, gave me permission to use his remarkable photographs in this book. Reg Crang allowed me to quote from his beautifully crafted diary and Eric Sellars also produced a detailed account of the U-559 incident. Indeed I am indebted to all members of the *Petard* Association and feel honoured to have been made an associate member.

I am most grateful to the director of trustees at Bletchley Park, Simon Greenish, for his full support. I wish him well in attracting the kind of finance that his vision for this internationally important heritage site deserves. Thanks also to his staff who have helped me in various ways, including David Steadman, Kelsey Griffin and Sue May. I also acknowledge the assistance given by Simon's predecessor at Bletchley Park, Christine Large.

I would like to mention the associates and relatives of all three men for the fabulous memories, documents and photographs which helped bring the Enigma heroes to life during our campaign and now also in this book. These will help to ensure that the men will live on in the minds of future generations. A special thank you to Sheena d'Anyers-Willis, Beryl Bauer, Colleen Mason, Margaret Kirk, Joyce Radbourne, Syd Lakin, and Norman and David Brown.

I owe a great debt to international best-selling author Robert Harris, whose comments about the three heroes helped motivate me to campaign on their behalf – as did his novel, *Enigma*. The team at The History Press provided much assistance, particularly Emily Locke, Amy Rigg and Jennifer Younger.

My sincere thanks also go to: T. Adey, L. Allsop, F. Andrews, D. Ansell, J. Aran, J. Arch, R. Arnold, E. Ashley, D. Atkin, M. Atkin, P. Atkin, N. Atkins, Baddesley WMC, H. Bagnall, A. Baker, Commander P.A. Balink-White, the Revd Alan Barrett, J. Bedwell, R. Bennett, D. Bindon, the Rt Revd Michael Bourke, Boots the Chemist, N. Bovey, A. Brightman, A. Brown, H. Brown, S. Brown, J. Bryan, P. Bryan, J. Buckland, Mr & Mrs Burdon, D. Bush, Cambridge Stamp Centre, CAMRA (Tamworth), F. Carnock, K. Carr, F. Carter, J. Cassidy, I. Cauchi, M. Champion, B. Christian, T. Clarke, M. Clempson, J. Cocklen, Colin Grazier Hotel (M. Roberts, R. Lake), Commander C. Colburn, R. Collingwood, R. Collins, R. Cook, B. Coombes, C. Cooper, M. Cooper, J. Copeland, M. Corden, F. Cornock, Courage West Midlands, M. Courtney, K. Crampton, R. Crang, H. Craven, J. Crooks, J. Culshaw, W. Czwarkiel, Dewes Sketchley, E. Dickson, J. Dinwoodie, Cllr P. Dix, Cllr T. Dix, G. Dixon, J.K. & S.M. Dobson, Dosthill Cosmopolitan Club, Mr & Mrs Doyle, J. Draper, J. Driffield, M. Dunn, B. Dunn, C. Egerton, D. Ellingworth, P. Elliott, Dr M. Evans, Captain Featherstone-Dilke, Mr & Mrs Fisher, C. Fitzhugh, G. Forsyth, A. Freeman, D. Freer, W. Garlick, P. Gee, M. Gempson, A. Gibbons, J. Gibbons, I. Gibbons, P. Gosling, R. Gosling, C. Grainger, H. Graven, T. Grazier, S. Greenhall, E. Gregory, M. Griffiths, H. Growen, M. Guise, Y. Guise, T. Guise, M. Handle, N. Hadley, W. Hadley, M. Hakon, J. Hall, W. Hall, A. Hamnett, S. Hamnett, L. Hare, P. Harper, S. Harper, R. Harries, R. Harris, Harry Pounds Shipping Limited (Portsmouth), Mr & Mrs N. Haywood, P. Haywood, W. Haywood, D. Heath, L. Hemus, G. Heritage, K. Hewitt, I. Hilton, S. Hinton, W. Hines, K. Hitchiner, W. Hives, HMS *Emerald* Association, HMS *Porlock Bay* Association, P. Holliday, F. Holt, W. Hornsby, A. Howden, HSBC Tamworth, M. Hughes, S. Hughes, A. Hutchinson, P. Hutchinson, Imperial War Museum, A. Jackson, E. Jackson, G. Jackson, L. Jackson, P. Jackson, H. Jakeman, S. Jakeman, B. Jenkins, P. Johnson, Mr & Mrs Jones, J. Kester, Kingsbury Historical Society, J. Kingslake, Mr Lake, T. Langley, F. Lea, T. Lee, Ms Lees, M. Lees, Dr Lewis, Mr & Mrs Lewis, E. Lewis, J. Lewis, M. Lisher, V. Lisher, O. Lewis, Lloyds TSB, B. Lucas, M. Lucas, S. Lunn, V. Lunn, J. Mackness, D. Maugham, J. Maugham, P. Maryon, C. Mason, J. Matthews, B. Mayall, Mr & Mrs McDonald, McLeans Homes, W.

Meads, Merchant Navy Association (Tamworth), P. Meryon, Midland Bank, R. Miller, R. Morris, G. Morris, Mr & Mrs Moss, B. Myall, *Navy News*, the Revd Bob Neale, R. Norris, J. Oates, S. Olley, H. Olley, Mr & Mrs Olley, Captain C. Owen, S. Packard, M. Parsons, M. Passingham, E. Peat, P. Peel, W. Peet, Mr & Mrs Pennell, J. Perkins, Peter Hicks Associates, C. Pickering, Mr & Mrs Pitt, A. Polhemus, Mr & Mrs Pott, T. Potts, M. Powell, G. Preston, Prince of Wales Ex-Service Fund, E. Pugh, F. Pugh, I. Purslow, J. Purslow, W. Pytel, K. Radbourne, L. Ram, RASC, D. Ratcliffe, Rawlett School, J.K. Reavey, J. Reed, E. Reeves, Mr & Mrs Richards, G. Richards, J. Richardson, P. Richardson, M. Richardson, R. Roberts, A. Rogers, M. Romeril, S. Rothwell, Royal Air Force Association (Tamworth), Royal Army Service Corps, Royal British Legion, Royal Corps of Transport Association, Royal Naval Association (California), Royal Naval Association (Coventry), Royal Naval Association (Leamington Spa), Royal Naval Association (Shard End), Royal Naval Association (Tamworth), Royal Naval Association (Welshpool), Sainsbury's, E. Saunders, Mr & Mrs Scott, Cllr P. Seekings, A. Shakeshaft, B. Shakeshaft, R. Sharp, E. Shave, Mr & Mrs F. Shaw, J. Showell, A. Sidaway, J. Simpson, Mr & Mrs Smith, H. Smith, R. Smith, W. Smith, J. Stacey, Staffordshire County Council, H. Stevenson, Studio One, R. Sulima, Swaddle, M. Tallents, Tame Valley Building, Tamworth Beer Festival, Tamworth Civic Society, Tamworth Co-operative Society, Tamworth Heritage Trust, Tamworth High School Old Girls' Association, Tamworth Lions Club, Tamworth Music Centre Saxophone Ensemble and Junior Choir, Tamworth Sea Cadets, Tamworth Sons of Rest, R. Tanner, M. Taylor, R. Taylor, F. Thompson, G. Thompson, F. Thurman, J. Tiller, L. Tilley, M. Tilley, T. Tippings, D. Titley, A. Traves, F. Traves, O. Tucker, E. Turner, L. Turner, Two Gates WMC, H. Vann, J. Vernon, P. Vipas, Volunteer Band of the West Midlands Regiment, B. Wallis, R. Warner, A. Warren, G. Warren, Mr & Mrs Warren, D. Whitehouse, J. Whitfield, D. Williamson, Wilnecote High School, B. Wilson, K. Wilson, A. Winters, C. Winters, J. Wood, W. Wood, C. Woodlands, Woolley-Pritchard Sovereign Brass Band, Wrens Association (Colchester), Wrens Association (Norwich), J. Wright, M. Wright, E. Yeomans.

PROLOGUE

The only thing that ever really frightened me during the war was the U-boat peril
— Winston Churchill

For more than sixty years, the bodies of two British seamen have been entombed in a German U-boat on the bottom of the Mediterranean Sea.

Able Seaman Colin Grazier and Lieutenant Tony Fasson drowned moments after seizing Enigma codebooks from the sinking submarine. Their heroism shortened the Second World War by up to two years, saving unimaginable numbers of lives worldwide. Yet the men remained uncelebrated and barely known – even in their home towns.

For decades the huge importance of the material they had sacrificed their lives for remained top secret. Consequently the men were denied the recognition their courage so richly deserved. A sixteen-year-old boy, NAAFI canteen assistant Tommy Brown, who helped them seize the crucial codebooks, escaped their watery grave by a hair's breadth, only to die in a house fire just two years later. He never knew the massive significance of what he had helped his two colleagues to achieve – world peace.

Historians now acknowledge that the capture of Enigma material from the U-559 on 30 October 1942 was a pivotal moment in the Second World War. The documents enabled Britain's brilliant codebreakers at Bletchley Park to unscramble German U-boat messages for the first time after a devastating ten-month blackout. The introduction of a four-rotor Enigma machine together with new versions of German codebooks (the short signal codebook and the short weather cipher) had blindfolded Bletchley for the best part of a year. The U-559 material put codebreakers back on track and thousands of enemy messages were being read each week by the end of 1942. From the autumn of 1943 until the end of the war in 1945, Bletchley Park was producing around 84,000 decrypts per month.

Intelligence arising from the deciphered communications was codenamed Ultra. The information not only revealed the positions of the Germans' deadly U-boats in the Atlantic, but also where they might be in a few days' time. It is estimated that this saved 500,000 tons of shipping in the first few months of 1943 alone.

Allied convoys bringing essential supplies including food from America to Britain could be re-routed to avoid lethal torpedoes and the tables were turned on the submarines. Under severe attack themselves, the U-boat wolf packs, which had previously been sinking our ships at twice the rate they were being produced, were eventually withdrawn by Admiral Doenitz, the commander of the German U-boat fleet.

The underwater menace which was threatening to starve Britain into an early surrender was at last averted. The codebooks taken from U-559 paved the way to victory in the Battle of the Atlantic, a battle which Churchill described as vital to the outcome of the entire war.

Despite all this, when the veil of secrecy surrounding the U-559 incident was lifted in the mid-1970s, no huge fuss was made of Grazier, Fasson or Brown. They remained very much the unsung heroes. In more recent times, Hollywood and the Imperial War Museum have failed to acknowledge these men who directly influenced the outcome of the Second World War, as have several authors and television documentary makers.

I was the deputy editor of Colin Grazier's home town newspaper, the *Tamworth Herald* in Staffordshire, and I never heard mention of him until 1998, and then only by chance. I was not alone. Very few people in the town were familiar with his name, not to mention what he died for. I was astonished by this widespread ignorance and decided to launch a campaign to gain proper recognition for Colin and to raise funds for a fitting memorial to be erected in his honour.

It soon became apparent that there were three unsung heroes involved and the *Herald* found itself carrying the torch for a defining piece of world history. The campaign was to last for many years and led to the newspaper winning the UK's three biggest prizes for campaigning regional journalism.

I didn't realise it at the time, but it was also to become the most amazing personal crusade of my life. I was invited to London to accept a special award on behalf of the three men from actress Prunella Scales. The Celebrities Guild of Great Britain's Unsung Hero Award was one of just six presented during a star-studded ceremony at a Park Lane hotel. It was the first time the Guild had made a posthumous award. More than 350 people, including many household names from the screen, stage and sporting worlds, gave a standing ovation to the men when the historic presentation was made.

I also had the honour of presenting the Duke of Kent with a memento of the campaign and received a special New Year's honour myself from the mayor of Tamworth. In December 2003 I had the privilege of being granted the Freedom of Bletchley Park, Churchill's secret wartime establishment where the Nazi codes were broken, for my work on Enigma. All this for highlighting a story that was sixty years old.

The climax of the campaign was the unveiling of a fabulous sculpture in the centre of Tamworth produced by acclaimed artist Walenty Pytel. The unveiling ceremony was an emotional day attended by close relatives and friends of the heroes, including several men who were on board their ship the very night they lost their lives.

In 2008 the hardback edition of *The Real Enigma Heroes* was launched at Bletchley Park where it was introduced by Shadow Defence Minister, Dr Julian Lewis. A few months later I was invited back to Bletchley Park to present Prince Charles and the Duchess of Cornwall with a copy of the book. I was also able to show them around an exhibition on the story in the newly restored Hut 8, an historic building which I had been given the privilege of officially opening to the public a few months earlier. Purely because of the Enigma heroes I have been on a journey full of incredible highs.

This is the story of a passionate newspaper campaign and the three men who inspired it.

Phil Shanahan, 2010

CHAPTER ONE

NOBODY MORE DESERVING

It is tragic that his sacrifice has gone unrecognised for so long in his home town, and I can't think of anyone more deserving of a memorial than Colin Grazier – Robert Harris

Deadline was fast approaching. The *Tamworth Herald* of 27 November 1998 was shaping up to be a solid if not startling edition.

Then a story landed on my desk which was not only going to change the shape of the newspaper that week, but my life for the next decade, and eventually even the very infrastructure of the town. It was the story that was going to grab me more than any other in over twenty years as a professional journalist – and I have worked on some extraordinary stories. It was without doubt the story that has had the biggest impact in the 160-year history of the *Herald* and one that has since been talked about throughout the world. It was a story that was destined to win the newspaper several national awards. It was to be featured on radio and television. It was to make headlines in *The Guardian* and even in half a million copies of the *Dallas Morning News*. It was to be referred to in the House of Commons and in personal letters by the Prime Minister and the Duke of York. It was also to come to the attention of Prince Charles and the Duchess of Cornwall. It is something that I will probably be associated with for life, and frankly I would be proud to be.

We latched on to the story through a chance remark made to one of our reporters. Rob Tanner had been sent to write a feature on retired miner, Frank Andrews, for the newspaper's nostalgia pages. During the interview Frank told Rob that a Tamworth man who had served with the Royal Navy during the Second World War had 'virtually won the war'.

I was highly sceptical when Rob returned to the office and passed on this claim to me. 'If a Tamworth man had influenced the outcome of the war, surely we all would have heard of him,' I replied.

I didn't doubt that the man had died heroically for his country, just that he could have had such an impact on world history. As a journalist you get used to hearing sensational claims, and to avoid being gullible you need to be armed with a fair degree of scepticism. I wasn't going to dismiss this out of hand, but I needed to research the facts before I jumped.

You could say I had serious doubts that sixty years after the Second World War I had only just heard the name of a local man who played a major part in bringing the conflict to an end. If this were true, surely the name of Colin Grazier would have been sung from the rooftops? The more we delved, though, the more intrigued we became and I began to realise that we could be dealing with an underplayed story of global significance.

We were getting close to our deadline and we hadn't got much time to investigate. It became immediately apparent that if what we had heard was true then Colin Grazier was

The first picture of Colin Grazier published by the *Tamworth Herald* at the news of his death and later when it was announced he was to receive the George Cross.

very much an uncelebrated hero. Certainly nobody had heard of him in our offices. We contacted other people in the town, including several councillors, and drew a blank again.

However, we did manage to contact Reg Crang in Dorset who was listed as the Honorary Secretary of the HMS *Petard* Association. The *Petard* was Colin's old ship and Reg was on board the night Grazier sacrificed his life for his country. Reg was the ship's sole RDF (Radio Direction Finding, later known as radar) mechanic. He confirmed what we had barely dared believe to be true.

Colin Grazier was just twenty-two when he set sail for the Mediterranean aboard HMS *Petard*. He had left behind his bride of just two days, Olive, in Tamworth.

Reg described how on the night of 30 October 1942, the *Petard* had drawn alongside the crippled U-boat, U-559, after an all-day hunt had culminated in the submarine being damaged by a depth charge and forced to the surface. As the German crew swam towards the *Petard* to escape the sinking submarine, Colin and first lieutenant Tony Fasson jumped naked into the cold, inky black water to make their way to the holed vessel. They were joined on board the U-559 by their young shipmate, Tommy Brown, who should not have taken part in the action on two counts – he had lied about his age to be in the Navy in the first place, and as a canteen assistant he was a non-combatant.

Colin and Tony passed German codebooks up to Tommy from deep within the submarine until it suddenly sank, taking the two men with it. Tommy was positioned on the conning tower when the submarine went down and managed to jump to safety. Two years later he perished in a fire at his home. Initially, we were told he had died rescuing his younger sister from the blaze, but his family later told us that this was incorrect. It had simply been a tragic fire which also claimed the life of his little sister.

For their bravery, Grazier and Fasson were posthumously awarded the George Cross and Tommy Brown the George Medal. Colin had played a part in shortening the war, yet all there was to remember him by in Tamworth was an old photograph hanging on the wall of Two Gates Working Men's Club, and the inclusion of his name on a memorial board in St Editha's Church.

As the main newspaper for Tamworth, we were primarily concerned with trumpeting the local man. Later, as our campaign snowballed, we were to champion Fasson and Brown too.

In our first front page story, Reg Crang explained that the entire crew had been devastated by the deaths of Grazier and Fasson. The survivors would be old men before they

ADMIRALTY

16th September 1943

MADAM,

I AM COMMANDED BY MY LORDS COMMISSIONERS OF THE ADMIRALTY TO INFORM YOU THAT, ON THE ADVICE OF THE FIRST LORD, THE KING HAS BEEN GRACIOUSLY PLEASED TO APPROVE THE POSTHUMOUS AWARD OF THE GEORGE CROSS TO YOUR HUSBAND, ABLE SEAMAN COLIN GRAZIER, FOR HIS OUTSTANDING BRAVERY AND STEADFAST DEVOTION TO DUTY IN THE FACE OF GREAT DANGER, WHILE SERVING IN HMS PETARD, IN A MOST SKILFUL AND SUCCESSFUL HUNT OF AN ENEMY SUBMARINE IN MEDITERRANEAN WATERS.

I AM EXPRESS THEIR LORDSHIPS' PLEASURE AT THIS MARK OF HIS MAJESTY'S HIGH APPRECIATION, AND THEIR DEEP REGRET THAT YOUR HUSBAND DID NOT LIVE TO RECEIVE IT.

I AM MADAM

YOUR OBEDIENT SERVANT

H.V.MARKHAM.

MRS. OLIVE M. GRAZIER
211 TAMWORTH ROAD,
KINGSBURY,
TAMWORTH.
STAFFS.

A letter, dated 16 September 1943, informing Olive that the King had approved the posthumous award of the George Cross to her husband.

The slogan used by the *Herald* to drum up support for the campaign to raise money for a memorial to Colin Grazier.

discovered the true significance of the events of that October night in 1942; the full facts remained under wraps for nearly four decades under the terms of the Official Secrets Act.

What I could not comprehend was the fact that nobody had since made a noise about Grazier, Fasson or Brown. They had changed the course of world history for goodness sake, and yet they had never received the recognition they deserved.

I began to think of my father, Jim, who died in 1996. How would I have felt if he had done what Grazier had and virtually nobody in his home town even knew about it? I felt a mixture of excitement at having such a story fall into my lap, but also a sense of sadness and anger about the way these men had been ignored. I was becoming emotionally involved and was about to take on the biggest professional challenge of my life.

Time for that edition was running out and I decided to splash the story on the front page. In doing so I broke a lot of journalistic principles instilled in me during many years in newspapers. It was not a current event. In fact the details had emerged years earlier. I could not understand why the *Herald* had not turned up the volume for Grazier then, nor why the town remained so ignorant of the full implications of what this man had achieved for the free world.

It seemed that not just Tamworth, but the whole country had been remiss, and we had a chance to do something about it. We had uncovered an event of international significance and few people appeared to know about it. To a journalist this was irresistible!

So on that November day in 1998 I launched a front-page campaign to honour our local hero. It turned out to be one of the best journalistic decisions I have ever made. We contacted the local civic society and explained the story. Chairman Gill Warren immediately offered her support and pledged £500 towards a commemorative plaque.

This was a good starting point and enabled me to use the headline: 'Recognition at last for town hero,' on the front of the *Herald*. However, it seemed to me that a plaque was hopelessly inadequate and I believed we should go much further. I decided to squeeze in a front-page editorial asking whether, given the enormity of what Colin Grazier had done, we should go further. The positive feedback I received was enough to convince me to really go for it, but even then I could never have imagined the momentous developments that would come about as a result.

When the campaign began, Colin's widow, Olive, was still alive. Sadly, her health was soon to deteriorate. One of my biggest regrets is that she did not live to see the overwhelming public reaction to her husband's heroism. Olive, who suffered from Alzheimer's disease in her final years, died before most of the landmarks in the campaign were achieved.

Her sister Joyce Radbourne later told me something that cheered me immensely. Joyce used to visit Olive in the nursing home where she spent her final days. She said Olive was in the main unaware of the efforts being made to honour her late husband. On one occasion, however, she suddenly noticed a feature we had published on the couple's wedding. She read the article, studied the pictures and welled up. Tears ran down her face and for a few moments she connected with what we were doing. I am very grateful for those few seconds.

The *Herald* did interview Olive once, shortly before her health declined. She was quoted in a *Herald* article published on 11 December 1998 saying that she would be 'proud and thrilled' to see a memorial to Colin in Tamworth.

The story of Colin and Olive's love makes his heroic death even more poignant. Their fathers fought side by side during the First World War and the young Olive and Colin played together as children.

In the interview, Olive said:

I lived in Bodymoor Heath and they [Colin and his father] would walk along the canal from Two Gates to visit us. We played together and grew up together and were close for a very long time. As the years went by, I went into service and Colin joined the Navy with his brother. We married at Kingsbury church and we should have been on honeymoon when Colin set sail on HMS *Petard*. It was so sad that he died like that. He went down so heroically. He was a wonderful man who always looked after others.

Olive was never to see the spectacular monument to the men that graces St Editha's Square in Tamworth today, but at least we knew we had her approval. It was so tragic that they had only enjoyed two days of married life together when Colin set off from Tamworth railway station to embark on a voyage which was ultimately to change the course of history.

I have since discovered that Colin acted a little strangely on the day he left his new bride at the station. As the train drew up, belching thick clouds of smoke, he kissed Olive and then firmly told her to leave and not to look back at him as the train pulled out. I suppose we will never know whether or not he had a premonition about the hugely significant voyage he was about to undertake.

As the campaign began to gather momentum, Colin's niece, Colleen Mason, came forward to give us her backing. She said her uncle was 'one of the nicest people you could ever wish to meet'.

She first heard about the *Herald*'s initiative from a man in her local newsagents and felt she just had to give it her support. She told us that there had been a small plaque to Colin at the former St Peter's Church in Two Gates, but she had lost track of it when the church closed. She also revealed how Colin's name had been read out every Remembrance Day and that a fresh poppy wreath was placed next to his photograph at the Two Gates Working Men's Club by the Royal British Legion. It amazed me how, unknown to us and right under our noses, a simple and moving ceremony was taking place each year, out of the gaze of the public eye, to honour the man who had helped to end the war. Talk about understated!

One of the men involved in that ceremony was Jim Welland, chairman of the Two Gates and Wilnecote branch of the Royal British Legion. Jim was later to become a very active member of the Colin Grazier Memorial Committee set up to steer our campaign. He told me how each year, while making an annual tribute to Colin, he would hear Olive crying in the background. He was forced to complete the words with a lump in his throat.

More and more people began to contact us about Colin. An old friend of his, Tim Wood, who emigrated to New Zealand, wrote to us from his home in Christchurch. The former RAF man said he wholeheartedly supported our efforts and claimed that without Colin Britain might have been brought to its knees.

The push to honour Colin received a superb boost in January 1999, when the *Herald* received twenty-three cheques totalling £555. Most of them had been sent by members of the HMS *Petard* Association after news of the campaign was spread by Reg Crang.

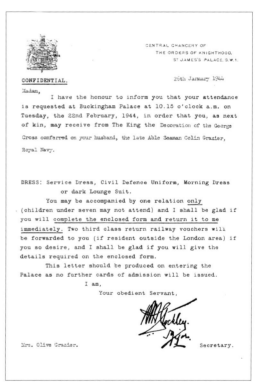

Above left: King George VI sent a signed letter of condolence to Colin's widow Olive, expressing his and the Queen's 'heartfelt sympathy'.

Above right: The invitation to Olive Grazier to attend Buckingham Palace so that she could receive Colin's George Cross from the King. Note the war hero's widow was only entitled to third class return rail vouchers.

Ref:
DNA3/CS/DD/5234

ADMIRALTY
BATH

1 1 NOV 1942

This is to Certify that

ACCORDING TO ADMIRALTY RECORDS

Colin Grazier,

Able Seaman,

OFFICIAL No: P/SSX 25550 ROYAL Navy

DIED ON 30th October, 1942 ON WAR

SERVICE

DIRECTOR OF NAVY ACCOUNTS

ROYAL NAVAL BARRACKS,
PORTSMOUTH.
9th November, 1942.

Dear Madam,

In confirmation of the telegram already
sent to you, I deeply regret to have to inform you that
your husband, Colin Grazier, Able Seaman, P/SSX 25550,
has been killed while on war service.

Please allow me to express, on behalf of
the officers and men of the Royal Navy, the high tradition
of which your husband helped to maintain, sincere sympathy
with you in your sad bereavement.

Yours sincerely,

COMMODORE.

Mrs. Olive M. Grazier,
211, Tamworth Road,
Kingsbury,
Tamworth,
Staffs.

Above left: The official confirmation from the Admiralty that Colin Grazier died on 30 October 1942, on war service.

Above right: The letter Olive Grazier received from the Royal Navy, informing her that her husband Colin had been killed in action.

Reg had pledged at least £100 on behalf of the association, and was proud that members had responded fivefold.

'This is more remarkable considering many of them never knew Colin, having joined the ship after he lost his life,' he said in his accompanying letter. Another donor, a Mr W. Smith, said the only reason his ship HMS *Magpie* was able to successfully sink German U-boats was because of the codebooks that Colin and Tony Fasson gave their lives for.

The story had fired me up in a big way, and I began devouring information on Enigma – the Germans' ingenious method of sending coded messages. One of the early books I read was *Enigma*, by best-selling international author Robert Harris. The novel was later made into a major film produced by Mick Jagger's film company and starring Kate Winslet and Dougray Scott.

The book amazed me and my eyes almost popped out of my head when I read the names Fasson and Grazier. I know the plot is a mixture of fact and fiction, but Harris was obviously determined to acknowledge the men whose bravery had such incredible consequences.

The *Herald* campaign gets under way.

The following extract from *Enigma* really hit home that we were on to something really worthwhile:

In September, 95 ships were sunk. In November 93…

And then came Fasson and Grazier.

Somewhere in the distance the college clock began to toll. Jericho found himself counting the chimes.

'Are you alright, old thing? You've gone terribly silent.'

'Sorry. I was just thinking. Do you remember Fasson and Grazier?'

'Fasson and who? Sorry, I don't think I ever met them.'

'No. Nor did I. None of us did.'

Fasson and Grazier. He never knew their Christian names. A first lieutenant and an able-bodied seaman. Their destroyer had helped to trap a U-boat, the U-459 [*sic*], in the eastern Mediterranean. They had depth-charged her and forced her to the surface. It was about ten o'clock at night. A rough sea, a wind blowing up. After the surviving Germans had abandoned the submarine, the two British sailors had stripped off and swum out to her, lit by searchlights.

The U-boat was already low in the waves, holed in the conning tower by cannon fire, shipping water fast. They'd brought off a bundle of secret papers from the radio room, handing them to a boarding party in a boat alongside, and had just gone back for the Enigma machine itself when the U-boat suddenly went bows up and sank. They went down with her – half a mile down, the Navy man had said when he told them the story in Hut 8. Let's just hope they were dead before they hit the bottom.

A few paragraphs later Harris touched on the significance of these secret papers and, like the above extract, it is based in fact, not fiction:

> At first glance they scarcely looked worth the cost of two men's lives: two little pamphlets the Short Signal Book and the Short Weather Cipher, printed in soluble ink on pink blotting paper, designed to be dropped into water by the wireless operator at the first sign of trouble. But to Bletchley they were beyond price, worth more than all the sunken treasure ever raised in history.

Again I was amazed that I had only just heard of Colin Grazier. After reading this extract I thought we should contact Robert Harris to see whether he would back our campaign. If we had the support of a prominent author, our quest would gain more credence.

I asked Rob Tanner to contact Harris through his publishers. The author's response was exactly what we had hoped for. We ran his comments on the front page of the *Herald* under the banner: 'It's time to honour our war hero', and a sub-headline stating 'Best-selling author backs *Herald* push to celebrate town sailor'.

Robert Harris was very supportive of our efforts and told us:

> It is tragic that his sacrifice has gone unrecognised for so long in his home town and I can't think of anyone more deserving of a memorial than Colin Grazier. Unfortunately, at the time of his death, not even his family could be told how significant his sacrifice had been. His actions enabled us to win the Battle of the Atlantic and change the whole course of the war. Without his bravery we wouldn't have been able to break the Enigma code and D-Day may never have happened in June 1944.

On the front page of that week's edition I had the confidence to write a bold opinion piece. It ended with a promise we were destined to keep in some style: ' … yet in Tamworth, Colin's home town, he is virtually unknown. The *Herald* pledges to change that sad fact.'

In January 1999, the Colin Grazier Memorial Committee met for the first time in the *Herald*'s offices. I was to chair the committee for the next five years. In addition to *Herald* staff, representatives attended from Tamworth's Royal British Legion, Royal Naval Association, and Civic Society. The *Herald* pledged £1,000 to the cause and the Civic Society confirmed its £500 donation.

Cash started to come in from that day onwards. A cheque for £834 was received from the town's Lady Meadow Restaurant. Owner Stuart Lunn had donated the proceeds from a string of charity bingo sessions. An early contribution also arrived from reader Yvonne Guise whose husband was killed in action in Singapore. Her reaction showed just how people were taking the campaign to their hearts. 'I grew up in the war and feel what Colin did was absolutely wonderful,' she wrote in a covering letter. 'When I looked at his face in the *Herald*, I could have cried because it is such a tragic story.'

In February 1999, a memorial tree was planted in Colin's honour in Legion Wood, Atherstone, North Warwickshire. The sapling was one of 1,346 planted in memory of individuals killed in the war. The Royal British Legion invited Colin's niece, Colleen Mason, and Sonya Grazier (widow of Colin's brother George), to carry out the honours. The *Last Post* was sounded and the event was attended by various branches of the Royal British Legion. The campaign snowball had started to roll.

CHAPTER TWO

THRILLED TO GET A GERMAN

I was thrilled to get a German in my hands and felt
like shaking him to bits – Reg Crang

To keep the Enigma campaign torch burning, I decided to publish a series of eyewitness accounts and use them periodically in the newspaper. Several people who were on board the night Colin and Tony died were still alive. It was obvious these survivors could provide us with dramatic first-hand reports of what had happened. I also felt these articles would help to build up a valuable, historic record of what took place.

Some of these accounts now form part of the Imperial War Museum's official Enigma records. Others are displayed in an exhibition about the campaign which will open at Bletchley Park in February 2008.

We launched the series with Reg Crang, who had risked disciplinary action for keeping a secret diary while on board the *Petard*. No other member of the crew was aware of this diary, even long after the war. It was compiled in a set of notebooks recording events soon after they occurred. Journals were forbidden by the authorities in case they should fall into enemy hands. Reg was able to write in complete privacy and maintains nobody ever suspected he was recording events. Reg's reflections offer a rare insight into life on board the *Petard*.

On 30 October 1942, the ship was one of four destroyers, also including the *Pakenham*, *Dulverton* and *Hurworth*, sent from Port Said in Egypt to investigate a U-boat sighting by a Sunderland aircraft off Haifa.

Reg had previously been made aware of the urgent need to capture a German submarine by his forceful captain, as he noted in his diary entry of 2 August 1942:

> The skipper called me to the bridge at 5am to talk about the poor results from the RDF. Pounding a clenched right fist into the palm of his left, he exclaimed: 'Crang, I want a U-boat!' I just muttered that I would do my best and escaped from his awesome presence as soon as I could.

The captain's words were still in Reg's mind two months later as sonar contact was quickly established with the U-559 and the destroyers began their merciless depth-charge attack. The dogged German commander of the submarine, Korvettleutnant Hans Heidtmann, used every trick in the book to avoid his pursuers and two of the destroyers eventually broke away, leaving the *Petard* in control with the *Hurworth* in support. During a ten-hour attack the ships unleashed 150 depth charges. The U-boat men were so traumatised, they later estimated that 228 bombs had exploded around them.

Left: Reg Crang, who kept a secret diary on board the *Petard*.

Below: This was the first view the *Petard* crew got of the U-559 after a ten-hour hunt forced it to the surface. The submarine's emblem can be seen on the conning tower, caught in the glare of the destroyer's searchlight. Robert de Pass, an officer on the ship, captured the moment for posterity.

Reg described the onslaught as 'ferocious':

The ocean shook violently again and again, with huge eruptions of seawater surging into the air. There was intense excitement among the crew for we all felt confident that our prey could not escape from this fierce bombardment. But no evidence of damage came to the surface and as the hours began to slip away our spirits began to droop.

The U-boat had dived to unprecedented depths, risking the lives of all its crew to escape the pounding from above. Ironically, Reg was later to become a submariner himself and only then truly appreciated the hell the German crew must have suffered that day. On one occasion his submarine *Tactician* suddenly went into an unexpected dive, and despite the efforts of the crew, sank to the bottom of the English Channel, resting on the mud.

After a period of extreme tension, the captain gave the order 'blow the tanks' and to the enormous relief of all the men inside, the vessel rose gently back to the surface.

Just imagine then how much more terrifying it would have been to be trapped in cramped, airless, stinking, claustrophobic conditions, and forced to dive to a potentially lethal depth to avoid oblivion. No wonder the occupants of the U-559 were so eager to get out once it surfaced at around 11 p.m., having been finally hit by a *Petard* depth charge.

Reg's diary entry for the night conveys both the excitement and the fear he and his crewmates felt when they realised the U-559 had been struck:

> I rushed on deck to see the U-boat caught in our searchlights. It was a frightening sight, a dramatic first view of the enemy. Someone shouted, 'stand by to ram!' I began to blow up my lifebelt even though I knew it had a bad leak. Then our pom-poms and oerlikons opened up on the conning tower, plastering it with shells. The U-boat was clearly in a helpless condition so we drew in alongside. It was awe-inspiring to be so close to the enemy.

Six decades later, Reg recalled more details which were reported in the *Herald*:

> I was standing on deck at the time and suddenly became aware of the unmistakable smell of diesel oil, quickly followed by a swoosh of turbulent water. Suddenly a searchlight snapped on and the conning tower was caught in a blinding glare. We were so close that we could plainly see a white donkey painted on it.

It has been claimed that the donkey, which appeared so sinister at that moment, was the result of a light-hearted moment among the German submariners. They had apparently eaten meat in Greece, which they thought afterwards might have been donkey and a joker amongst them had got out his paintbrush in an attempt to lighten the mood.

I now believe the emblem, which looks more like a horse to me, was the official symbol of U-boats in the same flotilla as U-559 – the 23rd Flotilla which was founded on 11 September 1941, under the control of Kapitan Frauenheim. The flotilla operated in the eastern Mediterranean. From April 1942, however, the U-559 became part of the 29th Flotilla which had been established in December 1941 under the command of Korvkpt. Franz Becker.

Its operational area was also confined to the eastern Mediterranean. The emblem of the 29th Flotilla was a donkey, but at the time of the incident the U-559 still displayed its old 23rd Flotilla logo, as can be seen in a photograph taken by Robert de Pass, one of the *Petard* officers, showing the turret illuminated by the ship's searchlights.

When the survivors began to jump into the water and swim towards the *Petard*, the sailors lowered rope ladders and netting to allow them to scramble on board. Taking up the story again in his diary, Reg said:

> The survivors started to scramble up the ropes but they were so shaken that it was an ordeal. One had terrible stomach wounds and got stuck on the ropes unable to climb further. His

comrades tried to help him but he slipped off and drifted away. I leant over and seized one man, pulling him from the water with a big effort.

I was thrilled to get a German in my hands and felt like shaking him to bits. But we pushed them all aft, many of them trembling from their ordeal. But they recovered quite quickly, some becoming cheerful and even arrogant.

They laughed outright at the diminutive size of one of our boarding party, who was only slightly larger than the rifle he was brandishing.

We learned later that the survivors totalled five officers (including the CO) and thirty-five other ranks. So they suffered very few casualties. But soon we were to learn of our own casualties, a tragic loss that left all of us speechless.

While the Germans had been swimming away from the stricken U-boat, Grazier and Fasson were swimming towards it. A boat had been launched to take a boarding party, including Tommy Brown, across to the submarine, but before it got there Fasson and Grazier had stripped naked and swum over to the U-boat. It was to prove a fatal decision for them both.

The boarding party led by Gordon Connell had come back without Tony Fasson and Colin Grazier. They had gone down with the U-boat which sank so suddenly that they were unable to scramble out of the conning tower. The first lieutenant had descended into the control room to rescue documents and secret coding material. This had been handed to Colin Grazier and then to Tommy Brown, who clung onto the U-boat casing while passing the vital material to the boarding party.

This party had just started to jump aboard when the U-boat sank, with the two gallant men still inside. Tommy Brown and Gordon Connell were able to scramble into the seaboat, but had to return with the devastating news:

> Jimmy [naval term for a first lieutenant], as we all knew him, was a real man's man, already a legend on the ship. Handsome and self-confident, yet deadly efficient, he was admired by everyone. He was ready with a joke or a smile for the humblest Ordinary Seaman. We cannot imagine that there is a finer first lieutenant in the Navy.

Interestingly, the very next entry in Reg's diary (31 October 1942) provides quite a contrast. 'Early this morning I was rough-handling Germans in the Eastern Med. This evening I find myself a hundred miles into Palestine, dining at a luxury restaurant and driving away in style in a taxi. Great life.'

CHAPTER THREE

HE CALLS US 'SUCKERS'

He openly calls us suckers for paying over the odds, knowing all the time that we can't resist what we have been deprived of – Reg Crang

Life on board the *Petard* was an emotional mix of peaks and troughs, as extreme and unpredictable as the waves she sailed on. At times she passed through the fiery jaws of hell, but on other occasions it was more akin to being on a pleasure cruise with sight-seeing trips in exotic countries and visits to theatres, cinemas and fine eateries. Near-death experiences were interspersed with naked swims in idyllic bays and fabulous sunsets. It was like an ultimate balancing act between joy and despair.

At a *Petard* Association reunion dinner in 2007, I was told that the antics of the ship's pranksters could push the boundaries at times – even in sacred places.

One of the crew, Sam Weller, was regarded as the joker in the pack. On one notorious occasion some of the men were invited by the Palestinian police to visit Jerusalem and Nazareth while the ship was being repaired. After a tour of the local bars, the lively and rather inebriated group was led to a dungeon packed with the 'skulls of the Crusaders'.

When the men got back on board, the outrageous Sam opened his jacket to reveal to his astonished shipmates a skull he had taken as a souvenir. It remained grinning grotesquely on a table in the mess for the remainder of the war. If any of the prisoners captured by the *Petard* had seen this macabre sight they might have felt they were fighting the devil himself.

There were also times when certain members of the *Petard* acted in a most ungentlemanly manner. The following extract from Reg Crang's diary shows that British hooligans are not entirely a modern-day phenomenon. This is what happened when the ship stopped off at Durban on 28 August 1942:

> Many of the crew were in a helpless state of drunkenness. Fights broke out and much blood was spilt. Several sailors reached the dockside in a state of collapse. They had to be carried on board. I shudder to think what the kind citizens of Durban think of this behaviour.

My favourite character on board the *Petard* has to be the ship's 'Buffer' (the chief bo'sun's mate) who is brilliantly observed in Reg's diary. He obviously had a personality the size of a house. I just love this entry from 1 June 1944 – particularly the saga of the shaved head:

> The Buffer has a fine old ice-cream racket going on which is paying off handsomely. He acquired several tins of ingredients from American destroyers in Trinco and has set himself up

There were many characters on board the *Petard*, but none bigger than 'the Buffer' who had a profitable ice cream racket going on board.

in business charging exorbitant prices. He openly calls us 'suckers' for paying over the odds, knowing all the time that we can't resist what we have been deprived of for many years.

The Buffer is one of the ship's characters, a cheerful ebullient extrovert who speaks plainly and tells you straight away what he is thinking, a real man's man. As a long-serving regular seaman he openly despises HOs – [hostilities only, i.e. conscripts] and has no time for anyone on the ship who is not actually firing explosives at the enemy.

Signalmen, telegraphists, stewards - but most of all RDF operators, he refers to as 'non-combatants', with the accent firmly on the 'bat' which is spat out in a derisory tone. Despite all this he is respected and popular.

The job he takes most seriously is painting the ship. Then he is at his most aggressive, a real bully who harries all the seamen until the task is done to his satisfaction. If he comes across a patch that has been missed, he finds the culprit and drags him to the spot. 'Where were you when this locker was being painted?' he demands. 'Were you on your holidays or something? Get a brush and do it again pronto.' Missed patches are always referred to now as holidays.

Members of U-559's crew, photographed at sea. Gunther Graeser, the submarine's engineering officer, is on the right. Courtesy of the Deutsches U-Boot Museum.

A line-up of the U-559's men as she lies in a Mediterranean harbour. Courtesy of the Deutsches U-Boot Museum.

Only once have I seen him nonplussed. Some weeks ago when we had a spell in harbour he shaved his head – completely. The change in his appearance was quite extraordinary. He was unrecognisable as the Buffer we knew, more like a gorilla and quite frightening.

We were standing in the morning in the wash house, doing our dhobying side by side. Suddenly I became aware of this stranger besides me, rinsing out his overalls. My first thought was that it must be a local from ashore, hired by somebody to do his chores. Even when our eyes met I did not at first know who he was. He just grinned in his pugnacious way and then I talked to him.

Later that day I was with the first lieutenant [Robert de Pass] in his cabin when an urgent signal arrived which needed a quick decision with the Buffer. Robert de Pass sent for him but was still studying the signal when he arrived, his cap removed as he came through the door.

After a while de Pass looked up but could hardly believe his eyes. He stared for several seconds at the Buffer, who began to shift uneasily from one foot to another. When at last he spoke, the first lieutenant said just four words very quietly. 'How revolting. Go away.'

The Buffer replaced his cap and departed without speaking, feeling I think aggrieved at having been so brusquely dismissed. He let his hair grow again after that.

I have spoken to Robert de Pass several times. He's tall and dignified and I can just imagine him saying those memorable words in his impeccable Queen's English.

CHAPTER FOUR

HITLER'S CHANCES DENTED

His failure to ensure the codebooks were destroyed was to considerably dent his nation's chances of winning the war.

Following his spontaneous heroics, Tommy Brown gave a detailed account of what happened on the night of 30 October 1942 to the Naval Board of Enquiry. I quote it in full here:

I got on board [the U-559] just forward of the whaler on the port side when the deck was level with the conning tower. I got on the conning tower. I first helped to make fast - three or four lines snapped until we made fast with manila [rope] passed from the ship. I went down below. The first lieutenant [Tony Fasson] was down there with AB Grazier. I carried a lot of books up and tried to make a line fast so I could get some more up. I left the others to do this and went down below again.

The first lieutenant was down there with a machine gun which he was using to smash open cabinets in the Commanding Officer's (Heidtmann's) cabin. He then tried some keys which were hanging behind the door and opened a drawer taking out some confidential books which he gave me. I placed them at the bottom of the hatch. After finding more books in cabinets and drawers I took another lot up. There was a big cabinet just above the CO's bunk.

The lights were out – the first lieutenant had a torch. The water was not very high but rising gradually all the time. I noticed this as it came over the steel ledge of the hatch. When I came up at the last it was about 2ft deep. There was a hole just forward of the conning tower through which the water was pouring. As one went down through the conning tower compartment one felt it pour down one's back. There was not enough coming through this hole to make out what was on the deck. There were plates stove in on either side of the conning tower.

I went below to the bottom of the ladder leading to the CO's cabin and on the other side the control room. The first lieutenant was trying to break some apparatus from the bulkhead in the control room. This apparatus was a small box about 18in long x 1in x 9in deep. We got it away from the bulkhead, but it was held fast by a number of wires which lead into the bulkhead. We could not get it free so we gave it up.

The water was getting deeper and I told the first lieutenant that they were all shouting on deck. He gave me some more books from the cabin. I took these up on deck, this was my third trip. These were passed into the whaler and when I looked down the hatch again the water was coming over the upper deck. I saw Grazier and then the first lieutenant appear at the bottom of the hatch. I shouted, 'you had better come up' twice and they had just started up when the submarine started to sink very quickly. I managed to jump off and was picked up by the whaler.

Hans Heidtmann, commander of the
U-559, survived the death of his submarine.

The commander of U-559, Hans Heidtmann, gave his version of events too, but not until
twenty-five years after the incident. Reg Crang obtained the captain's report, written in
1967, from the German U-boat archive in Wilhelmshaven.

Heidtmann, who was a prisoner-of-war until 1947, was at pains to justify the surrender
of his boat, describing his position as 'utterly hopeless'. Reg believes Heidtmann was
trying to explain away his failure to ensure the codebooks were destroyed by emphasising
that he expected the submarine to sink immediately after it was abandoned. In the report,
which Reg had translated into English, Heidtmann said:

> Subsequent calculations yielded that the boat had at least 35 tons of negative buoyancy. It
> is not understandable why it did not sink immediately, but rather stayed some time at the
> waterline, which I had to observe to my horror.
>
> It must be assumed that some leftover air had remained in the tanks, which, due to the list
> [of the submarine], had re-blown a proportion of the diving chambers.

Heidtmann also appeared to be critical of the British, accusing them of misusing a rescue
boat, which he said should have been tasked with picking up German survivors rather
than getting a boarding party to his submarine.

He made no suggestion that anything of value had been retrieved, saying simply that 'two men: one officer and a seaman, were shortly afterwards sucked into the deep with the submarine'.

The report concludes that in a 'hopeless situation, the commander avoided a final fight with automatic weapons and the consequent shooting of the crew'. So it would seem that Hans Heidtmann came out of the incident with some credit at the time, for preventing his entire crew from being wiped out in a gun battle (six of his men were killed and another man died later in captivity).

In actual fact his failure to ensure the codebooks were destroyed was to considerably dent his nation's chances of winning the war. In his report, he admits he gave the order to abandon ship, but pointedly emphasises that it should have been sunk by the engineering officer.

Hugh Sebag-Montefiore's book, *Enigma: The Battle For The Code*, refers to a member of the U-559 crew making a serious mistake in opening up vents to allow sea water to flood the submarine and take it down. In the rush to pull the levers operating the vents, the man forgot to remove the metal pins which were holding them in place, and the mechanism was damaged. So a different member of the U-559 may have been ultimately to blame. But the fact remains that, from Germany's point of view, Heidtmann was the man in charge of a disastrous encounter with the enemy. In 1943 he was awarded the Knight's Cross, a variation of the prestigious Iron Cross. It is questionable whether he would have received this honour with the benefit of hindsight.

Following his clash with the *Petard*, Heidtmann spent the next four-and-a-half years in British captivity, being held prisoner in Egypt, Canada and England. He was released in May 1947 and joined the Bundesmarine (the German equivalent of the Merchant Navy) in 1958. Heidtmann retired in September 1972 and died in Hamburg on 5 April 1976 at the age of sixty-one.

<hr />

The *Herald*'s 'fighting' fund continued to grow steadily and in February 1999 committee member Jim Welland organised a raffle to further boost the coffers. I really take my hat off to Jim for this, because he personally walked to Tamworth businesses, asking each to donate a prize. Jim, who championed the local British Legion poppy appeal for many years, came back with various prizes, ranging from a colour TV and a stereo to a barbecue and a signed Aston Villa football top. He had also secured a bottle of House of Commons whisky from Tamworth MP Brian Jenkins. The raffle money was eventually to finance an additional tribute to the Enigma heroes in Two Gates, Tamworth.

The following month, I was contacted by Tony Fasson's sister, Sheena d'Anyers-Willis, who lives in Scotland. Sheena was overjoyed that the *Herald* had started the campaign, as is apparent in this extract from her letter to me:

> I am delighted to see that the splendid *Tamworth Herald* has drawn the public's attention to the lack of a memorial to three heroic young men who gave their lives to defeat Admiral Doenitz's wolf packs in the Battle of the Atlantic.

Although my brother and I rarely saw each other during the war as I was serving as a Wren, my mother told me how he often used to talk of the respect he had for Able Seaman Colin Grazier, and I know she corresponded for some time with Colin's widow and mother after the devastating blow to them all.

I feel it is high time the courage and inspiration of these three were recognised, considering they saved thousands of lives in the Atlantic and saved this nation from starving, according to Churchill.

I shall be very interested to hear how Tamworth decides to inspire and create respect from younger people, and future generations to come. Congratulations on bringing the subject of the U-559 and the *Petard* men to public attention.

The campaign soon won the backing of the late Euro MP, Philip Whitehead, who had worked in the TV industry and acknowledged that we had struck the right note:

In my other life as a TV producer I felt that the one issue we failed to cover properly in *The World at War* documentary, was the Enigma story.

Only after the series finished did I discover that my own wife's aunt had been in the team at Bletchley. It was a well-guarded secret and you are quite right to seek proper recognition through the *Herald* for an authentic hero.

His words about television coverage of the Enigma saga were spot on. Channel 4 broadcast an excellent series called *Station X* – as Bletchley Park was known – over several weeks during the early part of our campaign. We were all gripped by it on the committee – but staggered when it came to an end without highlighting the importance of the three men we were fighting for.

CHAPTER FIVE

HERALD V. HOLLYWOOD

How long will it be before they claim they won the Battle of Britain as well? – Joe Bates

A hugely important moment in the campaign came about in June 1999, and led to a much-publicised clash with a top Hollywood film director. It was a defining moment. It put fire in our bellies and gave us all an even stronger sense of purpose. It created anger, extreme emotion and much controversy.

But even though it made us all livid, in hindsight it was the best thing that could have happened to us. It put us in the international spotlight! I am referring to the making of the film *U-571*, a Hollywood blockbuster directed by Jonathan Mostow, and starring such greats as Harvey Keitel, Jon Bon Jovi, Matthew McConaughey and Bill Paxton. The movie had the audacity to hand the Americans the credit for seizing Enigma equipment crucial to the outcome of the war.

Amazingly, I first became aware that this film was in production when one of our committee members stumbled onto the film set in Malta. Pensioner Joe Bates, a member of the Tamworth Royal Naval Association who regularly holidays in Malta, came across some mock ships in St Paul's Bay. This is how Joe described what happened:

> There was a lot of activity and I saw a U-boat conning tower on a raft being dragged out for filming. I knew what they were doing because it had been big news in the Maltese press. They even had real fighter planes swooping down and attacking the U-boat.
>
> A crowd had gathered to watch the stars as they came out of the trailers. As they walked past I asked one of the stars if they ever had heard of HMS *Petard* and he hadn't. I tried to tell him about the *Petard* and the truth about the Enigma code, but all he said was 'I'm just the U-boat captain.'
>
> A lot of people in Malta are concerned about it as Malta has a great tradition of serving with the Royal Navy. I am really annoyed and feel it is an insult to all men who served at sea. Now Hollywood has re-written history so they won the Battle of the Atlantic – how long will it be before they claim they won the Battle of Britain as well?

I was just as incensed as Joe, but I must admit the image of him remonstrating with American film stars brought a broad smile to my face. But this was scandalous. The Official Secrets Act had denied these men their place in history. Almost sixty years on, and just when we had started to do something about it, we hear that Mostow is planning a film showing Americans rescuing an Enigma machine and material that was to have huge consequences for the world. This was a further insult to the real stars of the drama and we were determined to give Hollywood a bloody nose over it.

Incidentally, it was not the first time British fury had erupted over Hollywood reshaping our proud history. The 1945 film *Objective Burma* starring Errol Flynn sparked similar emotion. It depicted the daring exploits of an American platoon fighting the Japanese in Burma and caused a diplomatic incident by omitting the significant British contribution to that campaign.

The film directed by Raoul Walsh was not released in Britain until seven years later and only then after a full apology had been issued by Warner Bros. When it was released it came with a new prologue emphasising Britain's role in the episode. All this controversy was apparently the result of a journalist kicking up a fuss in the columns of his newspaper – obviously somebody from the same school of journalism as me!

Mostow must have been aware of this, so how could he be so insensitive as to repeat the insult? It is true that America played its part in breaking Enigma, but it was more to do with producing better quality bombes (giant processing machines), which did help to break the Germans' coded communications, even after a fourth rotor was introduced on the Enigma machine. But the storyline *U-571* was stealing was 100 per cent British.

America and Britain have long enjoyed a special relationship which is now rightly celebrated at Bletchley Park. I stress that it was the country's film industry, not the nation itself, that we were at war with.

Colin's ex-shipmate, Reg Crang, was also predictably seething over Universal Pictures' intentions:

> They have changed everything to glorify the US role in the war. They have created an episode they were not involved in at all. I am very angry about this and the rest of the association is up in arms. It is disgusting that the United States is trying to steal the thunder from our heroes.

The situation was even debated in the House of Commons while the film was being made and fifty MPs signed a protest letter to the film company which agreed to acknowledge actual British Enigma successes in the end credits. Reg, however, felt this did not go far enough. 'Everyone will be leaving the cinema by the time it comes up,' he said.

By sheer coincidence Joe Bates had alerted us to *U-571* early enough in its production to make our own telling protest. At the next meeting of the Colin Grazier Memorial Committee, I sounded a battle cry to all the ex-servicemen present to collect protest letters from their various branches. They didn't need a second invitation! Afterwards I received protests from hundreds of people. The resulting package was enormous and I remember it cost £40 to post to Universal Pictures. I also included a large collection of *Herald* articles about the campaign and penned the following letter to the director of the movie:

Dear Mr Mostow

You are doubtless aware that your film *U-571* has become highly contentious in Britain.

The true heroes of the Enigma story were British servicemen. Their families, friends, and

Preparing to go to war with Hollywood. The author in the newspaper's press room with the protest package that was sent to director Jonathan Mostow containing *Herald* articles on the real Enigma heroes and the signatures of hundreds of people angry about the film *U-571*. The film falsely gave the credit to American sailors for capturing the Enigma codebooks.

fellow countrymen are both hurt and deeply offended by their heroics being attributed to fictitious American characters.

For several months now, the *Tamworth Herald* has become involved in a campaign to recognise a true Enigma hero, Able Seaman Colin Grazier, who has never had the glory he deserves – not even in his home town of Tamworth.

Even British versions of the Enigma story have failed to properly recognise the huge international debt owed to this man whose ultimate sacrifice effectively shortened the Second World War. My newspaper has joined forces with local ex-servicemen to raise money for a permanent sculpture to this extraordinary war hero.

Since launching the campaign we have become aware of the nature of your film and the feeling among the war veterans, some of whom knew Colin Grazier personally, is that a massive historic injustice is being perpetrated. So strong is the feeling that a petition signed by hundreds of their colleagues has been organised. This I have enclosed.

If your film could mention the names of Colin Grazier (and also Tony Fasson and Tommy Brown who were heroes alongside him) it would go a long way to healing the hurt. The veterans are currently working exceptionally hard to raise money for a lasting memorial in Grazier's home town.

Can I ask one thing of you? You are using the Enigma story for entirely commercial reasons. But surely it would be a gross injustice to the memories of the men who inspired your film to be simply ignored? Perhaps the least you could do is read the enclosed newspaper cuttings. A recent Channel 4 documentary of the Enigma story which did acknowledge other British Enigma heroes failed to mention him. A general caption at the end of your film would be insufficient – it really should include names.

The enclosed newspaper cuttings about Grazier's heroics include testimony from best-selling international author Robert Harris, and even eyewitness accounts of the day Grazier died. Please find time to read them – I am sure you could not fail to be moved by his forgotten story.

If you take the trouble to authenticate the details, you will discover that the actions of these unsung heroes ultimately saved thousands of lives worldwide.

I intend to publish this letter to you in the *Herald*, a weekly paid-for Midlands title read by approximately 90,000 people, and look forward to publishing your reply.

Yours sincerely,

Phil Shanahan

The articles in the *Tamworth Herald* had stirred up a hornet's nest and feelings were running high in the letters pages. I was also receiving numerous telephone calls from people wanting to vent their anger at Hollywood and wish us success with the campaign.

It was also at this time that Tamworth Borough Council came on board with a £1,000 donation to the cause. The council leader was Steve Holland and his comments in the *Herald* of 13 April 1999 show how Hollywood was inadvertently helping our cause:

The council is delighted to help. We think this is well worthwhile. I understand the Americans are now making a film in which they are claiming the credit, which has made everyone, including the council, very angry.

But at least here in Tamworth we will know the truth and there will one day be a memorial to this man who saved so many lives through his bravery.

We hope the memorial will be put up sooner rather than later so the truth about what Colin did will be there for future generations to see.

U-571 was creating a flood of anger which turned into rivers of support for us. It was amazing that the *Herald*, which had been producing headlines since 1868, was now beginning to be the subject of them elsewhere. This was particularly the case when Hollywood replied.

A letter from Jonathan Mostow dropped on my desk in August 1999. I spotted the small envelope immediately as it had his name on the front. It was handwritten, in a style very similar to his signature, and the letter it contained was not written by a secretary with a formal reference number at the top. It was obvious that the great Hollywood director had typed it himself.

This pleased me because I was half expecting a formal fob-off from one of his assistants along the lines of 'Mr Mostow thanks you for the interest in his film … etc.' The fact that he had handled it personally told me that he had been taken aback by my letter and it had exposed a raw nerve. We had obviously extracted pangs of guilt. This is the exact wording of his reply:

Dear Mr Shanahan,

Thank you for your letter of June 6 and the accompanying materials. I wholeheartedly agree that Colin Grazier, Lt. Anthony Fasson, Tommy Brown and the other members of the HMS Petard who boarded the U-559 are great war heroes who deserve the utmost honors. Their brave capture of a short weather cipher played an important part in Bletchley Park's efforts to break the Enigma codes.

Over the past year, there has been much written in the British press about our movie, *U-571*. Unfortunately, little of it has been accurate. In making the movie we have no intention of diminishing the importance of the accomplishments of Colin Grazier or any other members of the Royal Navy. Our film is a fictional account of World War Two US submarine sailors. It is inspired by two events which were distinctly American in nature: Operation Drumbeat, which was Hitler's devastating U-boat attack on the East Coast of the United States in 1942, and the US Navy's capture of the U-505 in 1944. In our movie we show as realistically as possible the psychological and physical effects of submarine combat on the men who served. The film depicts examples of daring exploits by courageous submarine sailors. The capture of the Enigma is but one element in the film.

Again, I wish to emphasize that our film is a work of <u>fiction</u>. And while our story is not about the Enigma per se, we plan to include in the film specific tributes to some of the actual British and American crews who were involved with captures of Enigma materials, including the crew of the HMS *Petard*. As much as I would like to single out individuals for specific mention, the large number of sailors and officers who were involved in these incidents makes it impractical to do so in a two-hour film.

As director of a movie that will reach a worldwide audience, I recognize that I have a moral responsibility not to rewrite history. I believe that I am fulfilling that obligation. It is my sincere hope that *U-571* will focus public attention on aspects of the Battle of the Atlantic that would otherwise risk slipping into the footnotes of history. I hope that young people particularly will see this fictional movie and be motivated to study about the real-life heroes who fought to preserve world freedom.

Sincerely,

Jonathan Mostow

To get a personal reply was quite something and would give the campaign plenty of publicity. But I was completely unconvinced by the logic of Mostow's defence. Firstly, why was the film a fictional account? Are the real-life stories not dramatic enough? Two men die retrieving information that changed the course of history and Hollywood finds its inspiration from two far less significant incidents – American in nature!

How can he possibly hope that people will see this fictional film and be motivated to study the real-life heroes? Wouldn't a better way to achieve that be to focus on the actual

JONATHAN MOSTOW

August 3, 1999

Mr. Phil Shanahan
Assistant Editor
THE TAMWORTH HERALD CO. LTD.
Ventura Park Road
Bitterscote, Tamworth, Staffordshire
B78 3LZ

Dear Mr. Shanahan:

Thank you for your letter of June 6 and the accompanying materials. I wholeheartedly agree that Colin Grazier, Lt. Anthony Fasson, Tommy Brown and the other members of the HMS Petard who boarded the U-559 are great war heroes who deserve the utmost honors. Their brave capture of a short weather cipher played an important part in Bletchley Park's efforts to break the Enigma codes.

Over the past year, there has been much written in the British press about our movie, U-571. Unfortunately, little of it has been accurate. In making the movie we have no intention of diminishing the importance of the accomplishments Colin Grazier or any other members of the Royal Navy. Our film is a fictional account of World War II U.S. submarine sailors. It is inspired by two events which were distinctly American in nature: Operation Drumbeat, which was Hitler's devastating U-boat attack on the East Coast of the United States in 1942, and the U.S. Navy's capture of the U-505 in 1944. In our movie we show as realistically as possible the psychological and physical effects of submarine combat on the men who served. The film depicts examples of daring exploits by courageous submarine sailors. The capture of the Enigma is but one element in the film.

Again, I wish to emphasize that our film is a work of fiction. And while our story is not about the Enigma per se, we plan to include in the film specific tributes to some of the actual British and American crews who were involved with captures of Enigma materials -- including the crew of the HMS Petard. As much as I would like to single out individuals for specific mention, the large number of sailors and officers who were involved in these incidents makes it impractical to do so in a 2 hour film.

As director of a movie that will reach a worldwide audience, I recognize that I have a moral responsibility not to rewrite history. I believe that I am fulfilling that obligation. It is my sincere hope that U-571 will focus public attention on aspects of the Battle of the Atlantic that would otherwise risk slipping into the footnotes of history. I hope that young people particularly will see this fictional movie and be motivated to study about the real-life heroes who fought to preserve world freedom.

Sincerely,

Jonathan Mostow

MOSTOW LIEBERMAN PRODUCTIONS
100 UNIVERSAL CITY PLAZA • BUNGALOW 72 • UNIVERSAL CITY CALIFORNIA 91608
PHONE: (818) 777-4444 • FAX (818) 866-0174

Hollywood movie director Jonathan Mostow's letter to the author, defending his film, *U-571*, against criticism that it gave the Americans the credit for capturing vital Enigma material instead of the British. Mostow said his work was a 'fictional account'.

heroes themselves? He then reveals that he is actually going to mention the *Petard* at the end of the film. If this film is nothing to do with the *Petard*, and is just fictional, why has he agreed to mention the *Petard* at all? Is conscience rearing its head again? He emphasises that the film will have a worldwide audience and he is aware of his moral obligation not to rewrite history. So why does the film have to do just that? The heroes who mattered most in seizing Enigma material were British, not American, as his film implies.

And how could I agree with a person who says he hopes to focus public attention on the real-life Battle of the Atlantic by producing a film which gives a false account? Maybe he would also suggest that I should concentrate on my favourite football team Stoke City by watching video clips of Port Vale in action.

Interestingly enough, unlike most people in Tamworth at the time, Jonathan Mostow had apparently heard of Grazier, Fasson and Brown. It seems their stories were not unknown to him but he was going to leave them unsung and create more American glory. How many people watching it would then delve into the real story of Grazier, Fasson and Brown? We were going to do our utmost to let the truth come out and focus on the facts. It was the *Tamworth Herald* versus Hollywood!

Despite Mostow's desperate attempts to justify the film to me, the man who wrote the screenplay for *U-571* several years later admitted to feeling ashamed of the movie. In August 2006, David Ayers told Radio 4's *The Film Programme*: 'It was a distortion … a mercenary decision to create this parallel history in order to drive the movie for an American audience.'

Ayers said he knew how significant the Enigma chapter was in British history and pledged, 'I won't do it again'. At least he had the decency to eventually admit what we all knew anyway. In one weekend alone, in April 2000, the movie netted more than $20 million for its makers. Sleep well Mr Mostow!

The spat with a Hollywood heavyweight meant that we were not going to be starved of the oxygen of publicity. Mr Mostow's clash with a weekly newspaper in the Midlands was subsequently featured in national newspapers and magazines, on television and even in half a million copies of the *Dallas Morning News*. It was all beginning to get a little interesting.

The *Navy News* was one of the first to carry reports of our campaign and the controversy with Mr Mostow. I would like to put on record my appreciation to this fine publication for all its invaluable help. I dealt mainly with deputy editor Anton Hanney and assistant editor Mike Gray. Both were wonderfully co-operative and I never had to convince them of the importance of our efforts. They backed us all the way with regular updates on our progress and the story struck a chord with their magazine's large and far-flung readership.

Reaction to our Enigma campaign had gone from local to national and with *Navy News* on board it was going international. A Munich-based U-boat association carried the full story on its website under the headline: *Statue für Enigma-code Helden geplant* (Statue for Enigma code heroes planned).

We began to receive letters of support from all over the world offering donations. They came from Britain, America, Australia, Canada and even the Philippines. It was remarkable. Not just Tamworth but people all over the world were following our drive to raise awareness of three little-known heroes. Very early on we even had a letter from Tamworth, Australia, saying that its residents were also proud of Colin Grazier.

Our crusade came to the early attention of *The Guardian* newspaper which carried a prominent page lead story headlined, 'Statue appeal for unsung hero who helped win war.' Richard Norton-Taylor's article quoted naval historian Ralph Erskine who succinctly summed up the importance of the incident which we were campaigning to highlight. 'Few acts of courage can ever have had such far-reaching consequences.'

The article also revealed that a plaque had been erected in Fasson's honour at a church near Jedburgh, Scotland, and quoted chunks of the letter which I had sent to Mostow, along with his reply. *The Guardian* could not get Mostow to comment and so relied on his letter to me.

Fasson's plaque in Bedrule church, near Jedburgh, vastly understates the importance of the mission that cost his life. It simply says:

In loving memory of Francis Anthony Blair Fasson, Lieutenant GC, RN.
Killed in action in an enemy submarine in the Mediterranean 30 October 1942.

Slightly more information is contained in a framed report on the wall of the same church:

At 15.50 hours on 30 October 1942, HMS *Petard*, of which Lieutenant Fasson was first lieutenant, commenced a hunt for a German U-boat in the Eastern Mediterranean. At about 22.00 hours, following a search in company with other destroyers, U-559 had surfaced and was being abandoned by its crew.

In a gallant attempt to recover Top Secret enemy codebooks, Lieutenant Fasson and Able Seaman Colin Grazier stripped off their clothes and swam across to the U-559. With the help of a very young NAAFI Assistant, sixteen-year-old Tommy Brown, the attempt was partially successful, but the seacocks had been opened. U-559 sank taking Lieutenant Fasson and Able Seaman Colin Grazier with it. Both were awarded the George Cross posthumously for reasons that could not be revealed at the time.

The plaque does not do justice to one of the key moments in world history, especially as it is described as only 'partially successful'. Apart from a framed photograph of Fasson and a replica George Cross in the Royal British Legion Club in Jedburgh, it was all there was to commemorate the three men, but you would have had to have stumbled well off the tourist track to find even that little trace of their story. It really was time something on a grander scale was planned for them.

I was contacted by Captain C.B. Featherstone-Dilke in September 1999, who told me he was the last naval officer to deal with Colin Grazier's citation. He was very interested in our push to honour the Enigma heroes and revealed that he had been dispatched by the Admiralty to meet the Grazier family in 1966 after they had written to request information about Colin's death.

He said he was so moved by their son's story that he personally convinced the Admiralty to release Colin's citation. This was more than twenty years after the action had taken place. This is an extract from the *Herald* edition of 3 September 1999 in which he describes what happened:

'With the end of the war, the Graziers sought to find out details of Colin's gallant act, but Ultra [ultra-secret classified Enigma intelligence] and the world of Bletchley Park were still top secret and the Admiralty declined to disclose any details,' said the captain, who was in charge of HMS *St Vincent*, a training establishment at Gosport at the time.

Some time in 1966 Mr and Mrs Grazier wrote to the commander-in chief, Portsmouth, to enlist his aid in finding out about Colin and to tell the Admiralty that, as they were by then 'getting on', they would like to ensure that the medal had a good home with the Royal Navy.

The commander-in-chief told me to do what I could to comply with their wishes and to give them every support to help. I therefore went up from Gosport and by appointment called on them at their home near Tamworth. This was greatly appreciated and I came away with the George Cross.

I then badgered the Admiralty at the highest level I could and they agreed to release the citation which had hitherto been top secret.

Captain Featherstone-Dilke had his trainees build a display case for the medal and the citation, and after a formal parade, attended by the Graziers, these were put on display in the chapel at HMS *St Vincent*. 'After lunch Colin's parents returned to Tamworth and were most appreciative of our efforts. To know after all those years what their son had done brought them great peace and happiness.'

It is good to know that the Graziers at least had this day to celebrate their son and credit must go to Captain Featherstone-Dilke for achieving this. But the citation did not reveal the full facts. Mr and Mrs Grazier were no doubt immensely proud of their son's bravery. Regrettably, they were never to fully understand the part he played in ridding the world of war. The need for secrecy was to deny them the knowledge of their son's full glory. The citation did not confirm that any material had been retrieved by the men, let alone the full implications of it:

Able Seaman
Colin Grazier
P/S SX 25550 GC.

Able Seaman Colin Grazier of HMS *Petard* was awarded the George Cross (posthumous) for outstanding bravery and steadfast devotion to duty in the face of danger during an action on 30th October, 1942. The award was gazetted on 11th September, 1943.

On the 30th October 1942 HMS *Petard* together with other ships of the 12th Destroyer Flotilla carried out a most successful and skilful hunt in the Mediterranean waters culminating

TWO GATES COUPLE PRESENT SON'S GEORGE CROSS BACK TO NATION

A *Herald* article published on 20 May 1966, included a photograph of Colin's father proudly showing off his son's George Cross which he had decided to hand back to the Navy for safekeeping. Colin's widow Olive is in the picture with her arm round his shoulder. The article described Colin's action as 'daring but unsuccessful'.

in the destruction of the enemy submarine U-559. During the course of the action, in which HMS *Petard* carried out four attacks, the U-boat surfaced. HMS *Petard* engaged her and finally took her in tow. The party was put on board led by Lieutenant Anthony Fasson R.N. who together with A.B. Grazier dived into the sea and swam out to the sub. They went down into the submarine to obtain information, a task they knew to be extremely dangerous as the submarine was sinking fast.

A.B. Grazier followed the first lieutenant over the side and boarded the boat with him in the shortest possible time. He stayed below working in the darkness with the water rising and knowing the submarine to be holed until too late to escape thus giving their lives in their eagerness to get vital information.

A *Tamworth Herald* article, published on 20 May 1966, reported that it was the first time the George Cross had ever been handed back to the nation. The story included a picture of Colin's father (who was also named Colin) clutching the precious medal during an annual get-together of the Wilnecote and Two Gates Royal British Legion branch. Colin's widow, Olive, is pictured alongside him. What struck me most about this article is the description of Colin's mission that they both obviously had read and no doubt believed to be true. 'At the age of twenty-two, he was one of two heroes of a daring but unsuccessful mission to capture important documents from a sinking German submarine.'

Fasson's plaque had described his final actions as 'partially successful' and now Colin's bravery had been deemed unsuccessful. I was so glad I had been given the chance to put the record straight.

In her history column, published on Bonfire Night in 1982, popular *Herald* columnist, Mabel Swift (who sadly died in 2007 at the age of eighty-eight), revealed what had prompted Colin's parents to return their son's medal to the country:

> Back in Tamworth, Colin's family went to work with renewed hope (following the award of the George Cross to Colin) – Dad in the coalmine and Mum in the munitions factory at Two Gates, where the Reliant factory is [it has since been levelled] and Olive making Spitfires.
>
> When at last the war was over, in 1945, Olive gave the George Cross to Colin's father. He wore it with great pride on Remembrance Day parades when he marched with his old colleagues of the 1914 war in which he had served in the army.
>
> But one day in 1966 a stranger called on the Graziers. He expressed an interest in the George Cross and offered them a large sum of money for it. There was a hasty family conference and it was unanimously decided that the medal should not be sold to any stranger.
>
> But a realisation of its value brought concern for its safety, and they decided to offer it to the Royal Navy for safekeeping.

I have since come across a few other references to Grazier's death in the newspaper's archives, but always a jewel of a story was underplayed. The subject was touched on a couple of times but never given much value in the news columns. It seemed always to have been confined to the history or nostalgia pages and was always buried way back in the newspaper. It is uncanny just how often this exceptional story had been underestimated and by so many different people.

Unfortunately, even when information on the U-559 incident passed into the public domain in the 1970s, these men were never given the attention I believe they had earned. The fact that Grazier was so unknown in Tamworth was a travesty. So was the lack of fuss made of Fasson and Brown. It was essential that we should now redress the balance sixty years after their deaths.

HMS *St Vincent* closed down in 1969 and Grazier's George Cross was passed to the Royal Naval Museum in Portsmouth. Captain Featherstone-Dilke thought it would be nice for the medal to eventually go on display at the town hall in Tamworth, so long as security was not a problem. But the medal never got to Tamworth. It turned up in a far more northerly place where Tony Fasson's sister, Sheena d'Anyers-Willis, spotted it by sheer chance.

On 14 December 1992, Sheena was invited to the Faslane naval base on the west coast of Scotland. She had been invited by a close associate, Admiral Sir Hugo White, to visit a submarine previously under his command.

On her way to lunch Sheena passed by a corridor with a glass cabinet containing naval memorabilia. A George Cross grabbed her attention and she was completely stunned to see it had been won by the man who died with her brother. 'I couldn't believe it,' she told me. 'I was just walking past and there it was in the corner.'

Colin Grazier's citation was there too, but nobody could shed any light on how the items had ended up in Faslane.

While driving home Sheena couldn't help thinking about what she had seen. She is the guardian of her brother's George Cross which is displayed in Edinburgh Castle. The more she thought about Grazier's medal the more she felt it was being kept in an inappropriate place. 'It seemed to me that it would be much better if it could be alongside Tony's medal in Edinburgh Castle,' she said.

Finally, but only after a huge amount of campaigning from Sheena, the Admiralty agreed to the move. In 1994 the medal was placed alongside her brother's in Edinburgh Castle where it remains to this day. Sheena had always felt very sad that her brother and Colin had been overlooked and her success in getting the medal moved at least helped to raise their profile. Sheena and I still exchange letters and telephone calls from time to time. She is a truly remarkable woman and I have a great deal of respect for her.

CHAPTER SIX

AN OUTSTANDING LEADER OF MEN

The reply came back 'I've something of vital importance here – I must risk it'. These might well come under the heading of famous last words – Captain Barry Stevens

Sheena d'Anyers-Willis told me an amazing story about her brother which happened before his Enigma heroics. It was something she only learned from other people years after his death.

Tony Fasson was a hero twice over for he had saved the lives of two Maltese stewards after his ship hit a mine. The stewards suffered the horror of being trapped in the engine room which was filling with water. Tony immediately dived in, despite not knowing whether the deck was intact below him, and held the men's heads above water until help arrived. The young naval officer was some man – as is evident in these touching tributes received by his family at the time of his death:

He was always so full of life and courage. It seems that someone very splendid has left the world. – Bethany Allen.

That delicious personality, radiating charm, happiness and complete understanding as he did. – Marian Minto.

Tony was always the tonic which you expect from someone who by nature was so full of zest and natural friendliness. I can not think of him unless it was laughing, and although I did not know how his life ended, I am certain that it was by doing whatever it was with a cheerfulness as infectious to his men, as it had been infectious to us all, during his lifetime. It would take more than a war to get Tony down. He will be missed by all whose luck it was to know him, and remembered as a character you could not help loving for the way he helped tackle things – no matter whether some mad-cap escapade of Dartmouth days, or the serious demands made on us today. – John Hayes, Royal Navy.

Of all the charming 'Ansons' Tony and Peter Medd could not help becoming two of my special favourites. They both had such outstanding qualities – particularly happiness and good nature, that they were quite irresistible. None that led such a grand life as Tony did, could have done anything else [referring to his most glorious death]. He will be terribly missed by literally hundreds of friends, for he was quite one of the most popular people I knew. – Admiral Anthony Kimmins, Royal Navy.

Tony always seemed to me to be typical of the best type of naval officer. He was so gallant. – Ian Johnston.

Left: Every inch the officer, Lieutenant Tony Fasson combined that rare talent of being a strong disciplinarian while maintaining his popularity with those under his command.

Far left: Tony Fasson always had a smile for his friends and colleagues.

My favourite tribute to him, though, was aptly straight from the heart of his best friend:

It was always Tony whose perpetual exuberance jerked me out of any lethargy and helped me to see the spice in life. Tony whose perfect manners were his and his friends' passport to any party. Tony whose quiet sympathy, often under a pose of the greatest intolerance – made him my dearest friend. I am glad to think that so much of Tony is immortal and will be with me wherever I am. And I am sure that it is in that way that he would like us to think of him – not vain regrets for what might have been. I am sure he died just as he would have liked to, in the full employment of his energies, just as if he had been hunting, or playing a game of rugger. – Peter Medd, Royal Navy.

The *Petard*'s sub-lieutenant, Gordon Connell, also paid a fine tribute to his honourable shipmate in his book *Fighting Destroyer*:

Tony had immense energy; he was a good athlete and took part in all the activities he promoted, football, hockey and the rest. He had the special knack of being able, without being patronising or without any loss of authority, to mix and relax with the junior ranks. A firm disciplinarian who could enforce the traditional and accepted code with understanding, a light touch and considerable charm; his decisions regarding punishment, often severe for breaches of discipline or leave-breaking, were accepted by the offenders without lasting aggression or umbrage against the first lieutenant. With the junior officers on the ship he was a genial and attractive companion; it was Tony who made life tolerable for those who may have fallen short of the formidable captain's standards.

In a confidential report to the Chief of Naval Information, dated 15 October 1945, Captain Barry Stevens of the 7th Destroyer Flotilla, Mediterranean Fleet (on board the *Pakenham*) gave his own account of the action for which Tony Fasson was awarded the George Cross:

The sinking of U-559 on 30 October 1942, provided in its last phase a shining example of devotion to duty; of coolness and of great human courage.

When this U-boat finally surfaced at one o'clock in the morning [other sources have put the time at 10 p.m. or 11 p.m.] HMS *Petard,* the nearest destroyer, went alongside in an endeavour to capture the U-boat and tow her into harbour. Unfortunately the U-boat was too badly damaged to be salved, and within half an hour she filled and sank.

It was during this last thirty minutes that we got so glowing and so typical an example of cold and calculated courage.

The first lieutenant of *Petard*, Lt Francis Anthony Blair Fasson RN, accompanied by Able Seaman Colin Grazier, dived overboard and boarded the U-boat in an attempt to salvage documents and gear, though they knew the boat was sinking, and worked in the darkness inside with water rising above their waists, to get everything possible out of her. Very much information about U-boat dispositions, and other secret matter were found and passed to those on deck.

Eventually, when it became apparent that the boat would sink at any moment, a petty officer stationed on the conning tower called down to Tony Fasson: 'You'll have to nip up quick, Sir, I think she's going.' The reply came back: 'I've something of vital importance here – I must risk it.' These might well come under the heading of famous last words.

The Captain (D) of the Flotilla at the time, now serving in the United States, mentions the very great love that officers and men of Lieutenant Fasson's ship had for him, and refers to him as 'an outstanding leader of men'. He adds:

'The final act of his life was typical of him and in writing to his family afterwards, I was able to assure them that deeply as his loss was regretted, his life was not wasted in view of the inspiration to all of us given by the coolness, courage and devotion to duty which he displayed at one o'clock in the morning of that dark October night. The award of the George Cross posthumously to this officer and rating were gazetted as, "For outstanding bravery and steadfast devotion to duty in the face of great and imminent danger."'

John Burman, a gun loader on the *Petard* for the first three months of its service, still has clear memories of Tony Fasson:

In his capacity of 'number one' he started the process of educating the green crew including myself and several other 'Y' [potential officer candidates] who he informed would receive no special consideration – in fact we would be under his scrutiny all the time. But unlike the commanding officer, he was a very understanding and fair leader of men. He soon commanded the respect of the entire ship's company for he knew his trade exceedingly well.

When the ship went in to the Azores to refuel and take on stores, he put me in charge of a party unloading bananas from a lighter alongside. Since bananas had not been seen in the UK for years, they were very desirable and, with this in mind, he instructed me to ensure that all of them made it safely into the wardroom stores. He told me he knew exactly how many there were supposed to be, an example of his humour.

Destined for a naval career,
Tony Fasson aged about thirteen.

When the ship's company was assembled each morning to receive his work orders for the day, he would emerge from the wardroom hatch often dressed in a silk robe, sandals and his cap – a dashing figure!

Tony was born in Edinburgh on 17 July 1913, and was the second son of Captain Francis Hamilton Fasson and Lilias Clara Fasson of Lanton Tower, Roxburghshire. The historic house situated in the Scottish borders was ransacked by the English after the Battle of Flodden in 1513. The stone tower survived the raid and in more recent times the building was restored by Scottish Heritage. Tony loved the house and would return on leave to enjoy hunting trips in the company of his beloved spaniel.

Lanton Tower was sold by Tony's elder brother James after the war. James reached the position of lieutenant-colonel of the Lanarkshire Yeomanry. He served in Singapore, but was captured by the Japanese and sent to work in the infamous Kinkaseki mine.

Tony attended the Royal Naval College in Dartmouth from the age of thirteen. He was an excellent rugby player (his father was a Scottish international) and went on to play for the Royal Navy and United Services. At Dartmouth he joined the Fleet Air Arm, and suffered a near-fatal crash when his Flying Swordfish ploughed into a field.

Sheena is understandably proud of the sheer courage her brother demonstrated in boarding U-559. 'What a lot of people forget is that as Colin and Tony swam towards the vessel the Germans were fleeing from it in terror,' she said. It's a point I've also thought about a lot. The Germans knew the precarious state their submarine was in and fled in blind panic. How do you then summon up the courage to go into the mouth of the very horror enemy sailors were so desperate to escape from? Special people indeed.

CHAPTER SEVEN

THEY FLY FORGOTTEN

Time, like an ever-rolling stream, bears all its sons away. They fly forgotten, as a dream dies at the opening day – Isaac Watts, based on Psalm 90

In the autumn of 1999 I visited the Imperial War Museum in London to see how it recorded the Enigma story. The museum had recently launched an exhibition entitled 'Enigma and the Codebreakers'. Surely there was no way this world-famous military archive was going to add insult to injury by also ignoring three British men who played such a decisive role in winning the war. Guess what? No mention of Grazier, Brown or Fasson anywhere. It was as if they had never been born. Yet this was an exhibition put on by our most prominent war museum and one which apparently gave the facts about Enigma. Did anyone care about what they did? TV documentaries, a Hollywood director and now even the Imperial War Museum had all ignored the role the men had played in history. I began to think I was unearthing a conspiracy of neglect, a sixty-year-old case of dead and forgotten heroes.

Strangely enough, Reg Crang once wrote down his fears of men being forgotten during his time on board the *Petard*. He had just attended a religious service at sea and the following words from the hymn 'O God, our help in ages past' had deeply affected him:

Time, like an ever-rolling stream, bears all its sons away. They fly forgotten, as a dream dies at the opening day.

Back in his cabin, a rather morose Reg took out his diary later that evening (11 October 1942) and wrote, 'On the ship men are very much alive – earthy, arrogant, humorous and full of vitality. To say that before long they will all be dead and even forgotten is hard to accept. What is the point?'

Nineteen days later, Fasson and Grazier were dead. The significance of their final actions was to be concealed from a nation that owed them so much. Reg's fears of *Petard* sailors being forgotten in the future had proved prophetic.

With an increasing sense of purpose I wrote to the curator of the Imperial War Museum, Robert Crawford, pointing out that the men had never been properly recognised and this was an opportunity for the museum to set the record straight. The more I thought about this the stranger it seemed. The museum houses the ultimate record of Britain's military triumphs and yet fails to adequately record a major turning point in the Second World War. Unbelievable!

'We are trying to make Colin's name well known in Tamworth, but his fame should spread far wider than that,' I wrote. 'Please help give him a higher profile.' This was a battle I was to repeatedly return to later in the campaign.

Among the people who sent in contributions during September 1999 was Mick Lucas, of Surrey, who was the leading torpedo man on HMS *Petard* from 1943-44:

> I joined the ship after she sailed back into Alexandria, so I never met Colin. I have nothing but happy memories of my time on the *Petard*. I saw more action on her than any other ship I served on.
>
> I think the *Herald* campaign is a wonderful idea and I hope it is successful. People should be made aware of the sacrifice Colin and others made to shorten the war. This campaign can make a difference.

We also received support from a Mr D. Bush, of Bognor Regis, who had read about the campaign in *Navy News* reports. Mr Bush served aboard HMS *Dulverton*, one of the ships that accompanied HMS *Petard* during the hunt for the U-559:

> I was an AB [able seaman] on HMS *Dulverton* and was with the *Petard* when the U-559 surfaced. We managed to pick up some survivors, including the U-boat captain, Hans Heidtmann. I only thank God I was not given the order to swim to the U-559 on that night.

Mr P. Haywood, of Wiltshire, contacted us to thank us for highlighting the Enigma story. 'I am sure there are a lot of people like me who didn't know about Colin Grazier,' he said. 'I hope you can build a suitable memorial to a very brave man.'

Shortly afterwards another veteran got in touch who had served with Colin Grazier. Douglas Freer was a petty officer on the *Petard* and was convinced we were on to a good cause:

> At the beginning of 1943 the Germans sank their peak number of Allied vessels – by the end of that year the Allies had sunk their peak number of German U-boats. That was because Bletchley Park was able to decipher the German codes without them knowing and this could not have been achieved without the recovery of those documents.
>
> Winston Churchill said, 'lose the Battle of the Atlantic and we will lose the war' – many say that Grazier and Fasson's recovery of the codes shortened the war, but many others say it won it.
>
> Grazier was a very reliable and dependable sailor and I have no doubt that if he had lived he would have risen through the Navy's ranks.

Douglas brought our attention to another incredible fact about the *Petard*. In addition to the part she played in shortening the war, she was the only Allied ship that had managed to sink submarines from all its enemy navies – German, Italian and Japanese. In Douglas's opinion this was mainly down to its remarkable captain, Lieutenant Commander Mark Thornton DSO, DSC. 'He was a very experienced officer who was committed to anti-submarine warfare and the rigorous training that he maintained was crucial to our success in forcing the U-559 to surface,' he explained.

The *Petard* lying at anchor during the Second World War. The photograph was taken between 1942 and 1945. During her service she sank submarines from all three enemy fleets, the only ship to do so.

The author Stephen Harper, who joined HMS *Petard* on her second commission in 1945-46, has argued that the ship is as important a piece of British history as HMS *Victory*, Nelson's flagship at the Battle of Trafalgar in 1805. Yet while the latter lies proudly in Portsmouth harbour, the *Petard* was unceremoniously scrapped at Bo'ness in 1967, twenty-five years after first sliding into the River Tyne. How could the government have let that happen? Even if the full facts had not yet emerged, someone in the know could surely have delayed its execution. A precious piece of our heritage was destroyed that year. The thought makes me sick to the stomach. That ship could now be a floating museum lining the banks of the Thames. What better tribute to our naval history than to have the *Victory* in Portsmouth, plus the *Petard* in London? What a dreadful waste of a glorious vessel.

By October 1999, the campaign had raised £6,000, much of it made up by small donations from all over the country. Mr W.T. Hives, who was a cipher machine operator, said he would regard it as a privilege if we would accept his contribution. He told us that he hoped our efforts would ensure generations born after the war understood what had been achieved.

Mr C.W. Granger, a naval veteran from Exmouth, wrote along similar lines:

> I would hope that the memorial will remind present and future generations not only of Colin's great bravery, but also of the number of local boys, many of them schoolmates, who made the ultimate sacrifice at sea in the Second World War, keeping their memory alive, now that we who remember them decline in numbers.

Letters like these were to flood in throughout the next few years and they certainly helped me to retain my focus.

The *Petard* waits her turn to be scrapped at Bo'ness in 1967.

The raffle organised by Grazier Committee member Jim Welland eventually raised £1,500, and a bucket collection at the re-dedication of the Fazeley War Memorial near Tamworth boosted our pot by another £200. By November of that year the appeal fund was just shy of £8,000. We even had a contribution from an ex-Wren, Betty Mayall, from Oxford, who had worked at Bletchley Park.

The campaign took a transatlantic twist when I was contacted by a journalist on the *Dallas Morning News*. The newspaper was chasing up the controversy stirred up in England by the forthcoming Hollywood movie *U-571*. Reporter Yvonne Barlow had been gauging reaction to the film in America and Britain and had heard about our brush with the film's director. I was subsequently quoted in half a million copies of the *Dallas Morning News*, putting the record straight on Britain's wartime exploits. If you had told me that a year before I would never have believed it. The campaign was certainly taking me into uncharted territory.

This kind of publicity was having a healthy effect on our fund and I felt the time was right to approach Staffordshire County Council for a donation. The then-leader of the county council, Terry Dix, is a proud Tamworthian, and it was he who broke the news to me that we were to receive £1,000. The amount matched the district council's donation and we were getting the kind of backing that I had hoped for – and just what these men deserved.

The decision had been made at a meeting held on Armistice Day and Cllr Dix told me that there had not been a single voice of dissent. I also learned that Two Gates Working

Men's Club was planning to rename its concert room 'The Colin Grazier Suite' after spending £50,000 upgrading it. Grazier's name seemed to be cropping up all over the town after decades of anonymity. It was wonderful.

We suffered a setback in early December 1999, when I received a disappointing letter from the Imperial War Museum concerning my request to put on a display about the unsung Enigma heroes. My letter had been passed to Nigel Steel, the head of the museum's research and information department. I felt a huge sense of disappointment as I laid the letter down slowly on my desk having noted its contents.

Mr Steel said the museum was constantly made aware of the many acts of bravery and sacrifice which took place during wartime, but regrettably could not display tributes to them all. He did, however, have some positive news about the *Herald's* Enigma articles and acknowledged the publicity they had attracted from other newspapers including *The Guardian*. Mr Steel pledged that all the *Herald* articles would be kept in a special file and become part of the museum's records on the Enigma story. 'In this way, although not featured in the museum's displays, you can see that Grazier is commemorated as part of our wider remit,' he said.

I suppose this was another step forward and the fact that our articles were to become part of the museum's Enigma collection could be regarded as an achievement. But I was too emotional to take such a distanced stance. All I could see was that these men merited much more.

I also wrote to Mr Steel saying that a hidden file containing a selection of newspaper cuttings was 'no way to record one of the most important war heroes the world has known'. I wrote spontaneously and my letter reflected my frustration. I told him what the *Herald* had achieved to date and added:

I will keep banging the drum for these men as they have constantly been deprived of the recognition they so obviously deserve…

I am proud that this newspaper has been a catalyst for all this, but it also needs bodies such as the Imperial War Museum to ensure these men get the international attention their wartime heroics deserve … The world gained from their actions but the individuals concerned missed out. I cannot believe there could be any individual acts in history that can be more deserving than this.

I fully appreciate the pressure of space on the museum's collections. But whatever space there is available should surely be used to highlight the actions of Grazier, Brown and Fasson, otherwise you cannot justify calling yourselves the definitive war museum when you fail to record a major turning point of World War Two?

To back up what I said, I quoted from a column I had read in the *Independent* written by Stephen Harper, author of *Capturing Enigma*. I included the following facts from that article:

1. The men's actions saved 500,000 tons of shipping during the first few months of 1943 alone.

2. Convoys were re-routed around areas where the U-boats were lying in wait and were subsequently sunk at such a rate that Admiral Doenitz, the U-boat commander, withdrew the remnant of his packs from the Atlantic.

3. Six weeks later the tide had been turned and the Battle of the Atlantic won. The build-up for the invasion of Normandy in 1944 was able to go ahead – otherwise it might have been postponed until 1946 and atomic bombs may then have been used in Europe as the technology would by then have become available.

I thought I had a strong argument and Stephen Harper also wrote to the museum backing up my comments. He had spent twenty-six years with the *Daily Express*, rising to chief foreign correspondent. Stephen had also served on the *Petard* during her second commission. 'I agree with your excellent submission and have sent off a letter to back you up,' he told me in a letter. 'While appreciating there are many heroes, many more unsung, of the Second World War, I suggest that the story of the *Petard* and her crew is quite unique. It really is time that this proud event in Royal Navy history was properly recorded and exhibited.'

I think we had given the Imperial War Museum plenty to digest, and it was eventually to lead to a long meeting with Nigel Steel in London.

CHAPTER EIGHT

IN ALL ITS SHINING GLORY

We were stopped in our tracks by the magnificent sight on the kitchen table. It was there in all its shining glory – The Colin Grazier Memorial

Championing the cause for unsung heroes of international significance is difficult enough in itself, but just how do you fittingly celebrate them? This was the question that faced us from the outset.

There have been many moments during the campaign when things just seemed to fall into place, as if by magic. The number of times it happened was uncanny. My connection with Walenty Pytel, a world-renowned sculptor, was an example of this. Walenty was to go on to create the most fantastic tribute to the three war heroes imaginable. Yet my connection with him was entirely unrelated to the Colin Grazier campaign.

A few years ago I went to Herefordshire to write a magazine feature on Walenty, whose work I had long admired. The background to all this is rather odd, but relevant as it directly led to Walenty creating the wonderful monument that now forms the centrepiece of Tamworth's St Editha's Square.

My mother-in-law, Ann, lived in Munich for twenty years, and we were regular visitors. Her husband, Richard, had family connections with Herefordshire and many years ago bought a beautifully crafted iron sculpture of an owl fashioned by Walenty.

For years there was a Walenty Pytel connection to our regular trips to Munich. One of Walenty's most striking pieces is situated near the entrance to Birmingham Airport. Called 'Take Off', it's a big, breathtaking sculpture of three egrets rising into the air with their wings intermingled. It was something I always looked out for when I visited the airport as to me it symbolised flight so perfectly. I would then arrive at my in-laws' house in Germany and admire the little owl for the duration of my stay in Bavaria. It was this bizarre link that led to Walenty producing the wonderful Colin Grazier Memorial. As I said earlier, there just seemed to be a pattern to events.

When I first contacted Walenty I had never heard of Colin Grazier, but when I eventually got round to visiting him for the magazine interview the campaign was in its early stages and I spontaneously began to talk to him about it.

Walenty is widely regarded as one of the world's finest metal sculptors, with much of his work being displayed in prominent public places. His biggest piece to date is the enormous 'Fosse Sculpture' which stands proudly outside JCB's headquarters in Rocester, Staffordshire. Made entirely from JCB excavator parts, it was commissioned by Sir Anthony Bamford, who inherited the iconic British company from his father, and who is a collector of Walenty's work.

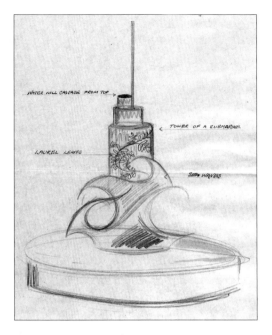

WATER MILL CASCADE FROM TOP

TOWER OF A SUBMARINE

LAUREL LEAVES

SEA WAVES

One of Walenty Pytel's propositions for the Colin Grazier Memorial would have resulted in a U-boat rising from St Editha's Square.

If the JCB sculpture is the biggest example of Walenty's genius, the most prestigious is surely the Jubilee Fountain Sculpture, commissioned by Parliament for the Queen's Silver Jubilee year in 1977. It stands 26ft high and features a selection of animals, birds and beasts, representing Commonwealth countries. It took eighteen months to complete.

After I spent a day with Walenty, gleaning material for the article, we sat in his kitchen with a glass of fine red wine and I began to tell him the story of Grazier, Fasson and Brown. Walenty was fascinated by the account and I asked him if he could come up with ideas for a suitable memorial.

He is mainly known for his animal and bird sculptures, and had previously only produced one memorial which consisted of a rising pillar with doves circling the top. Nevertheless, I was confident that he was the right man for the job, but I also knew he could charge much more than what we could afford and might not have the time to get involved.

The more we talked, however, the more interested Walenty became and I got the feeling I had sold the story to him. He was particularly grabbed by the fact that these men had achieved so much, and yet been celebrated so little. I was beginning to feel I was in with a chance. As Walenty dropped me off at the railway station he promised to give the matter some thought and put a few sketches in the post. I left feeling elated at the thought of commissioning a sculptor who had produced work for the Queen. Maybe we were on our way to doing something very special for the Enigma heroes.

Several weeks passed and I heard nothing from him. Then, on the very morning of the next committee meeting, an envelope marked urgent arrived by special delivery. It contained five different pencil sketches of the Colin Grazier Memorial for us to choose from.

At that time the idea was to make the sculpture the focal point of a fountain. We thought the water connection was apt for a tribute to seamen. However, it was an element we were later reluctantly forced to drop after consultation with the local council. We were advised that vandals might put soap suds in the water. I protested, pointing out that such features grace many towns throughout the country and are a constant joy to the eyes and ears of residents and visitors alike. I had recently enjoyed a night out in Stratford-upon-Avon and I urged the council to investigate how much the attractive steel fountain near to the Royal Shakespeare Theatre cost to maintain. The council took my advice and reported back that the local authority was coughing up a small fortune each year to repair damage caused by vandals. I had shot myself in the foot!

All the drawings Walenty submitted were highly imaginative, some featuring sea horses and swans. One of them would also have been a touch controversial, but I am sure it would have attracted huge publicity. It consisted of a U-boat conning tower decorated with laurel leaves, rising from the waves.

As I passed the drawings round to the committee members, one in particular caught our attention. It was of three anchors held together by a mass of chain. I immediately thought the anchors beautifully symbolised not just Grazier, but all three men. It also had a serene elegance about it. The others were more elaborate and sea horses and swans didn't quite seem appropriate, nor did the idea of a U-boat rising from the middle of Tamworth town centre. This one definitely caught my eye and thankfully every member of the committee agreed. We had made our choice.

After the meeting I wrote to Walenty and told him our preference. He sounded a little surprised, and I wondered if we had ignored his favourite design. Only when the sculpture was finally unveiled several years later did I discover the reason for his reaction. Apparently he had spent quite a bit of time on the other designs and then just before sending them in the post suddenly thought he had not given us quite enough choices. He rushed off another sketch of an anchor design, almost as an afterthought and included it with the others. He was then somewhat alarmed to hear that we had chosen that very design because he had yet to work out how he could pull it off from a practical point of view. The chain itself would weigh several tons and how on earth was he going to weld it all together? None of us realised the quandary he was in, but it was to turn out magnificently. He later declared the monument to be one of his all-time favourite pieces. Initially, however, it deprived him of many hours' sleep.

The weeks passed and more money came in. The fund was nearing the £10,000 mark when I contacted Walenty again to see if he had produced a working model of the sculpture. He asked me to come to Hereford the following weekend and assured me he would definitely have a miniature replica ready for inspection. I called him the following Friday and made arrangements to travel the next day. It was to be a memorable weekend.

My wife Claire and I arrived at Walenty's Queen Anne mansion at about midday. We drove slowly up the winding road alongside his private lake, admiring the various pieces of his work on display. We discovered the great artist in his workshop, dressed in his trademark holey pullover and jeans. He was looking flustered.

'I've made a start,' he said, pointing to various scraps of metal on the table, 'but I'm a little bit behind schedule. I'll definitely have it ready for tomorrow though.'

He then picked up a piece of rusty old chain and waved it in my direction. 'That represents the anchor chain for the memorial,' he said.

I have always been full of admiration for the man. He is gloriously eccentric and hugely talented. Just for a second, though, I began to doubt I was dealing with the most reliable person in Britain. He took us into his house, armed us with a drink, and we passed a pleasant hour or two with Walenty and his wife Mary. He suggested that Claire and I should go for a walk, and possibly stay overnight in a guesthouse. We hadn't planned to stay the weekend and fully expected by that time to be on our way home with a shining new model of the Colin Grazier Memorial safely ensconced in the boot of our car. We were both finding it hard to believe that the rusty heap in the shed could be transformed into anything remotely impressive. It required an enormous leap of faith.

Still, I did have complete confidence in the man's ability and we set off for a walk in the Herefordshire hills as he had suggested. After a pleasant meal in a Hungarian restaurant, we checked in for an unexpected stay in a quaint guesthouse in Ross-on-Wye. For a while I managed to keep my mind off the current state of the proposed Colin Grazier Memorial.

Walenty had invited us to Sunday lunch and we were met with an exceptionally pungent smell of grouse soup wafting in from the kitchen. Just about everything Walenty eats is homemade, and he nearly always catches his own game. He had also prepared us some delicious sea trout fish cakes.

As we walked into his kitchen we were stopped in our tracks by the magnificent sight on the kitchen table. It was there in all its glory – The Colin Grazier Memorial!

There were no signs of rust. It was so understated and beautiful, standing on a simple metal base. It had changed from the rough drawing – he had obviously been forced to come up with a practical solution to the design problems – but it was ten times better.

The three anchors looked magnificent, with the chain draped around them in an apparently casual manner, but the effect was just wonderful to the eye. I could not imagine the chain taking up a more beautiful shape. It had a most illusionary quality, with the heavy anchors looking like they were suspended in thin air. It defied gravity. It was magical. I shook his hand there and then. I could hardly believe this was the heap of rusty metal I had seen only twenty-four hours earlier. I was dealing with genius.

On the way home we called at my sister's house in Stoke-on-Trent. I showed the model to her and my brother-in-law and told them they were looking at a future symbol of Tamworth, and a sculpture that would one day be of international significance. It seemed strange then to think that, but it has certainly turned out to be the case. They were amongst the first people to set eyes on the design and loved it instantly.

I took the model to work on the Monday morning and all the staff crowed over it. The following Thursday we hosted another committee meeting and we decided to add a sense of drama to the occasion. The *Herald*'s assistant editor John Harper and I took the model

Right: Walenty Pytel, creator of the three-anchor sculpture in Tamworth, takes a bow at St Editha's Church. He later described the monument as one of his favourite pieces of work.

Below: The Colin Grazier Committee stand in awe at the model for the proposed monument.

into the boardroom before the meeting and covered it with a sheet. Once everyone had taken their seats and were given refreshments, I made a theatrical announcement. 'Ladies and gentleman … This is the Colin Grazier Memorial.' I whisked off the sheet and the entire committee was transfixed! Funnily enough we had a photograph of us all taken with the model that day and we were all looking at it with our hands clasped as if it were the Holy Grail. It had that kind of effect on us.

At the next committee meeting a new member turned up who had strong connections with a top Midlands brass band – the award-winning Woolley Pritchard Sovereign Brass Band. Ray Jennings, whose son plays in the band, suggested we put on a concert with the proceeds going to the memorial appeal. Based in Smethwick, Birmingham, the band draws its members from across the Midlands. It has been featured several times on television (including an appearance in the TV drama *Dangerfield*) and has won a string of impressive awards. The idea was that the band would play music with a strong naval and military theme. I was very keen on this idea and agreed to hold further talks. It was to become the first major tribute to Colin Grazier in his home town.

CHAPTER NINE

A HIT WITH THE GIRLS

Colin was very popular in the playground, especially with the girls. He was exceptionally good-looking – Gwen Forsyth

To keep our readers tuned into the campaign and not become weary of the subject, I realised we had to convey the tragedy of the story in as human a way as possible. We had to create a sense of who Colin was, what he was like, and what he looked like. We, therefore, regularly appealed not just for photographs but also for people's memories of him. It was an exciting time, because piece by piece we started to rebuild a very special human being from scratch. He went from being just a name to me, to someone I felt I was starting to get to know. Our campaign was beginning to get a human core and people were relating to it.

Colin's wedding pictures, sent in by his sister-in-law, Margaret Kirk, were particularly poignant. Like any newlyweds he and Olive were captured beaming in the posed pictures outside the church. As the camera clicked away, none of the guests could possibly have realised that these were the last photographs to be taken of a man destined to shape history.

Colin and Olive were married at St Peter's and St Paul's Church, Kingsbury, on 25 July 1942. Margaret Kirk was just thirteen at the time, but still remembers him fondly. 'Colin was a very nice fellow,' she told the *Herald*. 'We are all proud of what he accomplished – he did a great job for his country and should be remembered.'

Just forty-eight hours after those pictures were taken, Colin embarked on a mission from which he was never to return. The world was to be thankful for that voyage, but he was to remain uncelebrated for decades. I was filled with a sense of purpose.

The pictures also showed Colin had been blessed with film star looks. I have often heard him described as 'the best looking lad in Tamworth'. It was incredible to gaze upon these final images of Colin taken on the happiest day of his life. I put out renewed appeals for more information on his life and personality. I was not to be disappointed.

We continued to open windows on Colin's life as more pictures and personal recollections came in. A member of his family, who asked to remain anonymous, sent me three incredible photographs. The first showed a happy and very young Colin disembarking from the *Petard* in his Mediterranean whites. Another rare image showed him engaged in some heavy rope work with a young naval colleague. Perhaps the most striking one was of a bare-chested and well-toned Colin loading the ship's gun.

Some of the anecdotes we received were equally fascinating. I published the memories of Gwen Forsyth, who confessed to having had a crush on young Colin, in an article headlined: 'Colin – the cheeky and impish boy who made my heart flutter'.

Left: Colin Grazier married his childhood sweetheart Olive at St Peter's and St Paul's Church, Kingsbury, near Tamworth, on 25 July 1942. Two days later he set off on a voyage from which he never returned.

Below: Colin and Olive pictured with their family on the happiest day of their lives.

Gwen, who went to Wilnecote School with Colin in the mid-1930s, said: 'Colin was very popular in the playground, especially with the girls! He was exceptionally good-looking.' She remembered that all the girls were after him because he made all their hearts 'flutter'. 'He was always full of life and very mischievous. He was constantly getting his ears boxed and being told off. He was very likable.' She added that he was just the type of person to become a hero:

It didn't surprise me at all what he'd done. He was a daredevil and always used to do things without thinking of the consequences. He was a very brave young man and we were all very sad when he died, but at the time we all thought he was just another victim of the war. I am proud to have known him and am extremely grateful for what he did. I think what the *Herald* is doing is brilliant and very befitting of Colin.

Colin's second cousin, Douglas Heathcote, who now lives in Wales, revealed that Colin had an extraordinary habit – drinking neat vinegar! 'He was a beggar for it. It was like beer to him. It was a little-known commodity in those days and he just used to like it.'

Douglas's parents ran a pub in the village of Warton called the Hatters Arms and Colin and his family frequently stayed there with them. He remembers Colin and Colin's older brother George coming home on leave from the Navy and turning up at the pub unannounced in their uniforms. 'They were heroes to us as we didn't know any other servicemen. They were put on a pedestal and idolised.'

Colin had a big influence on Douglas who himself served in the Navy for twenty-five years. 'He was a jolly, happy and friendly bloke. He was very considerate and would always bring little gifts for everyone when he visited home.' Commenting on Colin's ultimate sacrifice, Douglas added: 'My first reaction was that he was a bloody fool for volunteering, but someone had to do it and Colin was always a stop and a half in front of everyone else.'

In March 2000, the *Herald* published an interview with a close shipmate of Colin. Trevor Tipping, DSM, only knew Colin from June 1942 up to his tragic death at the end of October of that year, but in those few months together the pair became firm friends. He described Colin as 'a reserved sort of fellow but a good friend ... We were both on active service which certainly united us. I think the young conscripts looked up to us as we were more experienced and could teach them about life.'

Trevor also revealed that Colin was the quartermaster on the ship and as such was an important figure in many young lads' lives. 'Some of the younger lads didn't know how to prepare a meal, and of course, Colin could teach them how to,' he explained.

The two sailors also embarked on a mini-adventure together on what turned out to be Colin's final leave. After docking in South Africa in late August 1942, the ship was inundated with offers of hospitality from local families. Colin and Trevor spent five days together on a sugar farm. 'It was a terrific trip,' said Trevor. 'We spent the time driving around the farm, watching people work, and at night we had magnificent dinners in the house with brandy and cigars to finish. It was five days of fine living.'

A bare-chested Colin loads one of the ship's guns.

Above left: A young Colin Grazier wearing his Mediterranean whites.

Above right: All hands to the deck: Colin hauling a rope with a Navy colleague.

It was good to hear that Colin had experienced such good times, but Trevor also had vivid memories of the night Colin prematurely lost his life. Trevor was responsible for one of the *Petard*'s main guns. In fact he was one of the men who opened fire on the U-559 as it rose to the surface. He said he was concentrating so hard on doing his job that everything seemed to happen very quickly. He was not even aware that his friend Colin and the first lieutenant had gone down with the submarine until well after the incident.

It was about half an hour to forty-five minutes from when Colin left the ship that the others came back. I didn't realise at first that he had died and when I heard it was a shock. I felt terrible at losing a friend, but I realised that you are there to fight and people do get lost.

Trevor was delighted that the *Herald* had launched a campaign and added: 'Colin would have been very embarrassed by it at first, although I think he would have felt tremendously proud eventually.'

Our policy of appealing for eyewitness accounts was paying off in style and many more were to follow. At about the same time I received a reply from the Imperial War Museum to my frank letter about its failure to recognise the three men's part in the Enigma story.

Nigel Steel, the museum's head of research, had taken stock of our argument, and to his credit was beginning to open the door slowly to featuring this chapter of history. He said he would be interested in any material, such as letters or other artefacts, relating to the three men or the incident. While not making any promises, he appealed to our readers to send him details of any items of special interest.

CHAPTER TEN

A MUSICAL TRIBUTE

We had unveiled a hero who had touched all their hearts

The musical tribute to Colin Grazier, held in the town's Assembly Rooms on 1 April 2000, was a litmus test for me and the campaign. Up to that point I was pretty sure the story was having a big impact locally and that the Tamworth public was supportive of our efforts. But I knew a lot of interest was coming from all the over the country too, which made it difficult to judge the true extent of feeling in the town. I desperately hoped that local people would turn out to the concert in force. I couldn't face the thought of this event being poorly supported. It would be so insulting to the memories of the men.

We were doing everything in our power to make up for the fact that his heroism had been widely ignored for so long – for people to show they were just not interested would have been unthinkable. We would have some serious questions to ask ourselves. I am a big believer in letting readers decide issues. We had started the campaign because we believed the local community would back it and we knew it would only work if it caught their imagination. It didn't matter how passionate individuals like myself were about Colin Grazier. We needed the backing of the people of Tamworth.

As the day of the concert approached, my head was full of these fears and it was with an increasing sense of panic that I wrote a piece on the front page of the *Herald* urging people to prove they really cared about what these men had achieved. 'This historic occasion should be a proud night for Tamworth when we can celebrate our association with one of the world's greatest heroes,' I wrote in the *Herald* of 30 March 2000:

> I think it will be a moving and memorable occasion and I would appeal for anyone who has not yet planned what they are doing on Saturday night to consider coming along. It is a chance to enjoy some first class entertainment while at the same time show we really care about what this ordinary man from Tamworth did for the world. He gave his life in an act which shortened the war and saved countless lives.

My heart was in my mouth all day on the Saturday of the concert. My fears were exacerbated by the fact that many people would be paying on the door. So the weather could be an influential factor. I kept everything crossed for sun.

It absolutely threw it down on the night of the concert. It was raining so hard that we had to run from the car park to the Assembly Rooms. When I walked through the door with my wife, I held my breath in case the place was empty, but what a wonderful sight greeted me. The Assembly Rooms was packed out. There was a palpable buzz about the place. I felt goosebumps beginning to form. God bless Tamworth people!

Also in the audience were various civic dignitaries. Terry Dix, the leader of Staffordshire County Council, was there, as was the local MP Brian Jenkins and his wife Joan, Tamworth's deputy mayor. But to me the great thing was that the place was brimming with Tamworth people. Nearly 400 of them. And they were even having to turn away people at the door. The stage was decked out with Union Jacks. I had a great feeling that this was going to be a special night for Colin. The atmosphere was like the Last Night of The Proms.

In fact it turned out to be a night that will go down in Tamworth folklore. It was the night that Tamworth paid its first public tribute to its most famous war hero – six decades after his tragic death. He was a man who in real life shunned the limelight, but on that night he was a huge star in the eyes of his adoring public. They came to sing, to listen to the music, to wave their flags and programmes in celebration, but most of all to say thanks to their local hero.

That night they belted out *Rule Britannia, For Those in Peril on the Sea*, and heartily joined in the three cheers to Colin Grazier led by Tamworth Sea Cadets. But the most moving moment of all for me was when the audience stood as one in a minute's silence as a sign of respect. We had unveiled a hero who had touched all their hearts. It was a very special moment.

The Beatles once played in the Assembly Rooms after driving themselves to the venue from Liverpool. Their signatures are believed to be hidden under the plaster on the walls. Now it has another night to proudly look back on.

By the end of the evening more than £1,500 had been raised. The total included nearly £300 from a raffle held on the night and £173 thrown into a bucket near the exit doors.

Standards from the Royal British Legion, the Royal Air Force Association and the Royal Naval Association, were paraded at the start of the concert. The Woolley Pritchard Sovereign Brass Band lived up to its reputation as being one of the top twenty brass bands in the country. The room filled with rousing renditions of traditional and classical pieces, and stirring marches. There was a Glenn Miller section, a solo section and even a mass singalong. Interspersed with the music were snippets of the 'The Colin Grazier Story' narrated by Michael Woolley.

At the end of the evening Tamworth Sea Cadets formed a guard of honour the length of the Assembly Rooms' aisle and the standards were ceremoniously lowered in Grazier's honour. The concert ended poignantly with the *Last Post, Reveille, Sunset* and *Hearts of Oak*, bringing lumps to many throats. Tamworth had done him proud.

I wrote a review of the night which appeared in the next edition of the *Herald* and in an opinion piece I concluded:

> The people of Tamworth have proved that, despite the passage of time, they are determined to honour Colin Grazier in style. On 8 January 1999, the *Herald* pledged to make Grazier's name well known in the town and to raise money for a lasting monument. Thanks to your response, we are now well on the way to spectacularly fulfilling both these promises.

I didn't realise it at the time, but we were only just getting limbered up!

The campaign was in full throttle and a couple of weeks later Colin was honoured again in Tamworth when a £55,000 newly refurbished concert room was named after him. There was hardly a seat to be had at Two Gates Working Men's Club when the brass plaque was unveiled by the deputy mayor, Cllr Joan Jenkins. Sea Cadets and standard-bearers from Tamworth, Lichfield and Atherstone attended the ceremony. The evening kicked off with a faultless marching display led by Jim Welland. The club is just yards from where Colin Grazier lived.

The Assembly Rooms in Tamworth were decked out in flags for the first public tribute to Colin Grazier. The concert in April 2000 was a sell-out.

Above left: Tamworth shows its respect for local hero Colin Grazier with a minute's silence at the town's Assembly Rooms. It was the first time the town had publicly saluted its brave son.

Above right: The late Michael Woolley (left), leader of the Woolley Pritchard Sovereign Brass Band, hands over the proceeds from the musical tribute to Colin Grazier to the author and Ray Jennings who organised the concert. The evening raised £1,500 towards the memorial.

Above left: Colin Grazier's niece, Colleen Mason, who was named after him, pictured with her uncle's personal Bible.

Above right: A close-up of Colin Grazier's Bible, copies of which were issued to all people engaged in the defence of the realm, with a message from King George VI recommending they read the Book as a Divine source of comfort and inspiration.

Band leader Michael Woolley tells the story of Colin Grazier at a concert in his honour attended by hundreds of Tamworth people.

Our fund had reached a wonderful total of £11,500 and we were also getting some fantastic additions to our collection of memorabilia which we hoped would be of interest to the Imperial War Museum. One of the most interesting items was Colin Grazier's Royal Navy Bible owned by his niece Colleen Mason. It was given to Colleen, who was named after Colin, by her father George – Colin's brother. 'If giving the Bible will help towards getting an exhibition then I am happy to lend it,' she said.

Contributions continued to come in with a donation from the HMS *Emerald* Association, made up of men who served in the Atlantic during the Second World War.

CHAPTER ELEVEN

COMIC'S WORLD EXCLUSIVE

To this day, Sheena cannot understand how the story could have appeared in an adventure comic before being officially released by the British

The intense secrecy surrounding the capture of the codebooks from the U-559 meant the details did not surface for many years after the event, and even then it was just a slow trickle of information. In 1976, Gordon Connell, a former gunnery officer on the *Petard*, mentioned papers being taken from the U-559 in his book *Fighting Destroyer*, but at the time was unaware of their massive significance. We had to wait another twelve years to learn the truth about what had been taken. Surely this was *the* best-kept secret of the entire war?

In 1988, Ralph Erskine, an authority on naval signals intelligence, checked with the Public Record Office and Naval Historical Branch before writing about the *Wetterkurzschlüssel* (short weather key) and other documents seized from the U-559 in his paper entitled, 'Naval Enigma: the breaking of the Heimisch and Triton'. But none of the above can claim they were first to break the story to the world – amazingly the plaudits for that go to a boys' adventure comic published in 1969!

How on earth *The Hornet* got hold of the story seems likely to remain as big a mystery as any chapter in the Enigma tale itself. I would love to know the connections the editor of the comic had at the time and his motivation for running the story. It's a puzzle that will probably never be solved, but that schoolboys' comic broke the silence on what happened on the night of 30 October 1942, many years before the Official Secrets Act released its shackles on the truth.

I discovered this bizarre fact from Tony Fasson's sister, Sheena, who described how *The Hornet* of 5 July 1969 told the story in cartoon form on its front page – even revealing the names of the men involved in the top secret incident. It was the first public mention of material being taken from the U-559.

The comic was first given to Tony's older brother in Scotland a few weeks after it came out, when a neighbour's son bought a copy. The illustrations depict how the submarine was spotted on the surface by a British plane on dawn patrol in the Mediterranean. It describes how the news was passed to the Navy's flotilla which then began to attack the U-boat with depth charges. The cartoon, entitled 'The Secrets of the Sea Wolf', does not name the U-boat but does specify that it was the *Petard* which was involved. It goes on to quote the *Petard*'s captain saying, 'It's a chance in a million to grab its secret papers and documents. The Admiralty would be tickled pink.'

Presumably the Admiralty would not have been quite so amused by *The Hornet*'s exclusive. Fasson and Grazier are depicted boarding the sinking sub, where they find 'a goldmine of secret documents'. Tragically the men are lost. But the comic makes it clear 'the Sea Wolf had given up many secrets'. This was pretty sensitive material to reveal – dynamite!

The Hornet dispels any notion of its storyline being fiction by stating at the end that the two brave men involved were Lieutenant Fasson and AB Grazier, who were awarded the George Cross for their heroism in September 1943. 'I was shocked but also horrified when I first saw the comic as this meant the story had been leaked by someone,' said Sheena. Before the magazine was published, the Fasson family was only told that Tony and Colin had drowned in an incident involving a submarine. There had been no mention of sensitive documents being recovered.

Clearly German government officials at the time of publication were not readers of *The Hornet*, or they might have latched onto the possibility that their 'unbreakable' Enigma code had been solved by the enemy. In actual fact, up until the mid-1970s the German authorities continued to believe in the invincibility of their wartime system of scrambling messages. In 1974, Doenitz received the truth from historian Jürgen Rohwer, that the British had broken the German Enigma cipher and had been reading traffic from June 1941 to January 1942 and again from December 1942 until the end of the war. Doenitz replied that he had always held niggling doubts, but after the war had felt reassured of its invincibility by the lack of revelations from the Allied side.

The Hornet, a boys' comic sold for just 5d, gave away top secret information about what really happened on the U-559 in its edition of 5 July 1969.

Above left: The *Petard*'s emblem features the bomb from which it takes its name.

Above right: A nine-year-old Colin standing on the back row (third from right) with his classmates at Two Gates Junior School in about 1931. The picture was sent to the *Herald* by Barbara Sharpe (second row from the bottom, third from left).

To this day Sheena cannot understand how the story could have appeared in an adventure comic before being officially released by the British. She even asked the editor of *The Hornet* at the time, but he said he did not know the source. It is obvious that someone else was determined to give these men their due recognition long before I began to act on their behalf.

I continued to appeal for people's memories of Colin and, like pieces in a jigsaw, fragmented bits of his life kept dropping onto my desk. Colin Grazier was born on 7 May 1920, and joined the Royal Navy on 10 May 1938, as an ordinary seaman. He served on HMS *Ramillies*, HMS *Victory*, HMS *Excellent* and HMS *Hartland* before joining HMS *Petard* in June 1942.

The ship was constructed at Walker's shipyard in Newcastle-upon-Tyne and took two-and-a-half years to build. It was to have been called *Persistent* which would have been an apt choice given its determination to hunt down the U-559. The Admiralty report on the sinking of the U-559 specifically refers to the success of the action being largely due to the ship's 'persistence'. Curiously, for reasons I have never been able to pin down, it ended up taking its name from a 'crude bombing device likely to blow up in one's face'. At least that's how one dictionary defines the meaning of *Petard*.

Three hundred and eighty-eight feet long, HMS *Petard* was a speedy vessel capable of reaching 34 knots. On board was a formidable array of firepower: four 4in guns, a four-barrelled pom-pom, four 20mm Oerlikon (single-barrelled) guns, eight torpedo tubes and 100 depth charges. She weighed over 1,500 tons. The *Petard* was one of eight P-Class destroyers built at roughly the same time. The others were *Pakenham, Paladin, Panther, Partridge, Pathfinder, Penn* and *Porcupine*. Only three, including the *Petard*, were to survive the war.

Tony Fasson and his sister Sheena play together as young children.

Tony Fasson relaxes at home with a faithful friend.

Above left: The last photograph taken of Lieutenant Tony Fasson, in his shorts and cravat, as the *Petard* passed through the Suez Canal.

Above right: Sporting a beard, naval officer Tony Fasson enjoying a moment's respite from the heavy demands of being in charge on a warship.

There were 211 men on board the *Petard* during the conflict, including nine officers. That was around double the peacetime complement and put enormous strain on the ship's accommodation. The *Petard*'s pennant was G-56.

Another of our readers, Barbara Sharpe, sent us a poignant photograph of Colin taken with his classmates in about 1931. The picture was of all the children in Two Gates Junior School. He was about nine years old, just a normal innocent boy. Tragically, he was already nearly half way through his life.

I also received a lovely set of photographs of Tony Fasson from his sister. One showed him as a young boy, another as a young man shaking hands with his pet spaniel, and a third showed the time he briefly sported a beard as a young naval officer.

The most poignant photograph, however, was of him wearing just a pair of white shorts and a cravat. It was taken on the *Petard* as it sailed through the Suez Canal not long before he drowned with Colin Grazier. That was the last photograph taken of Lieutenant Tony Fasson.

Alongside the photographs we published some moving quotes from Sheena, who described her heroic brother as 'a wonderful man with a wicked sense of humour'.

'When he entered a room the whole place glowed,' she said. On a more sombre note she added, 'I'll never forget the day my family heard the terrible news. I was having a meal with my parents when my father took a call from the Admiralty …'

In May 2000, I received a letter from *Dallas Morning News* reporter Yvonne Barlow, the reporter who had previously written about my clash with Hollywood. Yvonne sent me a copy of a review of *U-571* written by America's most prominent film critic, Robert Ebert, which she said vindicated our attack on the movie. Ebert is a film colossus in America and is their equivalent of Barry Norman. He had written a review in the *Mail Tribune* which left no doubt as to his own stance on the film:

> This fictional movie about a fictional US submarine mission is followed by a mention in the end credits of those actual British missions. Oh the British deciphered the Enigma code too. Come to think of it, they pretty much did everything in real life that the Americans do in this movie.

I loved it. Thank you, Robert! This man has clout and he made these points even before the film reached British screens. I included Ebert's comments in an article and not for the first time let rip in the *Herald* with a few choice remarks of my own. I had yet to see the film personally, but launched another public attack on Mostow:

> In my opinion *U-571* should never have focused on a bunch of make-believe Hollywood characters. It should have been a fitting tribute to the actual people whose deaths had massive consequences for the world – the very people whose bravery inspired this movie which, incidentally, is set to rake in millions of dollars. I wonder what the American public would think of a film which claimed the first man on the moon was a chap from Tunbridge Wells?

CHAPTER TWELVE

THAT DEADLY WEAPON – SOAP

*I find it amazing that an ordinary bar of soap can help to cripple a submarine in addition
to its capacity to remove grime and grease from the skin*

During the course of our campaign, the *Tamworth Herald* published many incredible
Enigma stories, but none more bizarre than the account of how one sailor used the most
extraordinary weapon imaginable to bring U-559 to the surface – a bar of soap!

Eric Ashley of Willenhall, in the West Midlands, was a torpedoman on board the *Petard*. He
described how the frantic U-boat crew had resorted to diving to the dangerous depth of more
than 500ft to ensure the *Petard's* depth charges exploded before they could do real damage.
Charge after charge failed to strike home until Eric was instructed to mould the soap in his
hands and force it into the depth charge aperture. Eric explained it along these lines:

> When a depth charge is dropped into the sea, a small aperture running through the middle
> of the depth charge slowly fills with water. When the required depth is reached and as the
> hole fills up, a spring rises to the detonator. The hole was filling up too fast and the depth
> charges were exploding prematurely above the submarine.

Eric explained the remnants of the soap would have to be washed out of the aperture
before it could start filling with water. Hopefully, this delay would mean the depth charge
would be at a much greater depth when the detonator was activated. They gave it a go
and, bingo, it worked first time!

I find it amazing that an ordinary bar of soap can help to cripple a submarine in
addition to its capacity to remove grime and grease from skin. Eric described the scene
after the U-559 was hit. 'The main thing I remember about that night is seeing the
sub come up, with a white donkey painted on the tower and the letters U-559. I can
remember thinking, "Thank Christ we've finally got it to the surface!"'

Once the U-boat surfaced and the survivors had been captured, the *Petard* attached a
tow rope to it with the intention of recovering the vessel. This took place while Grazier
and Fasson were still searching for material. When the submarine started to go under, Eric
was forced to sever the tow rope to prevent the U-boat pulling the *Petard* down with it.
He said:

> I was told to split the tow rope as we were in danger of going down with the sub. I thought
> all our men were off and it wasn't until later that we found out that Grazier and the
> lieutenant were still on board. We had a muster shortly afterwards and realised that the two
> men must have died.

U-559 in the Mediterranean. Courtesy of the Deutsches U-Boot Museum.

German prisoners from the U-559 are led off the *Petard* under armed guard at Haifa to be taken into captivity.

The crew took many German survivors on board, and they were later dropped off at Haifa in Palestine. Eric even managed to get a souvenir from the night. He kept a piece of a lifejacket from one of the Germans. It has an eagle emblazoned on it and the name U-559. Eric contacted us when he heard we wanted memorabilia relating to the incident. The item is currently in storage at Bletchley Park and will hopefully be exhibited there in the future.

The U-559 was built by Blohm and Voss in Hamburg and was commissioned in February 1941. Hans Heidtmann was the commander for all of her ten patrols. Before falling victim to a soaped-up depth charge, the standard Type-VIIC U-boat (one of 661 built) had suffered no previous casualties. But the U-559 had dished out plenty of punishment herself, causing the deaths of hundreds of Allied servicemen in murderous attacks on four supply ships (totalling 11,811 tons). She also sank the Australian destroyer HMAS *Parramatta* (II) on 27 November 1941. Only those on deck survived this bloody torpedo attack. A total of 138 people lost their lives, including all officers, after the *Parramatta* was torn apart by two violent explosions.

CHAPTER THIRTEEN

THE HIGHEST DECORATION

I am satisfied that AB Grazier and his colleague Lt Tony Fasson were granted the appropriate award – the highest decoration which can be awarded for an action not in the presence of the enemy – Secretary of State for Defence, Geoff Hoon

When Walter Czwarkiel, of Dordon, read about the bravery of the Enigma heroes in the *Herald*, he felt he just had to do something for the campaign. So the retired owner of a shop specialising in military collectibles put together a beautifully framed replica collection of the medals that Colin had won. He included a picture of Colin and the *Petard* and a braid from a Royal Navy cap. He then brought the collection to the *Herald*'s offices and presented it to me. 'I've been following the *Herald*'s stories for over a year,' he said. 'It has been fantastic and I just wanted to do something.'

Our initial thought was to offer it to Tamworth Castle as part of a planned exhibition on Colin Grazier. It never came off, however, and the medals remained on public display in the reception area of the *Herald*.

In September 2003, at Mr Czwarkiel's request, I handed the framed medals to Bletchley Park where they are now displayed. Walter's contribution shows how the story grabbed people in different ways. Sixty years after a man's death, hundreds of people felt compelled to act on his behalf – myself included.

In May 2000, the *Herald* commissioned a commemorative plate to recognise Colin Grazier and boost our appeal coffers. The plate was made of English fine bone china and included images of Colin, HMS *Petard*, an Enigma machine and the U-559. John Harper and I sketched out the design of the plate and a few words describing the importance of what Grazier and his shipmates had done.

Meanwhile, the Hollywood controversy was still raging with *U-571* being the current number one film in America. I was contacted by Carlton Television to see if I would do a piece to camera. The next day TV reporter Robin Powell arrived at the *Herald*'s offices with a camera crew. We initially based ourselves in the boardroom and Robin reassured me that we would have a small rehearsal first, telling me not to worry as it was not live. Just as he finished speaking, he received a call from his producer saying to continue with the planned piece for the evening news, but they wanted something immediately for the lunchtime headlines. They had about four minutes to get it done.

There was no time for any rehearsal. Talk about a tight deadline – the interview began the moment I sat down. The lengthier interview was more relaxed – except that Robin insisted on filming it slap bang in the middle of our newsroom.

A commemorative plate depicting Colin Grazier was produced to raise funds for the campaign.

The piece, which included clips from the film and interviews with the main stars, was shown in the Central region and as far away as Oxford. Other interviewees included author Robert Harris, Colin's niece, Colleen Mason, and *Petard* survivor Eric Ashley (the man who had stuffed soap into the depth charge pressure detectors to delay the operation of the mechanism). Eric urged people to boycott the film and to donate the price of the tickets to the appeal fund. This was particularly emotive and sparked a response.

Among those who sent in contributions to us as a result of the television coverage was Philip Elliot OBE, from Great Barr, Birmingham. After watching the news he immediately sent a donation of £100. A former Navy man himself, he said, 'I much appreciated the TV news report last week and compliment you on what you are doing. What Colin Grazier and his comrades did was very important. Just think of the fifty years of life he gave away for us. What he did really mattered.' The television exposure undoubtedly lifted the profile of the campaign.

One of the questions that I am repeatedly asked is why Fasson and Grazier were not awarded the Victoria Cross. I must admit it was something that had puzzled me initially and I was prepared to fight all the way to get their medals upgraded.

It has often been assumed that the George Cross awarded to the two men had been downgraded from the Victoria Cross to prevent the enemy being alerted to the importance of the mission. This is not true, and after discussing the matter with the Imperial War Museum and Royal Navy sources, I am satisfied the men received the appropriate medals, given the technical criteria. A person who receives a Victoria Cross must have been under enemy fire during the heroic deed. I am grateful to Tamworth MP Brian Jenkins who got me the final confirmation of this point from the highest level – the Defence Secretary, Geoff Hoon. And in answering the question, Mr Hoon, speaking on behalf of the Government, acknowledged the importance of the men's actions. This is how he answered Brian's letter questioning why the men had not received the Victoria Cross:

> Their action is widely regarded as having been vital in winning the Battle of the Atlantic, which itself was a precondition for the invasion of Europe in 1944. I am satisfied that AB Colin Grazier and his colleague Lt Tony Fasson were granted the appropriate award – the highest decoration which can be awarded for an action not in the presence of the enemy.

In a newspaper editorial, I stated that I was still at a loss to explain why bravery has to be classified in such a precise way, but given the rules I could not successfully attempt to get the men the Victoria Cross.

My views offended an old soldier who described what it was like to be under fire in an incredibly lucid and graphic way, given the writer was eighty years old. He certainly gave

Central TV reporter Robin Powell interviewing the author about the Colin Grazier Memorial Campaign at the *Herald*'s offices.

me a real sense of the courage required to selflessly help colleagues while guns blazed in all directions. However, I did not need convincing of this as I have great respect for our soldiers who have demonstrated such bravery in various world conflicts.

In my reply, I made the point that courage can also occur when there is no enemy fire present, for example, when a fireman goes into a blazing house to rescue children, or the teacher in Wolverhampton who defended her children from a crazed machete-wielding attacker and was left with terrible wounds.

I also believe Grazier and Fasson realised just how precarious their situation was when they boarded that submarine. The German crew knew there was danger too and were so terrified when fleeing the vessel that they forgot or ignored their orders to throw any secret documents into the sea before abandoning the submarine. Grazier and Fasson entered the U-boat after the crew had escaped, when the risk of its sinking was increasing with every second. Despite the enormous panic that surrounded them, they carried out an exhaustive search of the vessel, ignoring repeated warnings that it was in a perilous position. They got those Enigma documents and the world benefited, but it took levels of courage that I find hard to comprehend.

My problem with the medal issue is this. The Victoria Cross is considered the highest award this country can give to a serviceman. Certainly it is perceived as *the* top honour by the public. I truly believe that Grazier and Fasson deserve the highest award this country can offer. Who can argue with that? Surely the highest honour attainable should be based on the level of bravery involved and its significance, and not on a technicality, such as whether or not it was in the face of enemy gunfire. True courage can occur in a number of guises, but I was forced to accept I could not fight to have the medal upgraded, given the requirements. I remain dissatisfied with how bravery is classified, though, especially when I read that in 1943 the Honours Awards Committee had described the men's actions as 'up to Victoria Cross standard'.

CHAPTER FOURTEEN

HANDS OFF OUR HISTORY

Let's just hope we have kicked up enough fuss to make Hollywood directors think twice in the future. Hands off our history!

When *U-571* was shown in Hollywood for the first time I was faced with a major dilemma. I was the obvious person to review the film for the newspaper and many people were interested in how I would react, having taken the subject so much to heart.

I hoped I would hate the film itself, not just for its theft of a British triumph, but also as a piece of entertainment. How could I promote a film that had done such a disservice to the heroes we were campaigning for? It would really serve my purpose for the film to be an artistic flop. On the other hand I had to give an honest opinion. To my horror, while watching the film I found the action gripping. The submarine sequences were brilliantly filmed and the director managed to create a tangible, claustrophobic tension, especially during the depth charging scenes. Undoubtedly Jonathan Mostow is a brilliant director.

The plot centres on a group of Americans who attack a stricken German U-boat for its Enigma treasures. They are forced to hijack the vessel and end up in a cat and mouse battle with a German destroyer. The film is stronger on action than character, although Matthew McConaughey does a good job as the square-jawed officer who finds himself leading the operation. Harvey Keitel plays his second-in-command, an old seadog. The film contained some farcical moments that I was happy to highlight, such as the ridiculous sequence where a German prisoner, despite being chained up on board the submarine, still manages to escape and wreak havoc. But the truth was this was a very watchable adventure movie and I was going to have to say so.

After some soul searching I did find a way round the problem. I headlined the review, 'A Stunning, but Unforgiveable Film' to immediately set the tone. The sub-heading was a direct quote from my article, 'Insulting is Too Light a Word'.

I launched into the review by stating that *U-571* was 'a breathtaking portrayal of courage and terror at sea during World War Two'. In the next paragraph I pointed out that it was also 'a despicable act of theft on the part of Hollywood and an unforgivable insult to genuine British war heroes'. Then before even mentioning the film I listed the historical facts and stated that I made no apology for such a diversion – 'In this review at least, the facts are going to overshadow Hollywood make-believe!':

One of this country's greatest achievements was the seizure of codebooks from U-boats and the subsequent cracking of Enigma messages at Bletchley Park. The former involved life-sacrificing acts of daring, the latter brilliant minds working under unrelenting pressure. Grazier and his comrades got the key to unlock the code; brilliant individuals such as Alan

Turing were able to capitalise on it. U-boats were destroying our ships at twice the rate they were being built. At the same time the production of German submarines was reaching phenomenal proportions. Once the deciphered messages revealed to the Allies where the U-boats were they picked them off so quickly that Admiral Doenitz, commander of the fleet, completely withdrew the remnants of his wolf packs from the Atlantic. The invasion of Normandy was able to go ahead in 1944. Otherwise it might have been delayed until 1946 when nuclear weapons would have been developed and what would the consequences of that have been?

I threw in all this, plus a lot more. I certainly didn't need motivating. It was appalling that the Americans had made this film and then, in the end credits, mentioned an American ship which had also captured an Enigma machine in the same breath as HMS *Petard*. Even though the British were the first to do this, too. In 1941, David Balme, a twenty-year-old sub-lieutenant, led a boarding party from HMS *Bulldog* onto the U-110 and returned with an Enigma treasure chest including a three-rotor machine and precious documents. Jonathan Mostow paid for him to be flown to Hollywood to be wined and dined. More evidence that his conscience was pricking him? Balme later disclosed that Mostow had told him the story required American heroes to be a commercial success. 'I am at a loss to explain why Hollywood fails to appreciate how much people love a true story,' I continued:

> I am convinced that most people, including Americans, find the truth adds an edge to a storyline. Unfortunately Hollywood's spectacles are emblazoned with stars and stripes. The capture and subsequent cracking of the (naval) Enigma codes were definitive moments of the Second World War, but both were British breakthroughs. So instead of an extraordinary true account, we got Hollywood lies.
>
> Ironically the real life story was made for Hollywood. Able Seaman Colin Grazier had been married for only two days when he left his new bride Olive following a tearful farewell at Tamworth railway station. He was just twenty-two years old with film star looks, and went off to save the world with an incredible act of daring which would have put superman in the shade. Alongside him was the handsome gentleman officer Lt Tony Fasson. And at their side was little Tommy Brown, just sixteen years old, who had lied about his age to get in the Navy. He was the only survivor of the incident which changed the course of world history. He died just two years later in a house fire. Could any story be more dramatic than this?
>
> Hollywood, however, set sail on a fictional course: an American submarine crew is sent on a mission to steal a vital Enigma machine so important that it could change the outcome of the war. [Sounds familiar?] But just to make things really exciting, a bunch of German sailors are sent to help their U-boat compatriots. Oh, and surprise, surprise, the weather throws everything at them too!

While Hollywood has been guilty of stealing other nation's achievements on several occasions, Britain's record is not spotless. The Americans were the first to officially break the sound barrier in 1947, but kept it a military secret for several months. It was finally announced in 1948, the same year the RAF broke the sound barrier and claimed it as a 'first'. In 1952, the British Oscar-winning film *The Sound Barrier* gave the impression that the breakthrough was British in nature. The film won the USA's award for Best Foreign Film of the Year which must have been pretty galling for the US aviators.

In addition the Polish contribution to cracking Enigma codes has often been overlooked by British writers. The British did solve Shark (Bletchley Park's special name for Triton, the four-rotor Enigma codes used by U-boat HQ to communicate with the U-boats), but it was a decade after the Poles had cracked the early Enigma codes.

I was sorry that Mostow ignored my suggestion that Universal Pictures should make a donation to our appeal fund. The film was one of Hollywood's most successful, raking in millions of dollars. A few thousand dollars towards our memorial would have been a mere drop in the ocean to him. Although the end credits did refer to real British missions, I was disgusted that neither our heroes nor the brilliant code-crackers at Bletchley Park warranted a mention. The former gave their lives for the cause, the latter were geniuses who achieved something which even decades later the German government still regarded as humanly impossible.

I still don't know how Mostow had the gall to defend his film with such passion. In his letter to me he described his film as fiction and even underlined the word. I have seen him in subsequent interviews insisting it was not based on American or English events. When grilled on television he is a slick performer, skilled at dodging the most persistent questions and at defending the indefensible. I'm convinced that if the Americans had achieved what the British had during the Second World War the film would have opened with the caption, 'Based on True Events'.

Secretary of State for Culture, Media and Sport Chris Smith added his voice to the growing chorus of disapproval, as the film swept across Britain. During an interview with *GMTV* he said:

> I was at Bletchley Park a couple of weeks ago, looking at where the Enigma machine ended up and the work that was done, fantastic work, to shorten the war by months by the heroism of people who stole the machinery. Then to tell us that it was the Americans who did this is a little galling. It's something I will be taking up with colleagues in Hollywood next time I see them. I think that one of the things that needs to be made clear is yes, you're in the entertainment business, but when people see your movies they're going to come away thinking that it's information, not just entertainment.

Fine sentiments indeed! I only hope he did have that word with Hollywood. However, I doubt that it had any impact because in 2004 I heard that Hollywood was planning to bring out a movie on the Battle of Britain. Yes, you've guessed it – the 'true' heroes were to be a squadron of American pilots. Let's just hope we have kicked up enough fuss to make Hollywood directors think twice in the future. Hands off our history!

Government heavyweights such as Geoff Hoon and Chris Smith had already backed our heroes, and now it was time to bring them to the attention of the top man himself,

Prime Minister Tony Blair. The link was to be Tamworth MP Brian Jenkins and again the controversial *U-571* film was the catalyst.

Tony Blair's acknowledgement of the significance of what Grazier did came about after a group of MPs tabled a Commons motion calling for a boycott of *U-571* on the grounds that it 'detracted from the valour of the British sailors concerned'. Mr Blair was responding to a point made by Brian Jenkins during Prime Minister's Questions. Mr Jenkins asked:

> Does my right honourable friend agree with my constituents and the many ex-servicemen that the Hollywood film *U-571*, which portrays American sailors retrieving the Enigma machine and codes, is an affront to the memory of British sailors who lost their lives in this action? I refer in particular to Lieutenant Tony Fasson and Tamworth-born Colin Grazier. They were both awarded the George Cross posthumously, and were both local heroes.

Mr Blair responded: 'The two people he mentions fought with great distinction and bravery. Of course, we honour their memory. We hope that people realise that those were people who sacrificed their lives in order that this country remained free.' Afterwards Brian told us he was delighted to have flagged up Grazier's name at the highest level. He said: 'Colin Grazier was a very young man, who lost his life committing an act of bravery. His was the sort of story that couldn't be made up, and this film should not be passed off as a work of fiction. The local community can also feel aggrieved.'

Our coffers had swelled to around £12,000 in June 2000 with the most recent donations coming from Swindon and the Isle of Man. Most of these had contained angry notes about the Hollywood film.

Following renewed appeals for new material on the Enigma story, Colin Grazier's second cousin, Beryl Bauer, provided us with a gem of a picture. It was on the cover of a postcard which Colin had sent to her from Australia. Written in his own hand, the cover is a photograph of him and a naval colleague while on leave in Australia. It was taken on the Harbour Bridge in Sydney in about 1940. We have never discovered the identity of the man pictured with him. Beryl says Colin was more like a 'big brother' to her. 'I loved him dearly,' she said. 'He taught me how to play darts, dominoes and cards. He even taught me how to swim at Tamworth baths.'

Beryl's family used to own the Hatters Arms in Warton village and it was always the first place that Colin would visit when he came home on leave. Beryl always looked forward to seeing him. 'Colin was a wonderful character with a wonderful nature. He treated everyone the same. He had a good sense of humour and was always up to tricks.' Beryl compared his looks to the actor Victor Mature. Interestingly, Colin once told her that he had been invited to Hollywood once the war was over. She is still uncertain whether he was joking or not.

Colin wrote to Beryl at least every other week, while he was at sea. 'He was always encouraging me to make the most out of school and do really well. He was thrilled when I got my scholarship for Atherstone Grammar School. He would never say where he was or what he was doing though.' Beryl says the family is proud of the role he played in shortening the war. 'We are in awe that he volunteered to do something like this, but looking back that was Colin all over.'

Right: Colin visited Sydney with a shipmate and had a picture of them taken on the Harbour Bridge for a postcard which he sent to his second cousin Beryl Heathcote in Tamworth.

Below: The other side of the postcard sent to Beryl with the caption, 'Looking down on Sydney from the top of the Harbour Bridge,' and signed by Colin.

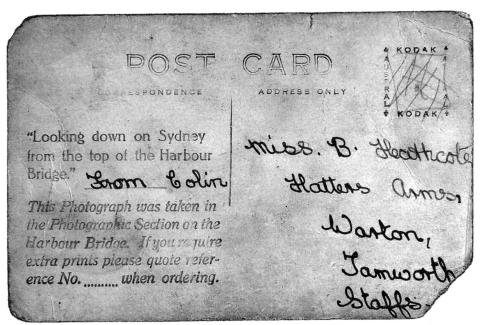

Beryl is incredibly happy that the men have now gained proper recognition. Grazier's name is so well known today that she has become something of a celebrity in Tamworth. When she moved home, her partner John introduced her to the new neighbours as, 'Beryl, Colin Grazier's second cousin'.

Beryl's celebrity status was also heightened when she was invited to appear in a Channel Five programme hosted by Gloria Hunniford. The *Herald* also played a significant part in the show, providing much of the background information. Researchers from *Open House with Gloria Hunniford* sent a car to our offices to pick up a thick wad of *Herald* articles.

Once again the Hollywood film was at the centre of the debate and Beryl was invited to give her views via a telephone link. Guest speakers were the film critic Alexander Walker and Dr Julian Lewis MP, who in 2002 was made Shadow Defence Minister with responsibility for the Royal Navy. Dr Lewis pointed out the historic inaccuracies and said: 'In 1942 two extraordinarily brave seamen refused to come out of a U-boat until they had retrieved as much information as possible. This resulted in them being taken to the bottom with the ship.'

I didn't realise it at the time but Dr Lewis had also been taking the fight to Hollywood and played a big role in at least getting a reference to the British seamen at the end of the film. David Balme, the first man to capture an Enigma machine, comes from Dr Lewis' constituency and knows him well. Julian later invited Beryl Bauer and me to an unforgettable day at the House of Commons.

In front of the television cameras, Alexander Walker remained unaffected by the rewriting of history. 'It's a fictional film and I rate it very highly, even better than *Gladiator*,' he said.

As a newspaper we had been successful in piecing together Grazier's personality and appearance, through publishing photographs and memories, and thanks to one of our committee members we even managed to bring his house back. If the old cottage had remained intact I would have loved to have seen it established as a mini-heritage centre. Sadly, Colin's home, like his ship, had long since been destroyed.

One of our committee members, Mary Edwards, is a talented artist and has produced many historical paintings of the old Tamworth she once knew. She was very familiar with the row of cottages in Two Gates where Colin and his family lived and decided to sketch out the scene. The pencil drawing is now the only record of a group of houses demolished in the 1970s and is testimony to both her artistic ability and power of memory. The cottages stood on Watling Street near to the crossroads of the Tamworth and Dosthill Road (A51). It is where Colin was brought up and lived right up until his marriage to Olive.

'Nobody seemed to know where Colin lived, but I did, even though it had been pulled down,' said Mary. 'We couldn't find anyone to produce a picture of the site so I decided to draw it from memory. I've tried to be as accurate as I can.' Colin's terraced cottage can be seen in Mary's picture with the front door open, and Colin is the small boy coming out of a shop.

A drawing by Mary Edwards of the cottages in Two Gates, Tamworth, where Colin Grazier lived as a boy. Colin is seen outside the shop. The Graziers' house is the one with the door open.

Mary went to the same school as Colin and she can clearly remember seeing him around the village. Mary's role on the committee was not just confined to recreating Grazier's home. She was an influential member of the committee and, despite being in her eighties, could certainly command attention.

I remember an incident which clearly demonstrates her strength of character. The issue of where to place the sculpture commemorating the three Enigma heroes took up a great deal of our time. We were determined to secure the best spot in Tamworth and I spent much time dealing with this matter. Throughout the campaign I invited representatives from the borough council to attend our monthly committee meetings in the *Herald* boardroom. Almost without exception they became as hooked on the story as the rest of us were.

Our two preferred locations for the monument were the Castle Grounds and St Editha's Square – the two most sensitive spots in Tamworth. We believed anywhere else would be sidelining our heroes who were already woefully in the shadows. On many occasions I had reminded the committee that we should never become sidetracked by lesser locations, something Mary took on board in a big way.

At one of our meetings, a council official was asked to give an update on our choice of sites for the memorial. His manager had given the unfortunate chap a couple of alternative suggestions to relay back to us. The first suggestion was a roundabout near to Sainsbury's, just yards from the *Herald*'s building. Despite its proximity to our offices, I thought this was a hideous idea. It was away from the old heart of the town and would be surrounded by busy traffic and almost impossible to walk to. Getting to the monument to read the plaque and quietly contemplate what these men had achieved or to lay a wreath would be a nightmare. The location was also noisy and lacked dignity. It would have been insulting to Grazier and his colleagues.

I was storing all this up to say once the man from the council had completed his pitch. Mary, though, put an abrupt end to the suggestion with one word and one gesture. The man had barely finished speaking when she brought down her fist so hard on the table that we all jumped in unison; simultaneously she roared, 'Noooooooo!'

You could tell by her expression she was not to be argued with and that was the last time we were ever urged to consider low-key positions for our memorial. Don't get the impression, though, that Mary is a fire-breathing dragon. Nothing could be further from the truth. She is a gentle, charming woman who like the rest of us cares deeply about this story. She just wasn't prepared to compromise on location.

To enhance the main monument, we commissioned a handsome bronze plaque to attach to its steel base. It was created by Wiltshire-based Peter Hicks Associates which has worked on a number of high-profile projects throughout the country. The plaque alone cost £1,000 and contained embossed images of Colin, U-559, HMS *Petard* and an Enigma machine. It tells briefly the importance of the codebooks which Grazier, Fasson and Brown retrieved from the U-559. We also spent £500 (from the proceeds of Jim Welland's raffle) on a resin replica of the bronze plaque to be placed on a brick plinth on a new housing estate named after Colin Grazier in 2003.

CHAPTER FIFTEEN

CHAMPIONS OF ENGLAND

It was the equivalent of Torquay winning the FA Cup

The *Herald* received some excellent news in July 2000 which was to direct more attention on the story of the Enigma heroes. A few weeks earlier I had spent a great deal of time painstakingly entering our campaign for the most prestigious awards in the UK's newspaper industry, the Regional Press Awards organised by the *Press Gazette*. The awards that year attracted big-name sponsors including Camelot, Virgin and Sheaffer.

Over forty judges, including several national newspaper editors, had spent two days at the Press Association in London debating and discussing the merits of the entries. We were absolutely thrilled to discover that we were down to the last six in the Campaign of the Year category for the whole of the UK.

What makes the Regional Press Awards so sought-after, and consequently so competitive, is the fact that no allowances are made for size or stature of individual newspapers. So we were not just up against every weekly newspaper in the UK but were also pitched against every evening title in England, Scotland, Ireland and Wales. It meant we were taking on the giants of the industry whose resources dwarfed our own. Even to get on the shortlist is a big honour and, despite the cost of each ticket for the ceremony at the London Hilton being well into three figures, newspapers often book an entire table just on the basis of being nominated.

I thought we had won our cup final just getting to London. The *Herald* had never been on this shortlist before. It was to turn out to be the most incredible day of my career to date, but I came within a whisker of missing it. The day before the awards ceremony I was struck down with a violent sickness bug which I later discovered had affected several other colleagues. There did not seem any way I would get to London the following day. I was as weak as a kitten and at 5.30 a.m. I was still lying on the bathroom floor in a cold sweat.

Herald editor Sam Holliday and I had arranged to meet at Tamworth Railway Station at about 9.45 a.m. At 8 a.m. I called him to tell him to just carry on if I didn't turn up for the train. Somehow I managed to drag my suit on and drive via a chemist to the station. I looked and felt awful, but I was determined to try to get something out of the day.

When we arrived at the Hilton we were met by a waitress offering us a glass of champagne and the managing director of Northcliffe Newspapers, Alec Davidson, came over for a chat. Northcliffe had recently bought the *Herald* and we were now part of one of the biggest newspaper empires in the country including the *Daily Mail* and *Mail on Sunday*. Lord Rothermere is the chairman of the group and Alec Davidson was his right-hand man at the time.

When Mr Davidson met me he must have wondered how I could have possibly steered the campaign to the last six in the country. I felt so ill, I could hardly utter a word. My shirt was open and my tie was loose. I did a lot of nodding, probably in all the wrong places, and said very little. I looked as dishevelled as Ken Dodd.

The main awards room was dripping with chandeliers. There were gifts including Sheaffer pens at every place setting. I must have appeared to be the fussiest eater in Britain that day. I am told the meal was excellent but I could only play with the food on my fork and hardly ate a thing. At one point I took a tiny sip of wine and instantly regretted it. Just then a woman journalist from Glasgow asked me what I thought of the wine. I couldn't tell her I was in no mood to judge, so to fob her off I said, 'Wonderful'. 'We think it is absolutely foul,' she said, scrutinising me closely for a few seconds.

The ceremony was compèred by ITV's nightly news presenter Dermot Murnaghan. When it came to our category he gave a summary of each shortlisted campaign and I was proud to see a *Herald* front page reproduced on an enormous screen. Our rivals for the trophy were predictably heavyweights and had seemingly brought along all their executives. They included the *Sunday Life Belfast*, *South Wales Echo*, *Western Daily Press* and the *Nottingham Evening Post*.

Then came those immortal words, 'And the winner is … [I was resigned to it being one of the big boys as Dermot opened the white envelope] … the *Tamworth Herald*, and here to receive the award is deputy editor Phil Shanahan who masterminded the campaign.'

Our table was instantly bathed in spotlights as I staggered to my feet. As Sam and I made our way to the stage with *Simply the Best* blaring out of the PA system, we found ourselves walking towards huge projected live images of our faces. Given the way I was looking and feeling at the time it was not the best sight in the world for me! En route to collect the award I kept bumping into various groups of people sitting at circular tables, all of whom responded by thumping me on the back – a dangerous gesture given the way I was feeling.

'Please God don't let me be sick on the stage!' I thought. We collected the award from the editor of the *Press Gazette*, Philippa Kennedy, who told us the decision had been close but unanimous amongst the judges, which she said was a rare occurrence. I make no apology for describing all the above in such detail. The *Tamworth Herald* had just scooped the biggest honour in its 132-year history. We were the campaigning newspaper of the year for the whole of the United Kingdom and could say so on our masthead. It was the equivalent of Torquay winning the FA Cup!

I also think that the campaign category is one of the most satisfying to win. When Ian Dowell retired as editor of the *Birmingham Evening Mail* a few years ago he was asked to list the three most important things a newspaper can do. 'Campaign, campaign and campaign,' he replied. Having just won this award I was very happy to agree. I sat clutching that trophy on the train home and I felt wonderful despite feeling absolutely lousy. When I returned home, however, I received some sad news which brought me back down to earth with a bump. My uncle Frank had died in a London hospital after suffering a stroke.

Not surprisingly, the following week's *Herald* was full of the news of this fine victory. We used a big picture on the front page under the heading, 'Simply the best – in England, Ireland, Scotland and Wales,' and we devoted an entire page to the award inside. We all felt a great sense of achievement and champagne corks were popping in the office.

Above left: The trophy for the UK's Campaigning Newspaper of the Year comes home to Tamworth. *Herald* managing director Stuart Burkinshaw is pictured holding the trophy with Phil Shanahan. It was a champagne occasion in the newsroom.

Above right: The billboard says it all. It was the biggest honour in the *Herald*'s history.

The award attracted more attention to our work and I was interviewed about the success of the campaign on local radio. I felt confident that we would go on to do a lot more for these men. We were now involved in the 'Best Newspaper Campaign in Britain' but it is true to say that we were to go on and achieve far more spectacular results than those which had gained us this particular accolade.

The following year another underdog collected the top campaigning trophy. Don Hale, the editor of the *Matlock Mercury*, accepted the award for his determined fight to free convicted murderer Stephen Downing. Don had long held serious doubts about the safety of the conviction and was influential in getting his man out of prison. The part of Don Hale was played in a TV drama by the actor Stephen Tomkinson.

A few weeks after our national triumph I was contacted by Julian Lewis MP who made a generous donation to our fund. Colin's relative, Beryl Bauer, had been sending him *Herald* cuttings on a regular basis since meeting him on Gloria Hunniford's TV programme. Explaining why he had sent a donation, Dr Lewis said, 'I firmly believe that these two men should be remembered as the bravest of the brave.'

At the same time we were contacted by the local organisers of the Campaign For Real Ale group (CAMRA) who wanted to produce a Colin Grazier Ale dedicated to our hero at Tamworth's forthcoming beer festival. Representing the Tamworth and Sutton branch of CAMRA, Geoff Cross and Chris Fudge explained that a donation was to be made to our fund from every glass of beer sold from this range. It was more excellent news for us, especially as another five ales were also to be named on the Enigma theme.

We decided to run a competition for our readers to suggest names for these other ales in return for a string of prizes including a free pass to the festival, a commemorative glass and, of course, a bottle of Colin Grazier Ale. 'Colin's story has captured the hearts of many people and we wanted to link the festival with something in the town,' explained Geoff.

Twenty barrels of Colin Grazier Ale were to be produced by the famous Bass brewery in Burton-on-Trent with three going to the festival. Fittingly its alcohol content was set at 4.2 per cent to coincide with the year Colin retrieved the codebooks (1942). The other ales were brewed by the Old Cottage Brewery in Burton Bridge, Eccleshall Brewery, Beowulf in Yardley, More Beer in Somerset and the Church End Brewery in Shustoke.

I was invited to be a judge on the beer festival panel (something I have very little memory of). I remember thinking it was ironic that Grazier was to have a real ale named after him, given his preference for drinking neat vinegar. I told the organisers that on no account should the brewers be influenced by Colin's preferences for taste!

The diverse ways in which we would gain fresh insights into the story never ceased to amaze me. When we started selling Grazier plates, people would often have a particular reason for making an order and would enclose a written note about themselves. It turned out, for example, that a man living in Sutton Coldfield was one of a handful of men still alive who were on board the *Petard* the night it attacked the U-559. Leslie Hemus enclosed a note with his plate order saying he remembered seeing Colin around the ship on numerous occasions and had formed a high opinion of him:

> Colin wasn't a talkative fellow, but I saw him around a lot and he seemed like a nice bloke. It was terrible that he died because he was so young and had only just got married. He worked on a different deck to me, so I did not know him that well. I saw more of the officer who also died, Lt Anthony Fasson. He had reason to reprimand me once which he did firmly and fairly. He was a brilliant officer who was well respected by all the men.

The campaign was like one long chain reaction. Something big would happen and that would spark another major milestone. It was certainly the case when the *Press Gazette* decided to send a reporter from London to interview me for a national feature about the 'Best Campaign in Britain'.

Mary Stevens spent a morning with me at the *Herald* and I took her through all our cuttings to date. She was very enthusiastic and the article filled an entire page in the *Press Gazette*. It certainly captured the passion I had for the story. In fact, it did that rather too well, using the term 'obsession'. I didn't know which was my overriding emotion, being flattered or a little insulted.

The *Press Gazette* has a national audience and it wasn't long before the chain reaction effect produced another honour, not just for myself but also for the genuine heroes of this story. Among those who read the *Press Gazette* piece was former journalist Ella Glazer OBE, a founder member of the Celebrities Guild of Great Britain. The Guild raises money for good causes by organising events attended by some of the biggest names in sport, politics, drama, television and film.

The highlight of the year is a lavish ceremony in London attended by many stars at which just six awards are handed out to Britain's unsung heroes. Ella told me the Guild had decided to make its first ever posthumous award to Grazier, Fasson and Brown. After reading the *Press Gazette* story, the committee had decided that I should receive the award on behalf of the three men, because of my work connecting all three of them. She said the award would be presented by a 'household' name in front of a celebrity audience of around 350. The musical tribute to Colin Grazier was the first public celebration of the men in Tamworth and now they were to be celebrated nationally.

Shortly after hearing this exciting news, the *Herald* released the names of the ales to be introduced at the forthcoming beer festival. In addition to Grazier Ale, there would be Enigma Variation, Grazier's Glory, Two Gates Tribute, Ale the Hero and U-559 (a great beer to sink!)

John Harper, Rob Tanner and I were first to try the new Grazier Ale at the *Herald*'s offices. I've always been partial to a glass of real ale, but I am not in the habit of drinking beer at 9 a.m. at work. But that was the case when Geoff Cross and Gary Clay, from CAMRA, turned up in reception with the first of the bottled variety. We certainly got some strange looks from people in reception who must have had their preconceptions about journalists emphatically confirmed. The bottles were handsomely decorated with a label which *Herald* graphic artist Chris Patterson had designed. Geoff introduced it as a 'really tasty ale with a combination of hops that makes it unique'. He also gave me a few pointers on how to appreciate real ale in time to be a judge at the beer festival. I learned a lot that morning despite the fact that I had been in training for years for such an event.

The beer festival turned out to be a huge success with over 4,000 pints being downed. After plenty of careful consideration, taking into account aroma, colour, clarity, condition and, of course, taste, Two Gates Tribute (one of the beers named in honour of Grazier) was declared the winner. Colin Grazier Ale also proved a hit and we benefited from a £100 share in its profits. Thankfully, I took a taxi home that night, having decided to take my role as a judge very seriously indeed. Following such dedication to the cause, I was in no shape to drive.

Above left: A beer named after Colin Grazier was produced in his honour for a Campaign for Real Ale festival in Tamworth.

Above right: The *Herald*'s Phil Shanahan, John Harper and Rob Tanner, sup an early morning beer named after Colin Grazier with CAMRA representatives Geoff Cross and Gary Clay.

CHAPTER SIXTEEN

THE TIDE TURNS

Dominating all our power to carry on the war, or even keep ourselves alive, lay our mastery of the ocean routes and free approach and entry to our ports – Winston Churchill

We branded our series of eyewitness accounts of the events of 30 October 1942 'Survivors' Stories' and produced a special logo with the line, 'I was there the day a Tamworth man helped to change the course of history!' Sometimes I had to check myself about using phrases like that in case I could be accused of going over the top, but it really did sum up the significance of the action.

In September 2000, we spoke to another survivor, Jack Hall, who had served on HMS *Petard* as a submarine detector. Jack, who lived in Southampton, volunteered for the Navy in 1941 when he was just eighteen. It was his job to be on the lookout for enemy submarines and warn of where they were heading. He had vivid memories of the exhaustive attack on U-559:

> It was not my watch at the time and of course it was noon when we first started depth-charging it. It was such a beautiful day. The sea was as calm as anything and it was not chaotic at all.
>
> The depth charges were being dropped, and I was standing on the bridge watching as the mud from the bottom of the sea was being disturbed. Lt Tony Fasson shouted up to me, 'the maggots are coming up now' as a bit of a joke. He was a great guy.
>
> We dropped the scramble net ready to catch the U-559's survivors when the sub surfaced. We already had the boat for the boarding party ready. When U-559 surfaced, it was hit again and a big hole appeared in its conning tower. It all became a bit chaotic when the survivors started coming on board. Some of them were in a right state.
>
> I knew that some of our men had boarded the U-559, but I didn't witness them going on myself. The next thing I saw were the lights on the sub go out as it started to go down. Shortly afterwards, the boat returned and Tommy Brown told us that we had lost the lieutenant and Colin. It was devastating news, absolutely devastating. They should have come out of the sub, but they were so intent on getting everything they could lay their hands on.

Jack did not appreciate the importance of the events of that night until decades afterwards:

> We had no idea of what had been salvaged. The stuff was taken to the captain's cabin and took three weeks to get to Bletchley Park. When I found out, I realised it was more important than we could ever have imagined. Bletchley might just have been disbanded and possibly the war lost, or at least extended for much longer had it not been for the *Petard's* Tony Fasson, Colin Grazier and Tommy Brown.

Jack served on the *Petard* until September 1943 and was involved in many other key actions including the sinking of the Italian submarine, *Uarsciek*. He was eventually forced to leave the ship after being injured by an exploding shell and spent three months recovering. It was an horrific incident which has remained engraved on his memory all his life. Years later, Jack described in the *Herald* what happened to him:

> There was a shower of sparks, and then darkness. I knew we had been hit but I didn't stop to think. I darted into the starboard passage where emergency lighting had come on, blowing more air into my lifebelt in case of abandoning ship. Imagine my horror when I saw blood bubbling from a hole in my chest. I was literally breathing through that hole. I made my way to the sick bay above where the medical officer, a short Irish man [William Prendergast] saved my life by stopping the blood flow and dressing my wounds. He gave me an injection as I was in a state of shock.
>
> Shrapnel had entered my side and come out at the front and another had torn a groove across my back. Three other men had fared much worse. Two had been blown to bits and a man was detailed to gather up their pieces into hammocks to be stitched up for burial at sea. Another was so badly injured that he had to be transferred to a hospital ship and another had his arm badly injured.

The tragedy may well have been the result of friendly fire, with HMS *Warspite* being the most likely suspect, during a ferocious battle between British ships and German aircraft in the Gulf of Salerno. The event was also recorded in Reg Crang's diary:

> And then it happened. A 6in shell probably from the *Warspite*, exploded in the forward seamen's mess deck, right amongst the ammunition supply party to A and B guns. Two ABs [able seamen] were killed instantly and six others wounded, three seriously. It was a great shock to the crew but the defence of the ship had to be maintained. The air attacks went on and the guns continued to fire and ward them off.

Reg later added a sequel to that diary entry:

> Jack Hall, one of the badly wounded, was able very much later to tell us what happened to him. He was flown to a field hospital in Syracuse for initial treatment and then to other hospitals in North Africa. He made a good recovery for several months and was then shipped home to the UK to resume his naval service.
>
> Because he had lost all his personal gear in the action, he reported to the Asdic School at Dunoon in army battle dress, the only uniform available. He was quickly noticed by the Master-at-Arms. He asked aggressively why Jack was not in naval uniform. Jack bravely told the MAA that if he would only 'get out there where the real war was instead of playing the part of a barrack stanchion' he would understand the reason. Of course the MAA would not stand for this and Jack was promptly put in the captain's report. However, the captain was sympathetic and let him off lightly which is nice to know.

Jack later joined another destroyer, HMS *Middleton*, which also survived the war. He told us that it was as if he had his own guardian angel looking after him during those years. It's just so tragic that having survived all this he was eventually to lose his life in a car crash in 2006. But he had lived his life to the full and in later years became a valuable member of the Southampton branch of the Jubilee Sailing Trust where other members still fondly remember him and his tales of amazing adventures at sea.

Jack sent us a picture taken by Robert de Pass of German prisoners from the U-559 being taken ashore at Haifa. I am not sure whether any other photograph of this exists. He also fully supported our stance with the Imperial War Museum and suggested that Bletchley Park needed more material on this particular chapter in history. Jack was of the opinion that HMS *Bulldog's* role in the war had grabbed all the limelight in the annals of history, effectively stealing the *Petard's* thunder.

Speaking of his time on the *Petard*, Jack added, 'I am pleased to have been part of it. I made some wonderful friends. I was very lucky to survive and every day I have lived since has been a bonus.' I am sure that Jack would have been delighted to hear that an exhibition dedicated to the *Petard's* role in the Enigma story has now been opened at Bletchley Park.

His views on HMS *Bulldog* resonated with me because I have long felt that the ship has enjoyed the lion's share of the limelight, despite the fact it was the *Petard's* booty which sparked the breakthrough into Shark traffic. Don't get me wrong; the *Bulldog* rightly claims to have been involved in a very significant chapter in the Enigma story. In fact to describe it as one of the most significant incidents in the Second World War would be no exaggeration.

I am simply in awe of the courage of David Balme, a sub-lieutenant on HMS *Bulldog*, who at the age of twenty led a boarding party onto the captured German submarine U-110 in 1941. Balme is a British legend. He became the first person to seize an Enigma machine, along with documents containing secret settings and procedures for the transmission of coded naval messages. Grazier and Fasson did not live to describe the terror of being on an enemy U-boat that could sink at any moment. Balme did and his graphic description of how he felt at the time makes me admire him and the *Petard* men even more.

Balme's courage was definitely on a par with the men we were fighting for and it would be wrong to turn this into some sort of competition between them. We should be equally proud of them. But I feel the need to reposition the spotlight as I agree that the *Petard's* story has often played bridesmaid to the *Bulldog's*. It has been widely ignored while the significance of the U-110 capture has even been highlighted by Bill Clinton.

As far as I am aware, no American president has yet commented on the importance of Grazier, Fasson or Brown. Perhaps one day the likes of George Bush will visit their memorial in Tamworth to make up for that. I'm not sure if that will ever happen, but I'm certain that if it did, it would be no more than the crew of the *Petard* deserve. Some of them still feel the *Bulldog's* capture of Enigma material has been allowed to overshadow their own ship's achievements. If you put the Enigma story into its historic context, it is easy to understand their frustration on this matter. Without the *Petard's* triumph over the U-559, we may never have won the Battle of the Atlantic, and capitalised on David Balme's heroism.

In the first half of 1940, the Nazi U-boats were running riot in the Atlantic, so much so that it was dubbed their 'Glücklichzeit' (lucky time). Churchill knew the way to victory was to outwit them but the odds at that time were stacked heavily in the enemy's favour.

We needed to know what their commanders were saying and frustratingly the U-boats were incredibly 'chatty', routinely signalling where they were and what they were going to do. They reported on the weather, their fuel situation and even how many torpedoes they had left.

If only we could eavesdrop on them. The problem, of course, was that their Morse code messages had been scrambled by their incredibly complex Enigma machines and were utterly baffling to prying ears. The ingenious electro-mechanical machine, which looked like a typewriter, employed a system of three rotors (later extended to four) which shuffled messages to such a degree that they could only be unscrambled by a person on the receiving end employing exactly the same set-up. They would also require the prearranged key setting (which was changed regularly) to understand any communication. To British ears those Morse code messages were as incomprehensible as baby-babble.

Any intelligence that was gleaned from these transmissions was dubbed Ultra (ultra secret) in Britain and sent only to top officials such as members of the war cabinet and military chiefs, but the progress made at Bletchley often came too late to save ships and lives.

After the occupation of France which began in May 1940, the Germans were able to set up bases in ports such as St Nazaire (where incidentally the U-559 was once based). Logistically this meant their range was considerably extended and they could remain out on their murderous ocean patrols for far longer. Wolf packs preferred to converge on convoys at night and fire their torpedoes under the cover of darkness. Their periscopes were hard enough to spot in daylight. After the sun went down they were nigh on impossible to detect. There was little defence against them. Britannia did not rule the waves – Hitler did.

An average of 311,000 tons of Allied shipping was sunk per month between September 1941 and February 1943, with very few U-boats being destroyed in return. If it had been a game of cricket, the Germans would have been close to declaring. The pressure was increasing on Bletchley to make sense of U-boat chit-chat. Intelligence chiefs, receiving radio traffic deciphered at Bletchley Park, were desperate to tell convoys bringing essential supplies to Britain from America where they could avoid or attack U-boats. Too often it was a case of closing the stable door after the horse had bolted.

Bletchley's knowledge, however, was slowly building up. Information passed on by the Poles about the wiring of the military Enigma machine provided the first clues as to how it worked, and the seizure of Enigma codebooks from German weatherships led to a deeper understanding. A raid on the weathership *Muenchen*, for example, was to provide cryptanalysts with the June 1941 naval Enigma settings, enabling them to break the three-rotor naval Enigma cipher known as Heimisch (home waters). This allowed Bletchley's codebreakers to read German Navy Enigma messages at the same time that they were deciphered by the enemy. Previously it had taken Bletchley an average of ten days to derive the meaning from those messages.

An early insight into the workings of Enigma was also gained from a set of rotors taken from the pockets of a German U-boat sailor who forgot to throw them into the sea after the U-33 was destroyed in the Firth of Clyde. The clues were mounting up, but Bletchley really needed a lot of material in one go to begin to prise away Germany's grip on the Atlantic. It was made blindingly clear to every naval captain that getting material from U-boats was a top priority. But the Germans were constantly moving the goalposts as far as their Enigma system was concerned, making it ever more difficult to comprehend.

An up-to-date Enigma machine was desperately needed. Not only a machine, but ideally also entire sets of orders for the codebreakers to really get their teeth into and from which they could extract decrypts. An entire month's worth of Enigma settings would be just what the doctor ordered. If Bletchley could be handed the current day's Enigma key setting, plus all the accompanying tables and signals, it would be on its way to a major breakthrough. Capturing a U-boat with its Enigma documents intact was thus a top priority. Such a capture would require lorry loads of guts and mountains of luck. Fortunately neither was in short supply when HMS *Bulldog* stumbled upon the U-110, a vessel jam-packed with the all latest Enigma hardware and software.

On 9 May 1941, three destroyers, *Bulldog*, *Broadway* and the corvette *Aubretia*, were escorting a convoy south of Iceland, when *Bulldog's* Asdic operator reported contact with a U-boat. An awesome depth charge bombardment followed as the ships turned the tables on the U-110.

The submarine was soon damaged and Kapitanleutnant Fritz-Julius Lemp gave the order to blow the tanks. The wounded U-110 quickly surfaced, causing an angry bubbling of seawater. Its appearance did not win any sympathy votes amongst the British. *Bulldog's* captain, Joe Baker-Cresswell, reacted to the sight of his enemy in a way entirely in keeping with the name of his ship. In a blind rage, he decided to ram the enemy submarine.

Lemp still had blood on his hands after two fresh kills on the thirty-five-strong convoy. He was one of the most successful but controversial U-boat captains. The day after war had begun, he sank the passenger liner *Athenia*, causing the loss of 112 lives. The incident, 250 miles off Inishtrahull in Northern Ireland, was against the international rules of war at sea. It was also the first U-boat kill of the war. Lemp, regarded as something of a loose cannon, claimed he had mistaken the ship travelling from Glasgow to Montreal for an armed merchant cruiser. The vessel was carrying many women and children and the dead included twenty-eight neutral Americans.

Just in time to avoid a collision with the U-110, Baker-Cresswell remembered the value of preserving a U-boat. He completely 'lost it' for a moment, but he regained his composure in the nick of time.

Broadway, however, continued her own angry lunge towards the U-boat. Baker-Cresswell was horrified and in an act of desperation grabbed a loudhailer and screamed at the destroyer to stop. *Broadway* was in fact attempting another depth charge attack but the windows on the bridge had been damaged by her own gunfire and the captain, Lieutenant Commander Thomas Taylor, was unable to see the scene clearly. Again a catastrophe was narrowly averted, but like a spiny fish caught in an angler's landing net, *Broadway's* hull was gashed by the U-boat's metal fins.

As the submarine's survivors were blindfolded and bustled below decks, Baker-Creswell instructed his sub-lieutenant, David Balme, to organise a boarding party. Balme rowed over to the floundering U-boat with seven other men and clambered up onto the 'round and slippery' casing.

I spoke to David Balme in July 2007. I was fascinated to know just how he felt when he climbed down the conning tower into the U-boat, as he must have experienced the same terror as Fasson and Grazier did when they entered the bowels of the U-559. 'It was the most frightening experience of my life,' he told me:

> Very scary, indeed. I had to holster my pistol while I climbed down three vertical flights of ladders. I did expect to encounter Germans down there either setting the scuttling charges or opening the sea cocks to sink her. It was deathly quiet except for an eerie dim blue glow of the secondary lighting and a nasty hissing noise.

The anticipation of danger would surely have been enough to even melt nerves of steel, especially as Balme thought the vessel was about to be blown to bits. Remember too that he had no way of defending himself while climbing down the flights of ladders. No wonder he said his heart was racing so violently.

Once he discovered it was safe, he shouted for the rest of the men to come down and join him. There they remained for some time, calmly removing an Enigma machine and masses of secret papers. Balme says at one point during the operation Baker-Creswell sent somebody over with sandwiches for the Enigma rescue party. It conjures up the type of civilised scene which perhaps only the British are capable of creating in such testing circumstances. Maybe attempting to recreate the gentle atmosphere of a picnic helped to take the sting out of a tense and dramatic moment of war. 'I don't remember what sort of sandwiches they were, but I do remember that mine were wrapped in a white table napkin,' Balme recalled.

Balme had never heard of Enigma machines at the time, but he and his colleagues had grabbed hold of just about everything on the Admiralty's wish list. When intelligence officers met the *Bulldog* at Scapa Flow they could not believe their eyes when two fat suitcases packed with Enigma treasures were handed to them. Christmas had arrived early.

Back at Bletchley, experts worked relentlessly on the material and the results were far reaching. The documents which codebreakers received on 13 May, included the manual for the Offizier (officer grade) Enigma messages. These were special settings used for conveying important messages to U-boat officers. These later enabled Bletchley to decode more routine Enigma messages and so were significant for the remainder of the conflict.

Decrypts of German communications were now being reported to the Admiralty on average just thirty-four hours after they had been transmitted. Over the next seven months Allied shipping losses dropped from a monthly average of 200,000 tons to 50,000 tons and during this time more than thirty U-boats were destroyed. Balme was rewarded with the Distinguished Service Cross.

But while the *Bulldog's* contribution handed the Allies the initiative for a while, saving many lives, it was to prove only a temporary advantage. On 1 February 1942, the Germans introduced a new four-rotor Enigma machine (M4) with a cipher known as Triton. The Bletchley codebreakers gave it the name Shark. It created more havoc than Jaws! Bletchley was back in the dark and in deep despair. The consequences were to prove horrendous.

To top it all the Germans also brought in a new meteorological code, replacing the one captured by Balme and his men. Things could hardly get any worse, but then they did when the German equivalent of Bletchley Park, the *Beobachtungsdienst*, broke the Royal Naval code and began to understand communications between Allied warships.

Once again the U-boats ran amok in the Atlantic, blowing more ships out of the water than even before the *Bulldog's* capture of U-110. The average monthly shipping loss increased to a terrifying 500,000 tons. In June 1942, 700,000 tons were lost, in November the same year that figure reached 730,000. These losses were unsustainable and the future of Europe was hanging by a thread.

In early 1943 the number of operational U-boats doubled to around 400. You would have received very poor odds indeed on Germany losing the war. During that ten-month blackout Britain got closer and closer to the ropes. The knock-out punch was looming. Doenitz was a very happy man.

But he did not know about the *Petard's* capture of U-559 and a haul which included the new *Kurzsignalheft* (short signal book) and the *Wetterkurzschlüssel* (short signal weather cipher). The short signal codebook was used when U-boats transmitted details concerning convoys they had spotted. It reached Bletchley on 4 November 1942. The short signal weather codebook was used to reduce the length of weather reports. It proved to be the most valuable in breaking Shark, but inexplicably did not arrive at Bletchley Park until 24 November.

A lucky break several months earlier – again involving that decisive factor of human error – had given the desperate codebreakers a route into the new four-rotor system. In late 1941 the German U-boat radio operators must have been training for the new system, because one of them enciphered a message in a four-rotor Triton code. The operator on the U-131 sent a message on 17 December, 1941, which said: 'Am able to dive – have been hunted by four destroyers'. Immediately realising his mistake, he re-enciphered the message but this time using the current three-rotor key (a key was how an Enigma machine was set up on any given day, including which rotors were to be used and their positions).

There had been other security lapses, but this one was particularly devastating as it enabled cryptanalysts to establish the wiring of the fourth rotor. However, this was only to bear fruit when the new version of the short signal weather cipher was captured from the U-559.

This codebook provided cribs (a piece of cipher text from which cryptanalysts could guess the corresponding plain text) which were fed into a bombe machine, devised by mathematician Alan Turing. It could check through letter combinations faster than the human brain.

After nearly three weeks of feeding information into the whirring bombe wheels, a correct Enigma key was recovered. From this it was found that weather reports were enciphered with the fourth rotor always pre-set to just one position out of a possible twenty-six. Three-wheel settings were still being used for short signals rather than four-rotor settings. In effect, the Germans were treating the four-rotor cipher machine as a three-rotor Enigma.

Thus the codebreakers could immediately derive meaning from the messages on the existing bombe designed to process information from the three-rotor Enigma machine.

Once the weather reports were penetrated it was a relatively simple matter to read the highly-prized messages sent from HQ to the U-boats. It was discovered that the Enigma settings to encipher these revealing orders were virtually the same as those used for the short signal weather reports. The only difference was that the fourth rotor was set to one of the other twenty-five available positions. Having found the corresponding short signal weather key it was no great challenge for the mathematicians to find the position of the fourth rotor as it only involved checking twenty-five other possibilities.

The vital breakthrough into Shark signals had been made just six weeks after the U-559 was sunk. Within an hour of the success fifteen U-boat positions were identified. It was surely the most important Enigma capture of the entire war. The 13 December should be declared a Bank Holiday in Britain – it was the date in 1942 when Shark was cracked.

The relief and cheers in Hut 8, where intercepted U-boat traffic was analysed, must have been phenomenal when the breakthrough was made. For reading Shark saved an estimated 500,000 tons (and possibly as much as 750,000) of shipping in December 1942 and January 1943 alone. The enemy's mind could now be read and we were on the way to finally gaining the upper hand in the crucial Battle of the Atlantic.

It wasn't all plain sailing from that point, but thanks to the captures from the U-559 Bletchley was never to be completely in the dark again. It did, however, suffer some costly interruptions in reading messages during the fiercest phase of the U-boat war. The spring of 1943 was the most critical period of all with Allied convoys battling against at least 100 U-boats at any given time. It has been claimed that at one point we were even close to abandoning the convoy system altogether.

Bletchley Park was making its most significant progress in reading the four-rotor code at the very time that Doenitz was launching his biggest U-boat offensive. His aim was to starve Britain into surrender, by cutting off our supply routes. He estimated that he needed to sink 800,000 tons of shipping a month to defeat us. On several occasions he beat that target. In May 1942, the total German sinking of merchant vessels totalled a massive 834,164 tons. In June of that year, the figure rose to 834,196, and in November 807,754 tons of shipping was condemned to the seabed. Not all the ships were sunk by U-boats, but on average they accounted for a least 80 per cent of the total and maybe even another 4 per cent on top of that (attributed to 'unknown causes'). The documents from the U-559 had arrived shortly before the most savage clashes between convoys and U-boats. It was one heck of a climax – so imagine what the scenario would have been without the *Petard's* contribution.

Bletchley's so-called 'bad patches' (when they were unable to read U-boat wireless traffic) sometimes lasted for days with catastrophic consequences at sea. The destruction wrought by the U-boats on the convoys reached a hideous peak when twenty-one ships were sunk for the loss of a single German submarine. The U-338 inflicted the most damage – torpedoing four of the ships during a three-day shoot-out. The assault on the convoy, which took place in March 1943, was the bloodiest bout in the fight to gain control of the Atlantic.

It began when thirty-nine U-boats targeted two convoys totalling seventy-seven ships en route from Nova Scotia to Liverpool. The first convoy lost eight ships. It then joined up with the other group and a massive firefight ensued. During the month a total of ninety-five Allied ships were sunk. If such German dominance had been maintained we would have lost the Battle of the Atlantic. And without the *Petard*'s priceless cargo the German successes may well have continued.

The mental stress on codebreakers must have been unbearable – and one can only imagine how they felt when they heard details of the casualties they were unable to prevent. It was touch and go for some time as to who would become the dominant force at sea, but thanks to the U-559 haul, we were eventually to rule the waves again.

Between 13 December 1942 and 10 March 1943, there were only ten days when Bletchley Park could not decipher Shark communications. They were blinded again, though, when the Germans brought out a more complicated weather cipher, but this time it was the lesser of the *Petard*'s codebook prizes (the short signal book) that enabled the cryptanalysts to get back on track. From 10 March until the end of June all Shark signals were read on 87 out of 112 days.

By April 1943 Royal Navy ships were becoming more confident in launching attacks on German U-boats. Backed with information gleaned at Bletchley, fitted with better radar and accompanied by new escort carriers, they consigned fifteen submarines to the seabed during the month. The following month saw U-boats suffering even more. While Allied shipping enjoyed safer passages, forty from a total of 118 U-boats were put out of action. It was now seven months since the attack on U-559 and U-boat transmissions were being decoded daily.

The price was beyond what Germany could afford to pay, and at the end of May Doenitz (who had been promoted to commander-in-chief of the entire German Navy on 30 January 1943) ordered his U-boats to withdraw from the main battle zone of the Atlantic. After five weeks of appalling violence at sea the tide had decisively turned. The submarines headed to areas west of the Azores to lick their wounds. Doenitz later stated that the Battle of the Atlantic was lost in May 1943. It was a huge blow to the Admiral, who was said to have harboured a strong hatred of the British since being taken prisoner in the First World War, when he feigned madness and spent time in a mental institution in Manchester. He was to become one of Hitler's right-hand men and returned to torment his former captors in the next war.

For a time, the U-boats continued to stray into the Atlantic, but during the summer of 1943 they suffered more losses than the Allied ships they were despatched to sink. They were being sustained in the Atlantic by *milch* (milk) cows – huge iron nursemaids which refuelled the submarines. BP's information about their positions was not acted on at first, for fear of alerting the Germans to the fact their communications were being read. It was vital they were not provoked into tinkering further with the complexity of their Enigma system.

However, by November 1943 only one *milch* cow from a total of ten remained intact – the rest having been located and sunk, thanks to Ultra intelligence. By then other factors, such as improved air reconnaissance and the setting up of new Allied air bases in the Azores, could explain the increased attacks on the U-boat's feeding stations. Two months earlier Churchill announced that three months had passed since an Allied ship had been sunk in the North Atlantic. Cue endless cheering in the Commons.

The war had started with the U-boat crews feeling invincible, but now they were paying a shocking price. Out of 41,000 German servicemen in U-boats, nearly 26,000 were killed and a further 5,000 taken prisoner. The Royal Navy had lost more than 73,000 men – the vast majority in the Atlantic. Around 32,000 British merchant seamen lost their lives in that lethal stretch of sea. Seven hundred and eighty-four of the 842 operational U-boats were lost. The cost in lives was terrible but the stakes had been set even higher as this quote from Churchill emphasises, ' … dominating all our power to carry on the war, or even keep ourselves alive, lay our mastery of the ocean routes and free approach and entry to our ports.'

HMS *Petard*'s capture of Enigma documents led to destroyer captains being given vital information on where they could attack their once so elusive enemies. One captain with several kills under his belt was said to be so overjoyed about being able to hit back so effectively that he roused his crew with the strains of 'a hunting we will go' blasting through the ship's loudspeakers as he set out on U-boat tracking missions.

As the Germans' battle-scarred submarines headed for respite in the Azores, Doenitz put his defeat down to other things such as the Allies employing more effective hardware including long-range Liberator aircraft and improved direction-finding sonar and radar. Even fifteen years after the war had ended he remained confident that his Enigma system had not been compromised. While some historians have argued that factors other than Enigma intelligence contributed just as much to the eventual outcome of the war, there seems to be widespread agreement that solving Shark considerably shortened the conflict.

On occasions Bletchley Park had deciphered messages even before the U-boats to which they were directed had done so. Indeed, from the summer of 1943 the naval Enigma code was read without significant problems for the remainder of the conflict.

After the war there was a mass burning of secret documents at Bletchley Park including decrypts. I have tried to find out what happened to those special documents from the U-559. Nobody seems to know. I can only assume they were destroyed along with other evidence of Enigma having being solved. Bletchley Park was closed in March 1946.

One reason behind the drive to remove all traces of the codebreakers' successes was that Ultra was useful to British intelligence long after the war ended. Maybe certain countries were using enciphering systems similar to Enigma, leaving us with a head start in the intelligence war. One thing is for sure, a lot more secrets are yet to surface.

Historians are still finding examples of Ultra (digested intelligence from Enigma decrypts) being of use in post-war Britain, during the years when the government remained tight-lipped about its Enigma triumphs. Years after the war ended, ships' captains alluded to the fact they were still using the knowledge gained at Bletchley Park.

In 1951, for example, Captain Martin J. Evans of D4 Flotilla on HMS *Agincourt*, filed a report on his exercises at sea. In pencil he tantalisingly noted the following words on the document: 'Everything connected by Ultra cut out of this report as it was still the highest secrecy when I put this.' The document is held by the Imperial War Museum. I have also been told that there have been references to Ultra being used as late as the 1980s. Incredibly, nobody in Britain was aware of Bletchley Park's key role in the war until the mid-1970s. And as one Bletchley guide loves to point out to visitors today, 'Yes, the Germans did find out all about us … in 1974!'

We had to wait until the mid-1970s to get the first published works on what happened inside the walls of that famous mansion. The first really eye-opening account was Winterbotham's *The Ultra Secret* published in 1974, and the brilliant cryptanalyst Gordon Welchman's more detailed book, *The Hut Six Story – Breaking the Enigma Codes*, was not published until 1982. And even more staggering – it wasn't until 1991 that a movement swelled up to save Bletchley Park's grounds from being swamped with new houses which would have prevented it from ever becoming a museum.

A key benefit of reading German U-boat traffic was that the British could measure just how much they were hurting the enemy. Every effort was made to hide the fact they had broken into Shark. Decrypted messages were never read out to our own commanders over the airwaves. Often the British thought up ingenious alibis to explain devastating attacks on German forces.

Enigma enthusiast John Gallehawk, a guide and archivist at Bletchley, says that when codebreakers discovered the location of German vessels, a spotter plane would first be sent to the area, so the Germans would be provided with a logical explanation for the forthcoming attack on them. No major offensive was launched unless it could be explained in ways other than intercepted radio traffic.

The British also took full advantage of the fact that they knew some of their own coded messages were being read by the Nazis. So on the occasions they could not send a spotter plane, such as during inclement weather, they fabricated feasible explanations over the airwaves. They even invented a mythical Italian agent whom they often thanked for his vital information, and once sent a message offering him a pay rise after his tip-off led to a particularly successful attack.

John Gallehawk believes that without this victory at sea, it would have been impossible to get the supply lines in place to enable D-Day to happen. The war may then not have ended in 1945 and we could have suffered far more from the new V2 rockets. John said:

If the war had been delayed then by the time we had defeated Germany we may well have had a situation where the Russians were sitting on the Rhine. The story of post-war Europe may have been very different. It's possible the atomic bomb may have been dropped on Europe and not Japan.

When you compare the U-559 Enigma bounty to that retrieved from the U-110, you realise the more important of the two captures is also the less known. Each Enigma breakthrough was a vital link in the chain of discovery and provided the necessary foundations for the next layer of knowledge. All the captures could, therefore, be described as one huge team effort – a chain of equally important links. True, but it could also be argued that it was Grazier, Fasson and Brown who scored the winning goals for their team.

It is certainly time to celebrate the crucial part played by the *Petard*, and all her crew members. Once the Germans added that fourth rotor to the Enigma machine (making

Right: General Eisenhower was the most famous person to sail on the *Petard*.

Below: Eisenhower surveys the invasion beaches off Sicily from the safety of the *Petard*. The ship took him to a rendezvous with General Montgomery.

HERITAGE CENTRE

"PREMIERE"

The seizing of Enigma

The new Hollywood Film "U571" we know is fiction
and is an insult to genuine British heroes.

There is now a brand new documentary video
"CAPTURE ENIGMA - The True Story" that reveals how
the Royal Navy changed the course of the Battle of the
Atlantic by daring operations from Iceland to the
Mediterranean. This unique video also tells the true
Colin Grazier Story - at last.

The Heritage Centre is proud to present a Private
Tamworth RAFA "premiere" of this Video (approx. 60
minutes) at 8.30pm on the large Television in the
Heritage Centre, upstairs.

on THURSDAY-NOVEMBER 9

All members interested are welcome - Admission Free
Special Guest - Phil Shanahan Deputy Editor
of the Tamworth Herald and Chairman of the
Colin Grazier Memorial Committee.

Hollywood might have produced a fictitious film that was an insult to genuine British heroes, but in Tamworth they were determined to tell the true story. A video revealing the exploits of Grazier and the Royal Navy in winning the Battle of the Atlantic was 'premiered' at the Heritage Centre.

the code considerably more difficult to break), all the previous deeds of heroism would have been in vain had it not been for our trio. Bletchley's bombes were designed for three-rotor machines and were unable to cope. We could have lost the Battle of Atlantic, and who knows, even the war itself.

The truth is that however much progress had been made in codebreaking up until the U-559 incident, it would have counted for very little. The British cracked Shark mainly because of the information grabbed by Grazier, Fasson and Brown. Their heroism has had nothing like the publicity it deserves, but we were doing our bit and this book is a part of that too.

We quickly sold out of our first batch of Grazier plates – the last two having being snapped up by Commander Philip Balink-White MBE RN, who was living in Florida, and a woman from Malta – and more were ordered.

Soon afterwards, the *Herald* reported an incident of national importance which helped to keep the Enigma story fresh in the minds of the nation. This was the audacious theft of an Enigma machine worth tens of thousands of pounds from Bletchley Park. It turned out that the theft of the machine, which was eventually sent to TV presenter Jeremy Paxman, was the culmination of a hate campaign against Bletchley Park's director, Christine Large. Oddly enough, the Enigma machine was stolen on the night we held the musical tribute to Grazier, Fasson and Brown in Tamworth. That was something Christine picked up on when I first met her – perhaps she thought I had arranged the theft as a publicity stunt!

Another *Petard* man to step forward for our eyewitness series was Les Hemus, who had vivid memories from his days at sea. He was part of the *Petard*'s gun crew. It was his job to determine the range for shells aimed at enemy vessels. Les was not on deck on 30 October 1942, so he did not see all the events unfold. However, he clearly remembers how he reacted when he heard two shipmates had been lost:

I am not usually a sentimental fellow, but I did shed tears. They were smashing guys and I knew them as shipmates. We used to call Lt Tony Fasson 'Jimmy-The-One' which was always the nickname of the first lieutenant. Many of us were just 18 or 19 and it was a big experience to lose anyone.

Les also remembered the *Petard* taking on board its most famous visitor – American General Dwight Eisenhower. He came on board the *Petard* on 14 July 1943 to be taken around the various beachheads in Sicily to get first-hand reports of progress from local commanders. The *Petard* even escorted him to a rendezvous with General Montgomery. 'We took him to Sicily for the start of the landing invasion,' he said. 'We were all upset as we had to dress in full uniform, when we would normally wear overalls on ship!' Reg Crang described how Eisenhower became something of a celebrity on board:

He let the skipper know there was to be no special treatment. The lads liked him for that. When one young matelot dared to ask him for an autograph he replied with a 'sure lad' remark. Other chaps soon followed. When Jimmy [the first lieutenant] found out what was going on he nearly shaved off [naval slang for exploding with rage] and stamped on it straight away.

The General was taken on a tour of the British invasion beaches and Reg says that for a brief moment the ship came under fire. 'On our way round the coast an enemy gun fired three rounds at us. Each shot fell well short so there was no danger – but it made the General jump!'

Had Eisenhower stayed an extra day on board, he would have experienced a very unusual incident. The *Petard* was one of several ships sent to bombard the coast of Sicily, paying particular attention to a road carrying military convoys. A tank on the road fired a shell at the *Petard* which passed right through the ship, drilling a neat hole. It did more harm to the ship's dignity than anything else.

At a time when we were getting more and more information about the story, it was frustrating to see it being snubbed elsewhere. I mentioned earlier that Channel 4 had failed to mention our three heroes in a new series about Enigma. So it was refreshing when a video, *Capture Enigma*, was released which finally acknowledged the crucial parts they played.

The Tamworth branch of the Royal Air Force Association acquired a video of *Capture Enigma: the True Story*, produced by DD Video, and invited me to its Tamworth premiere. After the screening I was asked to give my reaction to the association, and told them how pleased I was to hear credit go to Colin Grazier at long last. I also said I was amazed it had taken so long for the men's story to be mentioned on film. This was the RAFA club but there was a huge respect for what their counterparts in the Navy had achieved. In fact, very early on in the campaign the club sent us a donation of £100.

CHAPTER SEVENTEEN

STARS SHINE FOR HEROES

Neil Morrissey raised my arms into the air as if he was a fellow striker spontaneously celebrating a goal

The evening of 12 November 2000 will remain etched in my memory forever. It was the night the Celebrities Guild of Great Britain honoured Grazier, Fasson and Brown. The gala evening at the Four Seasons Hotel, in Park Lane, London, was a glamorous event in the company of some of the biggest stars in Britain.

The Guild put my wife Claire and I in a hotel near to the venue and we were told a taxi would pick us up and take us to dinner. We arrived in good time on the Sunday afternoon and, after a leisurely stroll, I decided to have a relaxing bath. I was determined to try to unwind as I was nervous at the prospect of having to make a speech to such a large and distinguished audience. I got out of the bath about an hour before the taxi was due to arrive. As I began to put on my dinner suit and bow tie I discovered that I had forgotten to bring my cufflinks. This was made worse by the fact that my shirt had extremely long fold-back cuffs.

I stood there with about six miles of shirt protruding from my jacket sleeves, frozen in horror. Soon I was to accept an award on behalf of three men who brought the Second World War to an early close and I was in danger of standing on the stage with an elephant's trunk worth of shirt unfurling from my jacket – humiliation in front of a famous audience! It wasn't quite in the same league as what happened to Judy Finnegan (from the *Richard and Judy Show*) whose dress came apart as she took to the stage, but given the occasion it was not good at all.

I shot out of the bedroom, skidded into the hotel lift, then sauntered casually into reception, trying to remain calm. 'Do you sell cufflinks?' I squealed at the receptionist. 'No sir,' came the polite reply.

I ran over to the bar area and asked a waiter if he had any cufflinks I could borrow. He hadn't. Doing a fine impression of John Cleese at his most manic, I hurtled into the lift again and rushed back into my room screaming at my wife to come out of the bathroom and help 'sort me out'. We summoned a taxi and told the surprised driver to take us to a cufflink shop! Despite it being a Sunday, he did just that. It really got me out of a hole. I ended up paying a frightening amount for my cufflinks as it was a very expensive shop. I still refer to them as my 'Grazier cufflinks' and save them for special occasions.

We got back just in time for the taxi to take us to the Four Seasons Hotel. The black cab rolled up outside the front doors of the plush establishment and the doors were opened by uniformed doormen. Shortly after arriving, I had a brief but memorable conversation with a television scriptwriter. He was standing at the top of a grand marble staircase impressively framed beneath an enormous sparkling chandelier.

'Have you read Robert Harris' *Enigma*?' he asked me, after inquiring who I was.

'Yes', I replied, 'an excellent book. Superbly written.'

'Just brilliant,' he replied, nodding his head enthusiastically, and peering over the top of a pair of half-moon spectacles. Then he looked at me in a slightly conspiratorial way. 'This Enigma business though,' he whispered 'I can't understand a f★★★ing word of it!'

I was still digesting this when we walked into the reception area. It was as if a television had suddenly tipped out all of its stars from all channels including movies, sport, news and TV drama. The guests included *Men Behaving Badly* star Neil Morrissey, David Jacobs CBE, who was Master of Ceremonies, former *Blue Peter* presenter Valerie Singleton (she brought back many childhood memories for me), sports commentator David Vine, musician Larry Adler, TV cops Dempsey and Makepeace alias Glynis Barber and Michael Brandon, game show host Bob Holness, and actors Dennis Quilley, Saeed Jaffrey OBE, William Franklyn and Barry Foster. The world of football was represented by Hans Segers and Gavin Peacock. The Guild's organising committee read like an entry from Who's Who and included legendary concert pianist Stanley Black, Leonard Fenton (Dr Legg from *EastEnders*) and comedian Bernard Spear.

Only six awards were to be presented during the evening and each recipient was assigned a celebrity to tell their story and introduce them on stage. Mine was Prunella Scales, a major star of the stage and screen. This was somewhat of a coincidence because a couple of years earlier I had interviewed Prunella in her dressing room at the Alexandra Theatre in Wolverhampton for a magazine feature. In fact the interview had gone so well that Prunella asked if *Herald* photographer Paul Barber and I had time to share a bottle of wine with her after the formalities had been completed. I still have memories of that day and I know Paul has too. Paul was driving and couldn't do much more than sniff the cork. But I came out feeling rather relaxed for the time of day. Before we left, Prunella recommended a particular white wine for us to enjoy on Christmas Day. It turned out to be a fine choice.

When we left the theatre, she insisted on coming with us and led us to an exit door leading out onto the street. She stood there with us for a while and waved us goodbye like old friends. Pedestrians passed by the three of us without turning a hair. They did not realise that the immortal Sybil Fawlty was standing amongst them. A few weeks later I arrived home to find she had left a message on my answering machine with a few more pointers for the article. And here she was again, about to share in another memorable moment of my life.

Ironically this time our roles were reversed. Now it was her interviewing me with notepaper and pen and a very thorough job she did too. It wasn't the first link Prunella has had with the Enigma story either as she played the part of Alan Turing's mother in the TV adaptation of Hugh Whitemore's play, *Breaking the Code*.

The meal that night was sublime. I thoroughly enjoyed it, despite knowing I was soon to address over 350 people. After the meal I began to relax a little and summoned the courage to stand up and look around the room to get used to the sight that would greet me when I delivered my speech. It was one hell of a mistake. The fact that I recognised most of the celebrities on each table made it all the more daunting. I fell back into my chair, my heart going into overdrive. Claire poured me another large glass of red wine.

Five other people were to receive awards. They included an aid worker with nerves of steel who had driven lorries through hostile Bosnia and a woman who was one of the first people to answer the plight of Romanian orphans abandoned in a terrible state after the Ceaucescu dictatorship. I was in exultant company and only because of the bravery of other people.

I was the last to be called to the stage and Prunella gave an impressive build-up speech. She described how, despite their enormous contribution to the war, the three *Petard* men had remained virtually anonymous. She also quoted the words of naval historian Ralph Erskine who said, 'Few acts of courage from three individuals could ever have had such far reaching consequences.' She described how I had visited the Imperial War Museum and found no mention of them, even in a section dedicated to the Enigma story. Prunella then told the audience about the *Herald's* campaign and how it was beginning to bring the men to public attention. She introduced me by saying, 'Phil Shanahan, who has done so much to ensure that recognition, is here tonight to receive the Celebrities Guild award on their behalf.'

At that point I walked onto the stage and felt the hairs on the back of my neck prickle as the entire audience stood as one to applaud. The standing ovation continued for several minutes. As I accepted the award from Prunella I remembered the words of Tony Fasson's sister who told me to hold my head up high and think of how proud her brother would have been.

I did feel proud. It was one of the proudest moments of my life, but I also felt extremely humble. They were on their feet clapping three extraordinary heroes who had helped to end the war and I, a deputy editor of a weekly newspaper, was receiving it on their behalf. I felt it ought to be the Prime Minister at the very least representing them.

It also occurred to me just how privileged I was to accept this prolonged applause. I hoped that somehow they were watching and realised that this was all for them. God knows how they plucked up the courage that October night. Here was I overdosing on adrenalin at just the thought of speaking to a celebratory audience – just compare that to the bottle they needed to board U-559. I felt in awe of them. I had led a successful newspaper campaign – they had died in an act which historians say was a decisive moment in the Second World War. Yet my name had been engraved on the crystal bowl alongside theirs because I had been chosen to receive it.

It seemed unreal and I certainly had no delusions of grandeur. That evening I really felt I had been given a strong purpose in life – a mission to gain three brave men their rightful place in history. My speech was brief but summed up how I felt. 'To receive an award on behalf of three of the greatest war heroes the world has known is the biggest honour of my life,' I said.

As I spoke I recognised many faces at various tables, but for some reason I found myself staring straight at former Chelsea striker Gavin Peacock who was sitting in the middle of the room lifting himself up from his seat to get a better view. I concluded by saying:

Without these three men there may never have been a D-Day, and without them there might have been a nuclear war in Europe. Just think of the consequences of that. Yet their stories

Above left: Swapping trophies, Prunella Scales with a Colin Grazier commemorative plate and the author with the Celebrities Guild of Great Britain award he accepted on behalf of Grazier, Fasson and Brown.

Above right: Film star William Franklyn, Michael Brandon, of Dempsey and Makepeace fame, and actress Anita Harris applaud as Prunella Scales presents an award from the Celebrities Guild of Great Britain to Phil Shanahan on behalf of Colin Grazier, Tony Fasson and Tommy Brown.

have remained hidden for far too long. I believe the Celebrities Guild of Great Britain has done them proud tonight and I can't thank them enough for that.

I'll also never forget coming down from the stage after the presentations had been made. Neil Morrissey raised my arms into the air as if he was a fellow striker spontaneously celebrating a goal. The story of the men must have really grabbed his imagination. He was a lovely man, in one sense not too dissimilar to the character he played in *Men Behaving Badly*. He was the only male in the room not to be sporting a bow tie and he was out to enjoy himself. And good for him. At one point he danced exuberantly next to us, armed with a beer glass in one hand and a cigarette in the other. I half expected Martin Clunes to arrive on the dance floor on the other side of us with his arms whirring like windmills.

We discovered later in the evening that Neil spent his formative years in Stoke-on-Trent, my home city. Claire had also lived in the Potteries for a time, although we first met in Portsmouth where our respective newspapers had sent us on a journalists' training scheme. We talked quite a lot about our memories of the Potteries and I later gave him one of the Grazier plates I had taken with me. I handed out several that night including one to Prunella Scales. They seemed to have really taken the story to their hearts. Later on it was good to see Neil passing his Grazier plate round his table for everyone to admire.

At the end of the evening, despite its only being November, we all linked arms on the dance floor and belted out Auld Lang Syne. What a night!

A reader, who was very close to Colin Grazier as a child, sent us what we now believe to be the earliest picture of him in existence. She did not want to be named, but was responding to our request for new material to keep his memory alive. I felt quite emotional looking at the picture – Colin was photographed with his classmates at Two Gates Primary School and must have been about six years old. The woman who sent us the picture described her relationship with him as, 'so close we were like brother and sister'.

She remembered him as a lovely boy with a gentleness about him which made him stand out from the rest. She lived just across the road from the Grazier family. She and Colin played together at home and worked together at school. 'We first met at school and he became a special friend,' she remembered:

> I'll never forget when we got to senior school and we had poetry lessons. We each had to stand up and read a poem. Colin would always read 'Drakes Drum'. He had the sea in him even then. He was very well liked by the boys and the girls. Although he could be quite mischievous outside school, he always knuckled down and got his work done. He was great fun.

The two of them shared the same birthday, and she remembered receiving a twenty-first birthday card from Colin when he was in Singapore. 'We lost touch for about three years before he went into the Navy, but he still sent me postcards and birthday cards whenever he could.' She was desperately upset when she heard of Colin's tragic death:

> I couldn't believe it. It was such a tragedy, but then war was a tragedy. So many young men died. I wish that his father could have known about this campaign. I know that if Colin was around now he would just say he was doing his job. It is time that everyone knew how brave he was and what he did for us.
>
> I miss Colin a great deal, especially on our birthday. I celebrated my eightieth this year, as he would have done, and I thought about him a lot on that day – as I will do on every birthday.

Such recollections brought home how we were fighting for real people that everybody could identify with – people who had been wronged by being forgotten. Not characters from the imagination of some Hollywood scriptwriter, but the real Enigma heroes!

Another of Colin's school friends told us how he had discovered to his amazement that Colin had made his own job of deciphering German Enigma messages a whole lot easier. Leslie Hare attended Wilnecote School with Colin. In 1941 he joined the Navy and, as coincidence would have it, he became one of 350 specially trained people whose job it was to intercept Enigma messages and forward them to the experts at Bletchley.

He was unaware until 1998 that it was his former school pal that helped recover the very codebooks which made it possible for the new messages to be understood. 'The Germans had changed their code and we were in great trouble,' he recalled:

William Franklyn, Michael Brandon, Glynis Barber, Anita Harris, David Vine, Prunella Scales and Neil Morrisey pictured on stage with the recipients of the Celebrities Guild of Great Britain Unsung Heroes Awards for the year 2000.

The earliest picture of Colin that the *Herald* received was this one of him at the age of six with his classmates at Two Gates Primary School. It was sent in by a woman who asked to remain anonymous but said she was like a sister to him and shared the same birthday. Colin is pictured third from left in the back row.

We were unable to crack the new code for a very long time – the codes were unbreakable. Then we got the new codebooks, which I later discovered were retrieved by Colin Grazier. They were immediately dispatched to Bletchley for deciphering. Thereafter, nearly every message intercepted on that frequency could be decoded. We knew exactly what the Germans were doing and we followed their every move. It virtually ended the war.

Not surprisingly the Grazier connection came as a big surprise to Leslie. 'It sent a shudder down my spine. I have feelings of great sadness and at the same time immense pride for the actions of Colin Grazier, a great hero.'

As the newspaper for Tamworth, we were most concerned with Colin Grazier, but I was always aware of our responsibilities towards Tony Fasson and Tommy Brown. In fact, I felt a great need to shine a light on that whole underplayed episode in history. We were a local newspaper which was beginning to think in national terms when it came to the Enigma story. Through regular contact with Tony Fasson's sister in Scotland, we had unearthed many stories about him. It was information about Tommy Brown we needed next.

CHAPTER EIGHTEEN

OUR TOMMY

If anybody was going to volunteer it was going to be our Tommy. He was a brave lad
— David Brown

Shortly after returning home from the Celebrities Guild dinner in London, I received a letter from Norman Brown, one of Tommy's brothers, saying that he had heard about the award and wanted to thank me for all the work on the campaign.

Tommy was one of eleven children and I was amazed to hear that four sisters and three brothers were still alive and living in the North East. If I had known that I would have been in regular contact with the family about our progress. I asked Linda Ram, a *Herald* reporter, to write a feature about Tommy and I put her in touch with the family.

Over the years many reporters had become 'Enigma correspondents' but Linda, who is half-German, enthusiastically took on the role for the final three years. The Brown family gave her a lot of information on the boy who at sixteen became the youngest person ever to be awarded the George Medal.

Tommy had lived his short life to the full. He was so desperate to join the Navy that he lied about his age, being only fifteen when he first joined the crew of the *Petard* as a canteen assistant. When volunteers were called to go over to the stricken submarine, Tommy did not hesitate in joining in the action alongside his two senior colleagues. He even managed to break through the grip of the canteen manager who had tried to restrain him from joining the boarding party. The fact he had fibbed about his age to enlist emerged during an inquiry held shortly after the incident. He was 'distraught' when he received his discharge from the *Petard* in Alexandria. It was so sad that Tommy survived, only to die with his sister in a house fire in North Shields less than three years later.

Like the families of Fasson and Grazier, the Browns were unaware of the importance of the codebooks Tommy helped to get hold of, despite the fact that his mother and older brother Stan went to Buckingham Palace in 1945 to collect his medal from King George VI. Tommy was presented with an engraved clock by the rest of the *Petard*'s crew. It is now displayed at Bletchley Park.

'When he came home from the *Petard*, Tommy never let on about anything that had happened,' his brother David recalled. 'When we found out, years later, we weren't that surprised as he was such a daredevil. If anyone was going to volunteer, it was going to be our Tommy. He was a brave lad.'

David also revealed that on the night of the house fire in February 1945, Tommy, then just nineteen, was at home with nine of his brothers and sisters and his mother. The fire broke out in the sitting room where Tommy was sleeping. He was serving on board HMS *Belfast* as a senior canteen assistant at the time. The ship had docked on the River Tyne to undergo a refit, which enabled Tommy to go home to his family every night in nearby North Shields.

He was already dead when the firemen finally managed to drag him out of the smoke-filled room through a window. His four-year-old sister Maureen had also stopped breathing. The two are buried together in Preston Cemetery, North Shields.

We also discovered that Tommy had spent part of his life in the Midlands, in East Shilton, Leicestershire, where he went to stay with his uncle and worked in a footwear factory shortly after leaving school. He remained in the area for a year before returning to the North East to join the Navy. His brother Norman told us that it was about time Tommy had proper recognition for his own role in the war.

The *Herald* campaign sparked a permanent tribute to him in the North East. He had a road named after him in Tamworth, as well as a hotel bar room. He was also to have his name included on the main Tamworth memorial, in the reception area of Colin Grazier House and on a plinth in the new 'Enigma' estate.

Norman Brown sent me the first picture ever taken of Tommy to use in this book (he had previously sent me the last picture taken of Tommy in his NAAFI uniform). He is a chubby-faced toddler pictured outside the family's downstairs flat with Norman, Stanley and Margaret. 'Photographs of Thomas are few and far between, but this one is a gem,' Norman told me:

> In the early thirties, it had to be a very special occasion to have a snap taken of yourself. There was very little money about, and what there was had to be used for more important things like getting something to eat. However, it was not all gloom and doom. We were and still are a very happy family. I still see four surviving sisters, two or three times a week. I see my youngest brother Bert occasionally and my older brother David from time to time.

Sadly, Stan Brown died while this book was being written, but he was aware of all the developments to honour his heroic brother. Norman also told me that there was nobody on the planet who had known Tommy as well as he himself had. 'After all, three of us brothers shared the same bed in our early years. We had to as at first we only had a downstairs flat.' Norman always had the feeling that Tommy was special and would go on to achieve something remarkable:

> When we were growing up, I always used to think that North Shields would never be big enough for him and that he would have better and bigger things on the horizon. I think he would have made a great success of his life had fate not intervened.

Ginger Richards remembers how everybody got to know Tommy on board the *Petard* as he was the one who sold them cigarettes and drinks. 'He was a lively sort of boy. He fancied his chances a bit, but not in a bad way. He was very popular.'

In January 2001, I became aware that the Cambridge Stamp Centre was planning to produce a limited edition commemorative cover in conjunction with the HMS *Petard*

Above left: A chubby-faced Tommy Brown (left), aged about five, poses for a rare family portrait outside his home in North Shields in the early 1930s. With him are his brothers Norman (seated) and Stanley, and his sister Margaret behind.

Above right: Probably the last photograph taken of Tommy Brown, smartly turned out in his NAAFI uniform, when he was eighteen.

Association. The cover was to feature a beautiful painting of the heroes clambering onto U-559 with the *Petard* nearby and the German survivors swimming in the sea.

Military artist Michael Roffe had been commissioned to produce the painting. Each cover was to be signed by a surviving member of the *Petard* on board the night the incident took place. A small number would be multi-signed by all the surviving sailors. Because of my involvement in the story, I decided I would like to buy a copy of the multi-signed version and contacted the stamp centre to make an order. I spoke to Keith Astell at the centre and it wasn't long before we got chatting about the campaign. Between us we came up with an idea to raise more funds for the appeal. Keith said he was prepared to auction off the original painting used for the cover to the highest bidder. We set a reserve price of £600 and Keith pledged that any amount over £500 would be donated to our appeal.

The painting attracted lively bidding with much interest from the Tamworth area. The highest bid – a very respectable £2,000 – was made by Robin Norris who lives in the

Staffordshire village of Elford. Tamworth Borough Council also made a strong bid for the painting, hoping to keep it in public hands. Robin, however, delighted us all when he declared that he wanted the painting to remain on public display rather than keep it himself. It was a very generous gesture and one which I very much appreciated. The painting is part of the material we have handed over to Bletchley Park and is on the cover of this book. Mr Norris explained in the *Herald* why he wanted to hand back the painting to the public:

> Firstly, to help commemorate the selfless act of heroism by a Tamworthian, Colin Grazier, and his two colleagues. Their names should be remembered for always in Tamworth.
>
> Secondly, in memory of my late father who served all his adult life in the Royal Navy, going to sea at sixteen in the battleship Malaya at the Battle of Jutland, and throughout the Second World War in the cruisers Sheffield and Bellona.
>
> Thirdly, to give something back to Tamworth for all the kindness I have received since I arrived in the mid-1950s from Kent.

CHAPTER NINETEEN

ON THE MAP AT LAST

The names of the three men were now indelibly engraved into the infrastructure of the town

One of the ambitious targets we set ourselves was to have a road named after Grazier in Tamworth. I had gone public on this aim on several occasions. Then out of the blue I was contacted by McLean Homes, the developer of a new multi-million-pound housing estate.

Around 200 upmarket houses were being built on the site of the former Reliant factory in Wilnecote. This was a prime location as Reliant had put Tamworth on the map as the home of the famous three-wheeled Reliant Robin. The quirky car achieved legendary status in the television series *Only Fools and Horses* starring David Jason.

The housing development commands panoramic views of the Dosthill Valley with distant glimpses of the River Tame running through it. The new estate was called Kensington Gardens, but the developer was happy for all its roads to be named on an Enigma theme in honour of the town connection. This was fantastic news for us. Instead of getting just one road named after Grazier we had an entire housing estate at our disposal. After consultations with the developer we came up with the following names: Grazier Avenue, Brown Avenue, Fasson Close, Petard Close and Bletchley Drive. I also wanted Enigma Avenue, which I thought had a lovely ring to it, but for some reason the developer turned it down. What a shame. I certainly would have loved to live in Enigma Avenue. Still, I couldn't be greedy. Some were long roads and required numerous signs. It was a lovely tribute. The names of the three men were now indelibly engraved into the infrastructure of the town. They were becoming immortalised in Tamworth.

Shortly afterwards we managed to get another road named after *Petard* Captain Mark Thornton – Thornton Way. Thornton was a controversial character, adored by some, detested by others. He was a brilliant seaman, focused completely on capturing a U-boat, and ran his ship with discipline that occasionally spilled into cruelty. There are stories of him putting the lives of officers at risk by ordering them to swim in rough seas, being brutal to other members of the crew and maniacally shooting down flocks of seabirds. Tony Fasson's sister Sheena also believes he blocked her brother from taking command of his own ship, something which created tension between the two for a while.

John Burman wrote to me from his home in California with his memories of his terrifying captain. John's role was to help load the *Petard*'s 'B' gun, positioned just forward of the bridge, and he joined up with the ship shortly after she had been built in May 1942. 'I remember the tone of Lt Cdr Mark Thornton's welcoming address – he wanted to get back into the fight as soon as possible and he expected us to be ready very soon,' he said:

Tamworth Herald deputy editor Phil Shanahan, reporter Rob Tanner and assistant editor John Harper stand next to the historic road signs named after war heroes Grazier, Fasson and Brown, on a new housing estate in Tamworth.

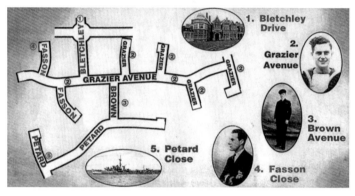

The *Tamworth Herald*'s campaign has put Grazier, Fasson and Brown permanently on the map with streets in the town named after the war heroes. Their ship, its Captain Mark Thornton and Bletchley Park are also commemorated on a housing estate.

I can still see him appearing on the quarter deck one morning dressed in his favourite crimson corduroy trousers, announcing to all and sundry that anyone able to catch him before he reached the bridge would be rewarded with an extra night's liberty at the next port. Of course nobody caught him.

Jack Hall, who also served under Thornton, described him as 'ruthless' and said that during exercises he would stand on the cross tree on the mast and hurl handfuls of iron bolts at anybody who had failed to spot another vessel on the horizon before he did. Jack remembered how Thornton tested the men by letting off a hosepipe in the stokers mess below decks, giving the impression that the ship had been hit. 'But our commanding officers needed to be ruthless to fight those U-boats,' he added in Thornton's defence.

This entry from Reg Crang's diary shows just how realistic Thornton's 'exercises' could be:

All hell broke loose with guns firing, crackers exploding, lights failing and sea water pouring in through hoses. In the midst of all this the ship's siren jammed open. The piercing shriek, tolerable only in short bursts, was driving people mad. In fact, the whole operation was so

The *Petard*'s captain, Mark Thornton, who ruled his crew with a rod of iron and was hell bent on capturing a U-boat.

realistic that poor Golding, the ward-room chef, collapsed and died. His body was sewn into a hammock and committed to the ocean.

Ginger Richards described Thornton as a big bloke, a bully, a madman and a brilliant seaman:

> He also had an absolute hatred of the enemy. He was never content with anything. He created emergencies which we thought were real. He'd even flood a compartment on the ship and it was frightening because we thought it was the real thing. But that was what would enable us to react properly to real emergencies. Thornton was the sort of man you would do anything for.

The most disturbing accounts I have heard about the *Petard*'s commanding officer refer to him callously mowing down enemy sailors when the *Petard* sank the Italian submarine *Uarsciek*. Thornton reportedly grabbed a machine gun and wiped out several submariners who the rest of the crew considered to be surrendering.

He had already got a taste for U-boat blood while he was in charge of the destroyer *Harvester* which sank the U-32 off the coast of Northern Ireland in October 1940. Thornton was awarded the Distinguished Service Cross for his part in the incident in which nine submariners were killed.

Eric Sellars, a petty officer on the *Petard* who worked closely with Mark Thornton, told me he was a misunderstood character whose brutality was motivated by an absolute determination to defeat the enemy. He believes that Thornton took the view that more Allied lives would be at risk in the long term if submariners were allowed to dispose of Enigma material, even if the enemy had ceased to return fire. It seems that the captain (with his privileged knowledge) appreciated that preventing the enemy from throwing Enigma documents into the sea could inflict serious damage on Hitler and reduce future Allied casualties. In that sense Thornton was right. It certainly might help to explain his no-nonsense approach to U-boat crews and the exacting standards he set for his men.

However, the ship's doctor, William Prendergast, became extremely alarmed about his captain's behaviour and is thought to have alerted the authorities. Thornton was removed from the ship some months after the attack on U-559, and the doctor's damning report on him has become a widely used explanation. It does appear somewhat ironic that the U-boat commander Hans Heidtmann, whose vessel gave up secrets which directly influenced his nation's defeat, should be honoured with a Knight's Cross, while the commander of the ship which captured them was apparently 'rewarded' by being removed from his post soon afterwards.

At the time Thornton told his men it was to do with eyesight problems, so we can only speculate as to the truth behind the decision. Eric Sellars believes his captain was taken off the ship to prevent his giving away highly sensitive information should he be captured at sea. If the Germans had known about the Petard's coup they would surely have brought about further devastating changes to their coded communications.

Eric says that Thornton went on to take up an important position in the submarine tracking room at the Admiralty. Whatever the facts behind his sudden departure, it was announced in January 1943 that Thornton was to be made a Companion of the Distinguished Service Order for his command of HMS Petard. The importance of the U-559 capture must have become very apparent by then.

The highly-strung Thornton was a key player in the U-559 attack and I believe he deserved recognition in the new housing estate in Tamworth. I have since heard several surviving members of his crew talk with great admiration, if not deep affection, about him.

Mervyn Romeril, whose job included acting as a lookout on the Petard, says his outstanding memory of the fanatical Thornton, is of him climbing up to the dizzy heights of the ship's mast while the vessel was in motion to look for submarines. 'That high up he was a like a little figure leaning back on the mast to balance himself. He was mad to get a submarine.'

The Thornton-fear effect on the crew made the Petard one of the most vigilant vessels on the ocean. She was the first ship to locate the Italian submarine the Uarsciek, but for me the biggest testimony to her remarkable lookout capabilities is the fact that on five separate occasions stricken servicemen were spotted in tiny dinghies astray on the ocean. This must be the nautical equivalent of finding a needle in a haystack.

On 21 November 1942, an eagle-eyed lookout on the Petard reported seeing a rubber dinghy in breaking waves while on route to Malta. In it were five RAF crewmen who had been shot down the day before. All owed their lives to the lookouts' observational powers as they were picked up by the Petard.

On 2 December 1942, the crew of an RAF Wellington bomber were spotted in another dinghy. An entire convoy passed by the desperate men. The *Petard* was the last ship in the line. The airmen had used up all their flares to no avail, and yet from a good distance away the keen *Petard* lookouts had glimpsed a tiny light from a small torch.

Three German airmen were rescued from a rubber dinghy on 14 July 1943, in the nick of time as they were in an extremely fragile condition. Unbelievably they were picked out in moonlight.

The fourth rescue, involving a dinghy being towed by a launch, was the most bizarre. Reg Crang noted the farcical incident in his forbidden diary:

We came across a launch towing a rubber dinghy. There were 12 men in the boat and to our great astonishment they were being threatened by the two men in the dinghy wielding machine guns. We lowered nets by which they scrambled aboard. Two from the launch were RAF officers, quite overcome with relief at being rescued.

They had a very strange story to relate. Their Beaufighter had been shot down yesterday by an Me109 and they had ditched in the sea. They had had time to launch their rubber dinghy and spent last night drifting in it. Just before dawn today they were nearly run down by the launch which contained twelve soldiers (ten Germans and two Italians), all making for Sicily. The launch took the dinghy in tow, but the two RAF men could not believe it when they were ordered to change places with the two Italian soldiers.

Even more amazing was the fact that the two Italians were allowed to take their tommy guns into the dinghy. There is no love lost between the Jerrys and the Itis and it appeared that the Germans intended to cut the dinghy adrift. The two Italians began to threaten the German soldiers and were delighted when they saw a destroyer approaching. They assumed it was an Italian ship coming to their rescue and were quite shattered to discover it was the British Navy after all!

Finally *Petard* lookouts noticed the crews of two German torpedo bombers on 12 September 1943, both of which had been shot down off Malta. Each crew of four had taken to a rubber dinghy, and all the men were hauled on board the *Petard*. It prompted Reg Crang to pay his own tribute to the ship's lookouts in his diary entry for the day. 'I think we have now rescued seven boats of survivors (thirty-seven men in all including twenty-eight Germans) a great tribute to our lookouts who are second to none in spotting small objects at sea.'

Thornton's death in 1983 led to the birth of the HMS *Petard* Association as his memorial service in London was attended by several *Petard* men who decided to form the organisation.

The man who eventually replaced Thornton, Rupert Egan, was an equally brilliant seaman. Reg Crang described him as, 'tireless, steadfast, resolute, and ice-cool in action'. 'The only words I have ever heard muttered against him was that he was too eager to take his ship into action! But the whole crew admired and respected him,' he said.

Unlike Thornton, he showed no outward signs on board that the responsibility was getting to him. The crew regarded Egan as a mentally strong character. So they were

THE REAL ENIGMA HEROES

shocked and horrified to hear that shortly after the war he ended his life by jumping from the balcony of a New York hotel.

All members of the Colin Grazier Committee were invited to the opening of Tamworth's new Enigma-themed housing estate and to be pictured with the newly made road signs. Three years later we were to go one better and erect a special plaque outlining the men's gallantry on a brick plinth in the estate. I often think it is very easy to lose sight of the meaning behind road names, but this will never be the case on this estate.

I always get a buzz when I see the various road names on the estate appear in *Herald* articles. Just reading about an achievement by someone who lives in Grazier Avenue, Fasson Close, or a house for sale in Brown Avenue or Thornton Way, shows how much their names have become part of the town. One of the first babies born in Tamworth in 2007 was to a couple living in Fasson Close.

In February 2001, I was surprised to be presented with a New Year's Honour from the mayor of Tamworth, Cllr David Foster. I had gone to the town hall to help *Herald* editor Sam Holliday and the mayor hand out honours to people who had made Tamworth a better place to live in. It is an event the newspaper has organised for several years and I was amazed to receive one of the honours myself in recognition of the importance of our campaign. It was gratifying, but I realised it was more a reflection of what the men had achieved.

Eric Shove's 'Survivor's Story' was published in the *Herald* in 2001. Eric was the *Petard's* leading telegraphist who spent most of his time sitting on the bridge communicating with other ships. Eric described how he felt during those dark days of war on the *Petard*. 'Looking back, I think I went through three phases. First of all astonishment, then fright and then lastly resigned to fate.' Despite being eighty-five when he spoke to us, he was still able to graphically describe the events of 30 October 1942:

> I was on the bridge when the U-559 appeared in the searchlights. The captain told Connell to go over to the sub, but Fasson said that he would go and he began stripping off all his clothes and then jumped into the sea. Grazier also volunteered and followed him across. [Connell later said that he owed his life to Fasson's decision to take over.]
>
> We were watching, waiting for them to come back. We knew they were still on the sub when we saw it go down. It was so upsetting to lose them. War is a very terrible, sad and strange time, but it should never be forgotten, which is why campaigns such as this are so important.

Eric won a Distinguished Service Medal for his time on the *Petard*. His story in the *Herald* was followed by the recollections of the late Douglas Freer.

Douglas, from Lymington in Hampshire, was one of 200 men who survived an air attack on HMS *Fiji* in the Battle of Crete. He was the Ordnance Artificer on the *Petard* with the responsibility of making sure all the guns and related equipment remained in good working order. His action station was on the bridge so he could be alerted to any problems with guns anywhere on board. This provided him with an excellent view of the unfolding drama on 30 October 1942. 'It was a game of cat and mouse with the hunter and the hunted. The sub was desperately trying not to be detected, and we were trying to find it. The atmosphere was calm. We were sailors and we all had a job to do.'

Decades later he was amazed to find out the significance of that day. 'I couldn't believe it when I found out. It is marvellous to think that by capturing the right submarine, we helped shorten the war. The *Petard* was a very important ship. It was, perhaps, the most effective destroyer of all time.'

Douglas sent us a copy of a letter he had received from Robert Harris, the author of *Enigma*. Douglas had attended a lecture given by Mr Harris and had attempted to question him on the importance of the *Petard* incident. He was unable to get his question across, but unperturbed he later wrote to the author to make his point. Robert Harris' written reply was further proof of the campaign's value:

> What a pity you were unable to ask your question as I would then have had an opportunity of paying tribute to the wonderful heroism of the crew of HMS *Petard*, who did indeed shorten the war and saved thousands of lives.
>
> It is a disgrace in my opinion that still, after all these years, the huge contribution of your late shipmates is not more widely known. I do make reference to the capture of documents from U-559 in *Enigma*, so I hope this goes some small way to redressing the balance.

In April 2001, I was contacted by well-known Tamworth restaurateur and prolific fundraiser, Stuart Lunn, who had produced a CD in honour of our campaign. Containing songs from local artists, the CD cost £6 to make and Stuart put £5 for each one sold into our kitty. 'We have got to get that memorial in the town,' he told me.

At about the same time I received £200 from Adrian Traves from the Philippines, which just showed how far the news was spreading. He made the donation in memory of his grandfather, Cyril Traves, who was coxswain of the *Petard* throughout her action-packed first commission. Reg Crang remembered Cyril as a key member of the crew, much admired by his colleagues.

Reg said this was particularly the case when the *Petard* was under attack by German Stuka dive-bombers, a regular occurrence in the Mediterranean between 1942 and 1943. 'The captain [Rupert Egan] would watch the Stuka throughout its screaming dive towards us,' said Reg:

> When he saw the release of the bombs – by which time the bomber was too close for comfort – he would snap out an order for a change of course to the coxswain which was followed in an instant. Both men remained ice cool while many of us trembled or winced beside them.

Cyril died in October 1999 at the age of ninety-three. His son had ensured that he had at least forged a link with our campaign.

In May 2001, I heard from a charitable trust which insisted on anonymity, but wished to donate £500 to our appeal. The letter stated: 'We act for a charitable trust set up for the purpose of benefiting good and charitable causes for the inhabitants of Tamworth and its surrounding areas. Patrons, who wish to remain anonymous, are aware of the *Herald* appeal and wish to help.'

We had received donations from all over the world and now we had a mystery benefactor. The money covered the cost of a bench with a brass plaque dedicated to the three heroes at the new National Memorial Arboretum which was being developed a few miles down the road near Alrewas. My joy at this gesture was tempered by the news that Colin's wife Olive had died.

CHAPTER TWENTY

WELCOME TO THE HOTEL COLIN GRAZIER

Interest in its Enigma theme was enormous

On the front page of its edition of 26 July 2001, the *Herald* announced another major development – Colin Grazier was to have a £1 million hotel named after him in the heart of the town.

Tamworth's fine old Georgian police station, a Grade Two listed building, was to be converted into a pub and restaurant with accommodation in seven bedrooms. The entire hotel was to be fitted out on an Enigma theme. The plans included naming the raised lounge area after Tony Fasson, and the lower bar after Tommy Brown. The Enigma links would eventually go far beyond this and the hotel later showcased the Enigma story on its walls.

I was chuffed by the news because I had contacted the developers to suggest it should be named in honour of Colin Grazier when I first heard it was to be converted into a hotel. I invited the Middlesex-based firm's operations director, Christian Stafford, to the *Herald*'s offices and took him page by page through one of my 'Grazier packs'. Assistant editor John Harper had come up with the description after watching me prepare endless Enigma information packs whenever there was an opportunity to gain more interest in the story. These packs contained copies of *Herald* articles and pictures that had been sent to us to help promote the men. As luck would have it Christian was looking for a strong local theme for the new hotel and had an interest in history. By the end of our meeting the Colin Grazier Hotel was well on its way to becoming a reality.

'It should be a marvellous thing for Tamworth that this is happening to a building which has been lying empty for the past two years,' Christian commented in the *Herald*. It struck me at that point that all our ambitions had been achieved with high interest. We hoped to have a street named after Colin and were lucky enough to get an entire estate themed on the Enigma story. We wanted a pub to be named in his memory and ended up with a hotel. We wanted to produce a fitting memorial and had one of the greatest contemporary sculptors on the case. Things were working out just fine.

In August 2001, Tamworth Beer Festival came round again and so did Colin Grazier Ale, which was once more produced by the Bass Museum Brewery in Burton-on-Trent. For the second year running the profits were to be donated to the campaign coffers.

The opening of the Grazier Hotel in September was a grand occasion. The lease had been taken up by Mike Roberts who had talked his brother-in-law Roy Lake into a management consultancy role. For several weeks beforehand I had been working closely with the management, preparing material which was to appear on the walls throughout the hotel.

We were still being sent pictures and memories of the incident to raise the profile of the men and my Grazier packs were thickening by the week. I spent hours at the photocopying machine. We took copies of everything before returning the originals in the post.

I must have driven *Herald* photographer Paul Barber round the bend with my requests for him to copy new photographs and *Herald* articles. He must have been relieved when the *Herald* invested in new technology which meant that material used in the paper was automatically digitally archived. In Roy Lake, in particular, I found a fellow Enigma enthusiast who left no stone unturned in his hunger for new material. He was constantly badgering me for more copies of *Herald* articles or old pictures to have framed for the hotel's walls. Our original idea was to use our collection to attract the interest of the Imperial War Museum, but the 'Grazier packs' were to prove vital in other ways.

The hotel became a fantastic tribute to the men, the Enigma story and indeed the campaign itself. *Herald* articles were everywhere – in the bars, eating areas, up the stairs and in all the bedrooms which had been named after each of the heroes, plus Captain Mark Thornton, Alan Turing and the *Petard*. Champagne and Grazier Ale flowed that night as that long-neglected building sprang back into life in some style.

Perhaps the most amazing thing of all was the fact that a live television broadcast was made from the hotel on the evening it opened. I don't know how many new commercial operations have reaped the benefits of free live TV coverage, but I know it must be exceptionally rare. *Central News* reporter Suzanne Page interviewed me in the bar about the background to the hotel. It was my second television appearance since the campaign started. Suzanne was also keen to follow up the story and asked me to keep her informed about the progress of the main monument. We didn't need any more evidence, but once again it showed how big the story of Colin Grazier and his colleagues had become. The hotel had got the right name and the interest in its Enigma theme was enormous.

Left: Tamworth shoppers strain to get a glimpse of the town's new £1 million hotel named in honour of Colin Grazier.

Below: The author is interviewed for TV about the opening of the Colin Grazier Hotel in Tamworth.

Colleen Mason (Grazier's niece) cuts the ribbon to officially open the Colin Grazier Hotel. To her left is Colin's second cousin, Beryl Bauer, and to her right, Olive's sister, Joyce Radbourne. To the left of Joyce is Stan Brown who was on the *Petard* on the night of the action.

Among the guests that evening were Colin Grazier's niece, Colleen Mason, his second cousin, Beryl Bauer, and his sister-in-law, Joyce Radbourne. The relatives were brought to the hotel in stretched limousines courtesy of the hotel management. Stan Brown (no relation to Tommy), who was on the *Petard* on 30 October 1942 was also there representing the HMS *Petard* Association. A large party of civic dignitaries was there too, including Tamworth MP Brian Jenkins and Peter Seekings, leader of Tamworth Borough Council.

Colleen cut the ribbon to mark the official opening of the new hotel and later said it had been a great honour for her Uncle Colin. 'I am just sorry that his parents never lived to see this day. It would have made them very proud,' she said.

Brian Jenkins described the hotel as an asset for the town and added:

It is such a shame that at the time it had to be kept secret for security reasons and the other priorities of the war caused us to temporarily forget. But at least we recognise, through the memory of people like Colin, the contribution that local people made towards freedom and democracy in Europe. So we should all feel proud that we can recognise them in the shape of the Colin Grazier Hotel.

Shortly after the opening of the hotel, I went to review the newly released film *Enigma*, based on Robert Harris' bestseller. This was a far more rewarding task than reviewing *U-571*. Very early on into the film three words were uttered which made a good movie great for me: Fasson and Grazier! They finally got a mention on the big screen – *Two men died for those codes, Fasson and Grazier*.

Oh joy! I think I missed the next five minutes of the film I was so excited. I kept turning to my wife Claire with a triumphant fist gesture, which soon got on her nerves big time. But I was celebrating a great cinematic moment. I had witnessed its sporting equivalent the previous month when England beat Germany 5-1 in Munich in a World Cup tie. It may be a strange comparison, but as a keen football supporter (Stoke City and England) I could see some similarities.

That victory in Munich more than made up for so many painful defeats and injustices in the past. The film was doing exactly the same. The men's lack of recognition had been addressed and this helped to lay the ghost of *U-571* to rest. Incidentally I received a joke email from one of my friends saying that the Americans were planning a new football film called '5-1'. Apparently it was to be about the extraordinary result the American national soccer team had pulled off against impossible odds in Germany!

Seriously though, it was great to hear the men get a mention even though it was far too brief. I did feel a bit aggrieved that Tommy Brown was omitted purely because he had not died at the scene.

Despite wanting more details of the men's heroism to be included, I was nevertheless pleased that Mick Jagger's new production company, Jagged Films, had at least acknowledged the real Enigma heroes. Like the book it was based on, though, the film concentrated on what happened after the codes were rescued and not before.

Wartime Bletchley Park is brilliantly recreated by director Micheal Apted and there are wonderful performances from Dougray Scott, Kate Winslet, Jeremy Northam and Saffron Burrows. I loved the atmosphere of the film, despite it being a little complicated to follow at times. Mick Jagger makes a brief Hitchcock-type cameo appearance as an RAF officer. Grazier and Fasson's inclusion was even lower key – but stole the show for me! But the plot did not go down well with the Poles who felt as sore as the British did after *U-571*. I had some sympathy with them too.

The storyline involves a Polish codebreaker working at Bletchley who treacherously attempts to reveal its secrets to the Germans. The Poles, responsible for so much ground-breaking work cracking the Enigma code, were most aggrieved, particularly as they were not even allowed to work at Bletchley Park.

As I was watching the film, another member of the committee, Arthur Shakespeare, was travelling on a coach bound for Leamington Spa for a fundraising evening hosted by that town's Royal Naval Association. Around thirty-five members of the Tamworth branch went to the 'Bell-bottoms Ball' that night and the evening began with a talk about the campaign. At the end of the evening we received a cheque for £350.

———◆◆◆———

Mervyn Romeril the 'lookout' was next to be featured in our 'Survivors Stories' series. He was desperately lucky to have survived the war as only a twist of fate had prevented his body from being amongst those thrown overboard in a sewn-up hammock as was the custom for fatalities on board.

One night, while the *Petard* was carrying out operations off the coast of Malta, Mervyn was moved from his usual position as part of the crew manning one of the *Petard*'s main guns, to act as a lookout on the bridge. A German fighter plane swooped over the ship undetected and wiped out the team of men Mervyn would have been part of. 'I should have been in that position. It sticks in my mind,' he said. 'I was looking aft. I saw these lights coming towards me. I couldn't hear the plane. Then I heard the noise of gunfire and I ducked under a shield in front of me.'

Reg also noted the terrifying incident in his diary entry for Easter Sunday (25 April) 1943:

A day I shall not readily forget. We were on another club run on a clear moonlit night. Off Pantellaria we were subjected to awful raking of cannon and machine gun fire from an aircraft which zoomed in low, unseen by our RDF or lookouts.

The whole of 'Y' gun's crew was wiped out, three killed instantly and the gun captain critically wounded. One member of the ammunition supply part was also killed and ten wounded, four very seriously. The injured included Lt Connell who had a remarkable escape from death in his exposed position in the director turret. A bullet pierced the top of his skull, cleaving a furrow before going on to shatter his binoculars. Yet he did not lose consciousness.

I went to see him in his cabin, his head swathed with bandages. The sense of shame I always feel when enemy attacks catch us unawares was made worse on this occasion … with four of our men lying dead I felt awful.

'Sorry to see you like this, Sir,' I stammered.

'Why didn't we pick it up?' he asked.

'It came in too low,' was all I could reply. He accepted that, knowing it was true … but I can't help feeling responsible and it is very hard to live with.

Mervyn clearly recalls the night, six months before his lucky escape, when the *Petard* finally landed its prize catch:

I can remember seeing the sub [U-559] come to the surface. I saw Grazier and Fasson dive over into the sea. The next thing I remember is seeing the sub go down, and the rest of the boat party getting away. I knew Lt Fasson, we all knew him, but I didn't know Colin much.

Now living in a retirement home in Bournemouth, he looks back with pride at what his ship achieved:

I feel that at least we had achieved something, that as a ship we did something to help. It was gratifying to know that I had done something useful, but nobody can appreciate what we went through.

I had to look out for periscopes. The U-boats hunted in packs. They knew the route of all the convoys and just lay in wait for them. It was pretty horrendous.

Mervyn left the *Petard* in 1943 and became a Fleet Air Arm pilot. He ended the war as an instructor, having enlisted as an eighteen year old in the Navy. His grandfather was a sea captain from Jersey and he had always wanted to serve at sea.

After the war Mervyn suffered from bouts of anxiety which eventually led to his early retirement. He partly put this down to pressure of work as a bank manager, but also acknowledged that its roots could well have been in the trauma of his experiences on the *Petard*. To this day he suffers terrible flashbacks and the sound of children screaming can bring back terrifying memories of shrieking Stuka planes attacking his ship:

Petard shipmates line up for the camera at a reunion of the HMS *Petard* Association in Bournemouth with the author, who was honoured to be made an associate member of the group. Seven of the men pictured were involved in the U-559 capture.

The noise those planes made was dreadful. Sometimes they followed the glittering trail behind the ship and used that as a line to attack us. Even when the bombs missed, we used to get covered in the sea spray. For years I didn't understand why children when they screamed do it at the same pitch as the screamers on those Stukas and why I had to come out of the supermarket when they were screaming.

Think of the guts it took for Mervyn to go on to become a pilot after that.

I was pleased to be invited to the *Petard* reunion of 2007, held over a weekend at the Savoy Hotel in Bournemouth. On the Saturday night there was a banquet, during which Mervyn became the star of the evening. After the meal he stood up and revealed he had a big surprise for us all. He told us how the *Petard* had come across the *Konstanz*, a Greek coaster masquerading as a hospital ship painted white with red crosses:

Some Germans on board were wearing white medics' coats, but it was just a façade. The ship was carrying arms from Italy to North Africa.

It wasn't on the Geneva list, which is how we knew it wasn't a hospital ship. We met up with it during a daylight patrol. It was circled by three destroyers, who put boarding parties on and I was chosen from the *Petard*.

We got over to the ship. There was quite a sea running then. Hands came across and we were hoisted on board. I landed on these two Greek sailors. They were very friendly and welcomed us with open arms. They told us they had been press-ganged by the Germans into gun running to North Africa.

When they saw the patrol, they ditched the weapons over the side. We went up onto the bridge. The other two boarding parties had rifles and we all crowded on the bridge and they started off for Malta. But we went round in circles. They said the metal on the rifles must be affecting the compass, so we marched off the bridge and it went on a straight course.

It was uncanny to be sailing through the Mediterranean in a blaze of lights after the blackout on our ship. I was given a new revolver from the store on the *Petard* but the safety catch was jammed. My job was to guard the engine room which I did with a gun that didn't work.

It took three days to get to Malta where we dropped off the German prisoners. I ended up going to shore on a motor boat kept on the ship. I found a German ensign in it which I shoved down my trousers. Because I was wearing puttees (webbing worn over trousers) it didn't fall through. I thought, 'They won't be needing this any more.'

He rediscovered the ensign shortly before the reunion, having forgotten about it for years. I sat with my chin on my knees when he suddenly produced the flag, in pristine condition, and announced he would like to donate it to Bletchley Park.

Various people began taking photographs of him with the flag unfurled and emblazoned with the sinister swastika. After a while I noticed a table of people looking quizzically in our direction, obviously a little suspicious of the organisation that was holding its reunion!

It was not the only amazing war relic that turned up that weekend. The next morning the late Gordon Connell's son, Mike, joined us for breakfast and brought with him a pair of binoculars which his father had found lying next to the body of a German officer on the upper part of the U-559's conning tower. Gordon Connell was a sub-lieutenant at the time and had been charged with overseeing the *Petard*'s sea boat that followed the boarding party to the submarine. The lenses were Carl Zeiss Jena and the swastika was engraved in the black metal casing. They still focused clearly, and it felt odd peering through the same pair of binoculars which must have been used for scanning the horizon for British ships.

Gordon Connell mentioned the binoculars in his book *Fighting Destroyer*, and Mike was allowed to play with them as a child. I spoke to Mike about the possibility of these also being put on display at Bletchley Park and it could now happen.

A few weeks before the reunion, the *Petard* veterans had tipped off Simon Greenish, director of Bletchley Park Trust, and me that two original treadplates bearing the ship's name were coming up for auction at Christie's on 16 May 2007.

In a short space of time we managed to cobble together several thousand pounds to put in a bid for the treadplates, but unfortunately lost out to a dealer. Together with the ship's bell, which I believe is still in private hands, they are the only known relics of that great ship.

Above: Petard look-out Mervyn Romeril reveals the swastika-emblazoned flag, which he hid down his trousers, to astonished former shipmates at a reunion dinner. He found the emblem on an enemy boat after boarding a German 'hospital' ship which turned out to be gun running.

Right: Phil Shanahan with a pair of binoculars taken from a German officer on the U-599 on the night it was destroyed.

Memories of life on board the *Petard* came flooding back during the weekend of the reunion. Ted Saunders, a gunner on the *Petard*, says his main memory is of U-559 survivors clinging desperately to the destroyer's scrambling nets. He said:

> There was no hatred against the ordinary man who fought the war. He was told what he had to do. The ordinary German was doing the same. There was no animosity. But one of the German officers opened a valve on his life jacket and squirted water in an Irishman's face. He thumped him and the officer fell back into the water. He had to be pulled back on the ship again.

Another image that has stuck with Ted over the years is the *Petard's* doctor, William Prendergast, operating on various people with a cigarette dangling from his mouth, a large line of ash about to drop off the end:

> He always had a fag in his mouth. One of the Italian prisoners [from the *Uarsciek* submarine] had a very badly injured arm and I remember the doctor had to cut it off. He asked one of us to throw it into the sea. It was grim, but it was war.

The *Uarsciek* became the *Petard's* second submarine victim after it was spotted lurking on the surface on 15 December 1942. The Italian vessel quickly dived and then fired its torpedoes at its approaching adversary. It was in the early hours of the morning and still dark, but the torpedoes created a phosphorescent wake and the *Petard* was able to dodge the oncoming tracks.

The *Petard*, along with fellow destroyer *Queen Olga*, were soon on the offensive and began depth-charging in earnest. The submarine rose to the surface and was caught in the blinding glare of the ship's searchlights. What followed, despite being another triumph at sea, was something which also left a bad taste in the mouths of some of the British sailors, as Reg Crang's diary so graphically captures:

As naked men emerged from the conning tower to drop on to the casing, both warships opened up a murderous fusillade of fire. No one on the decks could escape the slaughter.

After a long pause with no more firing, the *Petard* moved in closer. A few more naked men came out, we thought to surrender, but a machine gun on the bridge opened fire and began to pick them off. Our crew were aghast at what was thought to be the captain's [Mark Thornton's] own act of vengeance. Mercifully it soon stopped, but by now the *Petard* was so close to the submarine that it could not avoid a collision. With a sickening crunch the *Petard* half-rammed, half-climbed on to the hull of the submarine.

Then with engines astern it backed off; the fighting was over. Thought could now be given to rescuing the survivors instead of killing them. Daylight was just breaking and the Italian sailors began jumping in to the sea and swimming towards us. Many were crying out what sounded to me like 'Aiota', presumably 'help'.

A few, possibly injured or perhaps non-swimmers, drifted out of reach and beyond all help. It was pitiful to see. While we were hauling in survivors a boarding party led by Dunbar Nasmith, the first lieutenant, was preparing to tow the *Uarsciek* to Malta. When the party went down into the conning tower all thoughts turned back to the German U-boat in which Tony Fasson and Colin Grazier were lost. Could it happen again? No, not this time.

The *Uarsciek* was taken in tow and most of the boarding party returned in the whaler. They brought back codebooks, including a weighted sack of secret records found by the side of the Italian captain. He had been killed while trying to leave the conning tower to ditch the sack.

The tow got under way and we began attending to the survivors. They were so friendly and pleased to be saved, quite different from the Germans we had picked up. In fact

The ship's chain-smoking doctor, William Prendergast.

Above: Italian prisoners from the submarine *Uarsciek* are escorted off the *Petard*.

Left: A whaler returns to the *Petard* after its crew boarded the Italian submarine, the *Uarsciek*.

they were just like us! We had a few in our mess and they soon produced photographs from their wallets which they had managed to save. One was so proud of his girl back home, such a pretty girl smiling, it seemed, just for him.

The triumphant return to Malta, though, was somewhat ruined as the battered submarine had to be cut free when it began to sink. It was in danger of pulling the *Petard* down with it and so the crew were deprived of being able to triumphantly show off their prize in Malta. But Reg says the sense of theatre was preserved to some extent, thanks to the capture of the *Uarsciek*'s flag:

We reached Malta in the late afternoon. Word of the action had somehow got round and a large crowd of Maltese had gathered for our entry. When the skipper ordered the Italian flag to be waved they broke into loud cheers. But many of us did not feel like gloating over our success. I do not think I shall ever forget the cry of 'Aiota' from the drowning men.

CHAPTER TWENTY-ONE

TAKING FIGHT TO WAR MUSEUM

There was a sickening, reverberating clang as the German instrument of destruction left its mark on the Herald's *assistant editor*

In October 2001, John Harper and I set off to London for a meeting with the Imperial War Museum's head of research, Nigel Steel. The meeting resulted from our lively exchange of letters about why Colin Grazier's story was not properly documented at the London archive.

I had become increasingly frustrated with the museum's lack of action in rectifying the situation and had made some hard-hitting comments to Mr Steel both in letters and comments in the *Herald*. I hoped that by meeting him face to face and taking him one of my 'Grazier packs' I could make the museum more enthusiastic about exhibiting items on the subject.

The meeting was very successful. In spite of my previously aggressive stance, I found Nigel Steel a thoroughly professional, nice man, who cares deeply about history and the Imperial War Museum. However, right from the beginning he made us aware of the immense competition for space in such a prominent museum.

We did not lie down easily and, I must say, John and I were highly motivated salesmen that day. I painstakingly took Mr Steel through a 'Grazier pack', demonstrating how the public had taken the campaign to heart. 'The widespread public reaction to this incredible story is an indication of the interest your museum could attract by including these three men,' I told him. We constantly drove home the point that any museum dedicated to the subject of war could surely not ignore such a turning point in one of the biggest conflicts in history.

At one point, Mr Steel mentioned that space could at least definitely be found in a drawer on the subject in the Imperial War Museum North in Manchester. He had suggested this in a letter before and my reply had been, 'A hidden drawer is no way to treat unsung war heroes.' Although it is said that beggars cannot be choosers we were still not prepared to entertain this. It just seemed so inappropriate.

Mr Steel kept emphasising the pressure on space. We kept stressing the importance of the story and the public interest in it. We pressed our case firmly, but the atmosphere was very congenial, though a compromise was hard to find.

The meeting lasted several hours and to be fair we did feel we were making inroads. Mr Steel assured us the *Herald* articles would form an important part of the museum's records on the Enigma campaign in the Department of Documents where they would be accessible to researchers. This was great news in itself and an achievement that we can remain proud of, but we kept pushing for a permanent exhibition on the *Petard* story – particularly focusing on the courage and significance of Grazier, Fasson and Brown.

Above left: Phil Shanahan brings the campaign message right to the heart of government, riding the London Eye to make his point.

Above right: Gunning for recognition for war heroes, *Herald* deputy editor and assistant editor Phil Shanahan and John Harper with Nigel Steele (left) outside the Imperial War Museum in London.

We were taken on a tour of the museum and I asked Mr Steel to think hard about how he could use the story in a permanent exhibition. By the end of the day I had the strong impression that the door was creaking open a bit. Meeting Nigel Steel had also enabled me to appreciate his stance and I had more sympathy for the enormous pressure on the museum to display fresh artefacts. However, I still felt that a way must be found.

Mr Steel acknowledged the significance of the material the campaign had unearthed and its potential as an exhibition. He was very interested in some of the items we had put together, including Colin's Bible and the piece of life jacket from a U-559 survivor. But in the end he implied there was only one way in which all this could form part of the museum's permanent collections – if we could somehow obtain Colin Grazier's George Cross to form the focal point of a display.

The museum had a section dedicated to George Cross holders and if we got Grazier's George Cross, we could include other items with it in a small glass case to give a flavour of the story and also mention HMS *Petard*, Fasson and Brown. This, he told us, was the only possibility of finding space anywhere in the museum.

John and I left London thinking that we had achieved something important. From a seemingly inflexible position the museum was now trying to think up ways a display about the men could be organised.

The day was to hold some particularly painful memories for John. While the three of us had been striding through the museum's artillery collections, he had failed to notice the barrel of a huge German field gun protruding across the museum's floor. Not used in anger for decades, the gun was about to inflict a great deal of pain on an old adversary. There was a reverberating clang as the German instrument of destruction left its mark on the *Herald's* assistant editor. John had become temporarily distracted by another fascinating nugget of history from Mr Steel, when the accident happened. Despite being unable to speak coherently for some time, he did Britain proud by bravely continuing the tour on distinctly wobbly legs.

John is a keen historian, and his weekly column in the *Herald* is popular with readers. After our meeting he took me on a tour of his favourite parts of London and I could not have wished for a more informed guide. We walked for miles. Unfortunately the soles of John's feet protested and soon began to sprout blisters. At one point the pain was so bad he was forced to remove the offending shoes and wrap his feet with handkerchiefs. When we boarded the train home, John also applied a cool handkerchief to his forehead. I doubt if many people have emerged from a day out at the Imperial War Museum so much resembling a wounded soldier. Nevertheless, he had enjoyed the day as much as I had.

A few days later I received a letter from Mr Steel which confirmed the progress we had made. This is an extract from that letter:

> It was very useful to be updated on the progress of your campaign to honour the memory of Colin Grazier GC and to increase public awareness of the long-lasting importance of his actions and those of Anthony Fasson GC and Tommy Brown GM on 30 October 1942, in rescuing the *Wetterkurzschlüssel* and *Kurzsignalheft* codebooks from U-559 before it sank.
>
> Your account of the burgeoning momentum of the campaign and your clear success in achieving both goals was inspiring and I truly admire the persistence that you and the Herald have demonstrated over a considerable amount of time in securing for Grazier, Fasson and Brown, the national recognition they deserve.

He went on to stress that the artefacts we had collected would form the basis of a very good display but added that the George Cross would be essential to complete it:

> As you know from our meeting, the Imperial War Museum remains keen to help you in your campaign and would be delighted to be able to commemorate Colin Grazier in its galleries if an appropriate way of doing so can be found. I view this as an ongoing goal and I look forward to pursuing it together.

I was pleased that the museum was becoming more interested in promoting the story. I still felt that the three war heroes deserved a permanent home in a world-famous museum. However, circumstances were to propel me in a different direction. In the first place, I had a fundamental problem chasing Grazier's George Cross. We would obviously have to speak to the people at Edinburgh Castle, but even then I would face a moral dilemma. Sheena d'Anyers-Willis had gone to great lengths to get Grazier's medal placed alongside her brother's in Edinburgh Castle. I wrote to Sheena suggesting to her that by separating the medals we would be able to tell the story in two places, not just one. Also, I thought we could get a replica to remain alongside Tony's in Edinburgh.

Sheena replied that because of everything that we had achieved she would agree to this so long as the remaining relatives were happy about the arrangement. I could sense, however, that deep down she was sad about the prospect of the medals being separated. Because of this and because of Sheena's sterling work in getting Grazier's medal removed from obscurity, I decided to put this part of the campaign on a back burner. It also suited me to do so because of my other commitments. I was aware that the following October (2002) would be the sixtieth anniversary of the day the codebooks were captured.

Reg Crang told me this was a significant milestone and in particular for the surviving members of the *Petard*. He emphasised how significant this occasion would be to the men who were now in their eighties and nineties. He was also planning to hold the *Petard* Association's annual dinner in Tamworth the night before the unveiling of the memorial.

I knew exactly what Reg was saying and from that moment onwards all my attention was focused on the monument itself. We still needed to raise more money and there was also the matter of getting planning permission for the sculpture. A lot of organisation was still required and we had to give people notice of when the big day would be so they could arrange accommodation.

This turned out to be more difficult than I had imagined, and even now I'm not quite sure how we managed to pull it off. So I was happy to put the issue of a permanent display to the men on ice until after the memorial was in place. In addition, the Enigma campaign was only a tiny part of my responsibilities at work. I was so busy on other newspaper business that I could only give it my full attention towards the end of each week, and yet I was taking calls on the subject almost every day. Towards the climax of the campaign, especially, it became extremely challenging trying to fit everything in. It would have been tough enough if that had been the only thing I had to concentrate on.

As it turned out, it was a good thing that the issue of Grazier's medal was put back because it paved the way for Bletchley Park to house our exhibition. Who knows, in the future Bletchley Park may well be the place to reveal many more secrets about Britain's Intelligence War. For example little is yet known of the work at GCHQ (Bletchley Park's successor) during the Cold War. As a museum, Bletchley Park is in its infancy. It was not until the 1970s that the huge significance of the place was even hinted at.

After the war its very existence was in doubt, and it was only in 1991 that a movement began to save the wartime codebreaking centre. Unlike the Imperial War Museum, it does not have the same degree of pressure on its exhibition space and remains hungry for new and interesting exhibits. It seriously lacks money but has great potential to expand its collections. It seems strange that, having at last whetted the appetite of the Imperial War Museum, we became more involved with Bletchley Park. But where more fitting a place to display our contribution to this remarkable story than the very building where the codes the men died for were finally cracked?

Like the campaign and like the Enigma story itself, Bletchley Park has come to the fore in recent times and is at the cutting edge of history. It is ludicrous that its future is not guaranteed, in that it has to fight hard for every penny, receiving no funding from the government. However, my hope is that it will secure a prosperous future, and rightly so. Bletchley Park deserves a front row seat in British heritage and I'm sure that it will go on to attract huge numbers of visitors from across the globe.

During the war it was a powerhouse of intelligence, a real production line, a factory pushing out intelligence on a scale never seen before in any war. What better symbol could there ever be of the brilliance of human beings? It is a place with the potential to inspire generations of people, with concrete proof that the word 'impossible' is an impostor in the dictionary. At Bletchley there was no ceiling on what could be achieved by the human mind, even when it was working in the most pressurised conditions imaginable. It was also an institution which capitalised on the sheer courage of people like Grazier, Fasson and Brown. Thus it linked many aspects of human qualities – brain, brawn, spirit and guts. Every step must be taken to ensure that Bletchley Park receives the necessary finance to preserve and enhance it as a museum. A Britain without Bletchley is unthinkable!

As well as being the perfect place to display the material we had amassed, Bletchley didn't require the medal as a prerequisite to promoting the stories of our three heroes. That was to become even more important to me when I started researching this book and asked Sheena to sketch out her memories of the day she happened to stumble on Colin Grazier's George Cross.

One particular part of her account of that day at Faslane made an impression on me. While driving home Sheena says she 'asked' her brother what he would like. She said the following words came to her, 'We died together and our medals should be together.'

Despite our breakthrough with the Imperial War Museum, I had not got the heart to try to separate the medals after that. As I have previously pointed out, there seemed to be a set pattern to this campaign, a sense of things being meant to be. I had not pursued Colin's medal just after the opportunity to do so arose. Instead I became preoccupied with getting the final arrangements in place for the memorial to occur in time for the sixtieth anniversary of the great event. And it was at that very anniversary that I forged strong links with Bletchley Park representatives.

Let me make this clear though. I still hope that one day the Imperial War Museum does celebrate this part of history and I will always be willing to help it do so. I still believe it is remiss of the museum not to highlight the three men. A compelling exhibition on one of the most important actions of the Second World War does not, in my opinion, need Grazier's George Cross to be effective. I also hope one day to see a permanent exhibition on the story in Tamworth.

The Imperial War Museum's loss has now become Bletchley Park's gain and it has instead received some wonderful artefacts, some of which might have to be held in storage at least for the time being. I'm sure that Grazier, Fasson and Brown would be proud of the fact that their profile has been raised at Bletchley. I know that their former shipmates most definitely are, and it was my pleasure to help Bletchley Park highlight their story. I hope that in future more of our campaign material can be displayed there.

———◆◆✕◆●———

It was announced in November 2001 that proceeds from a concert at the Queen Elizabeth Mercian School in Tamworth would be handed to the committee. The event was organised by peripatetic music teacher, Jane Maugham. An audience of around 300 people was entertained by more than 100 of the town's finest young musicians. The concert added £1,000 to our kitty.

There were a variety of performers, including adults, and the evening consisted of solo acts, duets, a woodwind group and the Tamworth Music Centre Saxophone Ensemble and Junior Choir.

At the start of the evening, details of the heroism of the three men were given out. Afterwards Jane, who had been following the *Herald*'s campaign with keen interest, said: 'Hopefully the concert helped to raise awareness of Colin's and his comrades' glorious achievements.'

CHAPTER TWENTY-TWO

A LUCKY SHIP

The Petard *was a lucky ship – Stan Brown*

Stan Brown lives about half an hour's drive away from Tamworth. He is one of the men who fired in anger at the U-559 crew seconds after the submarine surfaced. Reg Crang had previously put us in touch with him and he had represented the ship at the opening of the Colin Grazier Hotel. Stan lived just outside Birmingham and had a selection of pictures and memories to share with us.

Grazier Hotel management consultant, Roy Lake, suggested that I might like to accompany him on a visit to the Browns' house. We spent the morning with Stan and his wife, and just as we were about to leave, they asked if we fancied a bite to eat. They led us to the kitchen where a superb buffet was beautifully laid out.

They were the perfect hosts and it was as if they had been expecting VIP guests. That struck me as so odd. Both Roy and I were thrilled to have been invited into the home of someone who was involved in such an important incident in British history. Stan operated the pom-pom gun on the night in question – a four-barrelled gun which fired shells:

> We were all at action stations trying to get the U-559 to surface and for me that was on the pom-pom gun which is just past the funnel in the middle of the ship. It is pretty high up, so I had a good view of what was going on. When the depth charges finally started to reach, I had a perfect view of the surfacing sub.
>
> The *Petard* had her searchlights on and we all felt relief that it was finally up. I didn't see that Fasson, Grazier and Brown had jumped over, but I knew there were men on the U-boat when it started going down. It was such a shame. They were well liked chaps.

Stan dubbed the *Petard* a 'lucky ship' and described how in 1943 she was engaged in heavy fighting in the Dodecanese Islands:

> It was terrible up there. We saw some really heavy battles. We had no air cover at all. The battle went on for about three months and, in that time, the enemy sank six destroyers. I think four cruisers were also damaged. We were fortunate that we didn't get hit – the *Petard* was a lucky ship.

Stan also remembered how in the winter of 1944, the *Petard* completed her unique hat-trick of destroying submarines belonging to all the enemy navies when she sank a Japanese submarine in waters off Ceylon.

The giant I-27 submarine had just sunk the merchant ship *Khedive Ismail*, causing the deaths of nearly 1,300 people. 'Nearly eighty British ATS (Auxiliary Territorial Service) women died that day,' Stan recalled. 'That Japanese sub must have been waiting for them. There were so many casualties because they were having a concert below deck on the ship. The *Petard* blew the sub to smithereens, right in front of our eyes. I felt lucky to be alive after that.'

The sinking of the *Khedive Ismail* was one of the worst disasters in history involving female service personnel. Seventy-seven women died. All the men on the Japanese submarine were killed, including Captain Toshiaki Fukumura.

The incident underlines the terrible life and death choices that ships' captains had to make during wartime. Imagine the dilemma that faced the captain of the *Petard* as the survivors were in the direct line of his fire. Should he just rescue them, or possibly save far greater numbers from being killed in future by attacking the fleeing submarine and consequently also the people waiting to be picked up? He went for the submarine, killing all its crew in the process, but also survivors from the *Khedive Ismail* who presumably thought they were about to be saved. One woman who got off the ship safely reportedly looked on in horror as her sister was killed in the depth charge attack.

Reg Crang dedicated a large chunk of his diary to the tragedy and was clearly disturbed by the events of that day:

Sunday 12 February, 1944: We were bound for Columbo in company with our sister ship *Paladin* and the cruiser *Hawkins*. This was a routine convoy operation, escorting five troop transports, including the very large *Khedive Ismail*.

On a quiet Sunday afternoon there was a general air of boredom – the usual idle chatter in the mess, enquiries of E.T.A., (expected time of arrival) and speculation about mail at Columbo. I decided to take a shower.

Suddenly there was a cry of 'tin fish!' But despite the urgency in the voice I was sceptical. It all seemed too unreal. For days there had been no action, not even a false alarm. I rushed for the door and there, not far away was a sight of horror. The *Khedive Ismail* had gone up! An immense cloud of steam, smoke and spray almost hid the stricken ship.

By the time I reached the RDF cabin the doomed ship had gone under. Out of the 1,500 on board there were pitifully few survivors, most of them clinging together on rafts and wreckage in an oily sea. The convoy dispersed rapidly while the *Petard* and *Paladin* raced to the spot from which the torpedoes were fired. We made contact immediately.

One of our depth charges exploded prematurely in mid air and fragments showered over our port side. Some even landed on the flag deck and I saw a wounded lad being led aft to the sick bay, his arm hanging limply at his side.

For a time we lost asdic contact and efforts were then made to rescue survivors. *Paladin* went into the main group while we circled round to provide protection against the lurking submarine. We lowered the motor cutter and one whaler to pick up the wounded and isolated survivors and ferry them to the *Paladin*. Each time we approached the main body of survivors there was renewed contact with the enemy submarine. More depth charges were dropped causing appalling agony to the group of men and women in the water. Whether by accident or design the submarine was taking refuge beneath them.

However, after a while it appeared to slink off. Contact was lost again and we had to widen the search area. An hour and a half after the *Khedive Ismail* had gone down we began to get anxious. No depth charges had been dropped for some time and our chances were dwindling.

I was standing on the Flag Deck looking out over the starboard quarter when in front of my eyes a conning tower emerged, suddenly and sinister. Shouts rang out, signalmen went mad and for a few moments panic reigned. The ship heeled over violently as we turned hard aport. I wondered if we would get round quickly enough to avoid torpedoes being fired from such close range. But we were soon bows on to her beam and then she was at our mercy.

Oerlikon and pom-pom fire from both ships strafed the conning tower straight away. Our main 4in guns also opened up, scoring several hits. But with such a low-lying target these guns would not depress far enough to really smash up the enemy. To our amazement several Japs clambered out of the conning tower onto the casing, evidently trying to man the single large gun there. But these were suicide tactics –the men were quickly cut down by our fierce small arms fire.

This was a big submarine and no mistake. It seemed to be armour plated by the way it withstood our gunfire. Badly damaged she must have been, but clearly she was not going to surrender or go down without a fight. She was still able to make five or six knots and seemed to be trying to get bows onto us to loose one last desperate torpedo attack.

Although our skipper was the senior officer the captain of the *Paladin* now decided to take desperate measures himself. Our sister destroyer backed off in order to work up speed for a full-blooded ramming of the Japanese submarine. As she was making her charge, some of our crew were filled with admiration at the sight and cheered her on. But Rupert Egan realising the extreme danger of the move frantically called for a stop signal. *Paladin* obeyed immediately and sheered away, in time to avoid possible self destruction, but too late to escape all damage. The submarine's projecting hydroplane tore a huge gash in the destroyer's belly. *Paladin* heeled over, taking in water and came to a full stop, out of action. It was now up to us.

Our captain now decided on an unusual, if not desperate measure himself. He took us in perilously close to the submarine so that we could drop depth charges right in its path. These were set to explode at a shallow depth so as to cause maximum damage. The explosions caused a spectacular eruption of giant columns of water all round the oncoming submarine. For its crew who by now would be at the point where they could take no more, it must have seemed that that they had passed through the gates of hell. Yet their vessel ploughed on, seemingly indestructible.

By now it was clear that there was only one means left to finish off the enemy – a torpedo. She would be destroyed with one blow. Conditions were all in our favour. We could take careful aim and choose the precise moment to launch it. Only one would be required – or so everyone thought. When it was dispatched we held our breath and waited … and waited. There was no explosion. It must have missed. Very strange but no matter, number two would bring it all to an end. But to our utter disbelief that also missed its target. So did number three, four, five and six. By that time our spirits had dropped and we became resigned to failure.

But torpedo number seven [only one remained after that] blew it up with a vengeance, a knock-out blow after a fight that had lasted some hours. The final explosion had been so great that no recognisable evidence of the submarine could be found. We would have to await the development of our photographs. Even without any spoils of war, our relief at the killing of a Japanese submarine was immense.

Now we were able to turn our attention to the plight of the *Paladin*. The first task was to relieve her of all survivors, some 200 altogether. There were only two Wrens, three nursing sisters (out of about 76) and a few British sailors and soldiers, while the rest were black troops en route to Burma.

The severely damaged *Arethusa* which the *Petard* heroically towed back to the safety of the port of Alexandria, despite coming under attack from German aircraft.

The survivors told us some heart-breaking stories. One petty officer said that when the *Khedive Ismail* was hit he had been standing on deck with his Wren fiancée. She had no lifebelt so he gave her his own and pushed her into the water. He then swam to safety but she was never seen again.

Another Wren was saved by a leading signalman on loan to the *Khedive Ismail* from the cruiser *Hawkins*. When the torpedo hit he dashed to the cabin which she shared with a friend. After trying unsuccessfully to push her through the porthole, he crawled through it himself. Then, standing on the slanting side of the ship, he pulled her out just before the ship went down. There was no time to save her friend, still in the cabin. For a long time afterwards the girl would not allow Howard [the Leading Signalman] out of her sight. She had developed a dread of the sea.

Stan Brown also remembered the *Petard* towing the damaged cruiser *Arethusa* over 700 miles back to Alexandria after it had suffered terrible damage during an air attack. This was another proud chapter in the *Petard's* story and happened when she was part of a formidable force escorting four merchant ships to Malta on 21 November 1942. It was a deadly run and the ships were subjected to intense aerial attacks from both German and Italian aircraft, many firing lethal torpedoes.

One of the planes scored a direct hit on the *Arethusa*, killing 157 of its crew and badly injuring many others, including the captain. The *Petard* towed her back to Alexandria in high seas and was subjected to further aerial attacks. All alone and handicapped by having to tow the badly damaged ship, the slow-moving *Petard* should have been easy prey from the air, but spiritedly still managed to fend off the attacks. When the ships reached the safety of Alexandria, all the survivors of the crippled ship lined the deck and gave their rescuers an almighty cheer.

A month after towing the *Arethusa*, the *Petard* brought down her first German Ju 88 bomber. Reg savoured the moment in his diary:

Great cheers went up as the Ju 88 having dropped its torpedo, strayed too close and got a bellyful of bullets. As it banked into a turn our pom-pom and oerlikons poured fire into its underside from less than 500ft. The bomber plunged into the sea quite near to us, turning over as it hit the water. Good shooting!

In December 2001, a visitor arrived at our newspaper, looking like a reporter from a bygone era. He was carrying what appeared to be an old-fashioned typewriter. In reality it was something far more interesting and valuable – a genuine, German, three-rotor Enigma machine.

Shropshire bookseller and publisher, Dr Mark Baldwin, is an expert in Second World War intelligence and codebreaking and had managed to buy one of the rare machines in Denmark. There are only about fifteen in public collections in Britain, including those at the Imperial War Museum and the National Museum of Scotland. Another thirty could be in private hands.

Dr Baldwin, a graduate of Cambridge University, travels the country giving lectures on the subject, including hands-on demonstrations of his own Enigma machine. The model he brought to the *Herald* was the type widely used by the German Army and Air Force.

He had been following our campaign from a distance, and decided to visit Tamworth to see the town's new Enigma connections and to photograph them for inclusion in his lectures.

The Enigma machine caused quite a stir in our offices, so I ushered him to a private room to give him some space. Nevertheless, we were soon tracked down by several eager hacks who had spotted his arrival and were keen to get their hands on the ultimate war relic.

The Enigma machine was developed in 1918 by Arthur Scherbius. Originally it was not designed for military use but for businesses to protect commercial or industrial secrets. Its function was purely to encipher and decipher sensitive messages being sent by international telegraph, thus preventing the telegraph operator from understanding, and revealing to others, the content of the messages he was transmitting.

When adopted by the German military, the machine was used to encipher and decipher messages being sent through the airwaves by wireless in Morse code. Its use could not prevent eavesdroppers from intercepting the wireless messages, but all they would hear would be an unintelligible string of Morse code letters. Because of the astronomical number of ways in which an Enigma machine could be set up, military experts had soon seen its potential as an instrument of war.

It had twenty-six letters and looked rather like a portable typewriter, but without numbers or punctuation keys. A lampboard was situated behind the keyboard with twenty-six round windows each bearing a letter in the same pattern as on the keyboard itself. Finally there was a scrambler unit. This had a fixed wheel at each end and three rotating wheels in the centre (rotors). When a particular key was pressed on the keyboard any other letter could light up and the pattern would only repeat after 17,576 key strokes.

During Dr Baldwin's visit to Tamworth, I drove him to the new estate named after the Enigma story and also to the Grazier Hotel. We sat in the bar with his machine on the table. A group of elderly people at the next table glanced over at us for a second or two, before continuing with their conversations. I am pretty sure they hadn't appreciated that the old 'typewriter' we were playing with was such a rare and influential part of the German war machine.

Dr Baldwin, a life member of the Bletchley Park Trust, was to play a significant part on the day of the grand unveiling of the Colin Grazier Memorial. Before that he was also booked to visit the town to give one of his lectures. Before he left us that day he told us the theoretical number of possible Enigma configurations:

3,283,883,513,796,974,198,700,882,069,882,752,878,379,955,261,095,623,685,444,055,315, 226, 006,433,615,627,409,666,933,182,371,154,802,769,920,000,000,000

Right: Dr Mark Baldwin brought a
rare Enigma machine to the Tamworth
Herald's offices to show to the author.
The enciphering device was so ingenious
that the Germans thought it humanly
impossible to unscramble the messages sent
on it, a belief they held long after the war
ended.

Below: Christmas 1942 in Alexandria and
the men of the *Petard* are in good spirits,
despite the perils facing them from the sea
and air.

Now that's what you call Enigma variations! The odds of winning the lottery are said to be around 14 million to one. The odds of cracking the Enigma machine were more like 150 million million million to one. This incredible machine was thus perfectly named – Enigma is Greek for riddle. The addition of a fourth rotor increased the number of possible permutations by a factor of twenty-six.

Christmas 2001 was approaching and in common with all newspapers we were looking for stories and pictures on a festive theme. Stan Brown had given me many photographs from his days on the *Petard* which we copied. Among them were some photographs taken on the *Petard* by Robert de Pass during Christmas 1942. It made for a lovely Christmas feature full of human interest – just the ingredients for keeping the campaign flame burning brightly with our readers.

It must have been very difficult being on a ship in a state of war at Christmas, but the pictures showed that the men, who despite desperately missing their loved ones, still managed to keep the festive spirit alive. Stan said the men had bonded deeply and made their own fun, putting the reality of the situation to the back of their minds. 'We did the best we could with the food and got merry,' he said:

> We all had to make the most of it and make the best of what we had. Everybody missed their families terribly, particularly at this time of year. It was a tradition in the Navy for the officers to wait on the crew at Christmas time. That was a great laugh and we really took advantage of it.

The *Petard* was docked at Alexandria in Egypt for Christmas 1942, only two months after the deaths of Tony Fasson and Colin Grazier. The pair were obviously very much in all their thoughts.

'There was plenty of food so it was all right. Looking back we were all very close, especially at that time of the year.'

CHAPTER TWENTY-THREE

THEY GOT MORE THAN CODEBOOKS

*I had that machine in my hands and I saw intelligence officers take possession of it in
Haifa. They got more than just the codebooks – Eric Sellars*

An officer on board the *Petard* the night the codebooks were seized from U-559 gave me
one of the most detailed and surprising accounts of the drama I was to hear.

Eric Sellars, from Brighton, was a petty officer on the *Petard*. As the senior officer in
charge of all anti-submarine equipment and detection, he played a key part in the attack
on the German U-boat. It was Eric who selected members of the boarding party given
the task of clambering on board the German submarine. He had a grandstand view of
the action that night.

Eric was also put in charge of the Enigma haul taken from the submarine and he hid
it in the ship's wardroom. At the time he had no idea of the huge importance of the
documents he handled that night. He joined the *Petard* as a Leading Seaman and was
qualified to senior level Asdics (Anti Submarine Detection Investigation Committee). He
was promoted to petty officer shortly afterwards.

By the time he joined the *Petard*, Eric had been involved in several dramas that sound
straight from the pages of a thrilling adventure comic. Eric had served on ships which
had destroyed three U-boats before falling victim to one in the most dramatic style. When
his ship *Khartoum* was torpedoed by an Italian U-boat, Eric was forced to swim three
miles to the island of Perim, off the coast of Yemen. He then boarded another ship (HMS
Kelvin) which pursued the Italian U-boat responsible for his misfortune and brought it to
the surface by peppering it with depth charges. After a short exchange of gunfire, it was
boarded and taken to Aden. Revenge was sweet, but that submarine was not to contain
such a priceless cargo as the U-559. Eric had also been involved in the sinking of four
Italian destroyers while serving on HMS *Khartoum*. He remembers 30 October 1942 'as
if it was yesterday'.

He clearly recalls handling the precious codebooks which had just been retrieved. It
was decided to let the enemy gain the impression that the codebooks had simply gone
down with the U-559.

Considering how many years have passed by, there is a reassuring level of consistency
between the various eyewitness accounts. Understandably, however, some of the details
do vary. For example, Eric agrees that the men stripped off their clothes to jump into the
sea, but says the accounts of them being completely naked are not true: 'Can you imagine
climbing aboard a metal sub, up an iron ladder and down iron rungs with no shoes or
clothes on whatsoever?' he asked me.

Petty Officer Eric Sellars had a grandstand view of the action and says he handled the secret papers captured from the U-559, and also an Enigma machine.

Where Eric differs fundamentally in his recollections of the incident, however, is that he is adamant that a four-rotor Enigma machine was also taken from the U-559. He insists that his senior position meant he was one of only a few people on board the *Petard* who knew about the capture of the machine. In fact, he says he personally handled the Enigma machine when it came off the whaler and, on the orders of Captain Mark Thornton, took it and the codebooks to the ship's wardroom.

He says that Thornton then summoned him to a secret meeting in the wardroom. There were about half a dozen men present and the captain explained to the group that they had been invited because they had the best overall view and knowledge of the action. Eric remembers Thornton saying that he wanted to check all the facts for a verbal report he was going to have to make to the Admiral in Charge and that no minutes were to be taken at the meeting. He also stressed the need for total secrecy.

Eric's revelation about taking possession of an Enigma machine is a surprising one, but cannot be lightly dismissed. As he points out himself, 'nobody on the ship could claim to have had a better view of what happened':

I was on the bridge of HMS *Petard* throughout the action, firstly as a major player in the detection and eventual capture of the U-boat, but also because I was in the position of being able to hear and see all that transpired. I had in my hands a magnificent pair of Navy binoculars after the U-boat had surfaced and I was never more than a few feet from the captain at all times. I had that machine in my hands and I saw intelligence officers take possession of it in Haifa. They got more than just the codebooks.

By a strange coincidence Eric found himself working in Bletchley Park after the war. He was a chief executive officer with Post Office Telecommunications which ran Bletchley Park as a training school, and says that while he was there in the 1950s it was confirmed to him that the Park had indeed taken possession of the U-559's Enigma machine. 'It must have been destroyed after the war, but it was common knowledge there at the time that Churchill had ordered Enigma material to be disposed of.'

When I told Eric I was writing this book he produced the following highly detailed and compelling account of the encounter with U-559:

Four destroyers [HMS *Pakenham*, HMS *Petard*, HMS *Dulverton* and HMS *Hurworth*] began a search and some time just after noon a contact was obtained. Three ships under control of HMS *Pakenham*, the lead ship, took up a standard triangular formation whilst the fourth ship, HMS *Hurworth*, was sent around the action to watch for any other trouble.

The triangular formation is a standard practice taught to senior officers at Asdic school when dealing with a single contact. Although few on the *Petard* have seen it used before, it was normal practice to me. One ship becomes the attacking ship while the other two ships remain at an angle and signal when depth charges should be dropped. For a short time because of the underwater explosions, ships automatically lose contact which is very quickly regained as the water clears.

None of the Asdic operators ever lost contact and whichever way the U-boat turned it was quickly picked up again. This type of action continued for a long time and it was obvious that the U-boat captain was a very experienced and skilful man. One of the favourite ploys is to go as deep as possible, come almost to a stop and wait. As soon as the sub's captain hears the depth charge throwers fired, he goes full speed ahead and escapes the worst of the explosion. It works very well but quickly wears out his batteries.

Meanwhile up on the surface the ships were rotating their attacks in turn so that whilst the attacking ship is at full action stations, the other two ships could go to relaxed action stations, allowing changes in operation and visits to the toilets, drinks, etc. The action continued for hours which was quite normal but really worried some of the ship's company who expected a quick result. The ship's great problem was running out of depth charges.

The efforts of the submarine to escape went on all day but its batteries must have been growing weaker and weaker, and when it came to our turn to attack again I was able to tell the captain that the U-boat was stopped and was resting either on or near the bottom. He asked if there was anything from my previous experience that we could do to get the submarine up to the surface as he knew that I had three successful U-boat sinkings before I joined the *Petard*. We had in the charthouse below the bridge a first class echo sounder normally used when navigating in unknown waters to keep a check on the depth below the ship.

I suggested to the captain that we switch off the Asdic set and find out exactly how deep the water was below the ship. It turned out to be 500ft. The powers that be had never realised that a U-boat could go so deep and our depth charges were not calibrated for such depths.

It was now totally dark but this could not affect the asdic operation. I told the captain, Mark Thornton, of a method we had discussed at Asdic school. If soap, the hard Navy type, was stuffed into the aperture of the depth charge detonator it would act as a delaying factor in firing the depth charge. Additionally instead of firing these depth charges in a pattern, I said if they were rolled over the stern together as one group, they would land on the seabed together and create one massive explosion. This is exactly what we did.

The seamen in charge of the depth charges set to as quickly as they could and eight depth charges were set up on the stern rollers.

The captain now set up the ship for an attack upon the U-boat, the normal way, but instead of proceeding at full attacking speed, he went in quite slowly and only when the depth charges had been given time did he increase speed.

Total success. As soon as the water had settled after the huge explosion I was able to regain contact and report to the captain that the submarine was blowing tanks and surfacing. I switched off the asdic set and dashed out of the cabinet to watch. Suddenly about 50 yards off the port side of the ship and in total blackness of the night the conning tower of the U-boat shot out of the sea. The Yeoman of Signals Chapman switched on his port side 12-inch signal lamp to illuminate the conning tower followed quickly by the switching on of the main searchlight.

Sub Lt Robert de Pass instantly took a picture with his ever-ready camera. The gunnery officer, Sub Lt Connell, gave the order 'all guns open fire'. Luckily only one of the four main 4in guns could be brought to bear and just one shell hit the conning tower and went straight through it. Had more been fired they would have destroyed the sub. As it was the U-boat was hit by a hail of small arms fire. The captain saw the U-boat crew were leaping overboard and making no effort to fight back. He saw instantly there was a chance of boarding the U-boat. He ran across the bridge and pressed the cease fire.

Mark Thornton made no secret that it was his aim to capture and board a U-boat. He and his first lieutenant, Tony Fasson, had regularly discussed how they would proceed if the opportunity occurred without anybody else being aware of the fact that they had been briefed about the importance of capturing secret material from any German vessel encountered and particularly submarines. Nobody else had any idea of what it was all about.

The captain gave the order 'launch the seaboat' and then turned to First Lt Tony Fasson and said 'off you go number one'.

The ship was still at full action stations which meant nobody else could leave their station until ordered to do so by their senior officer. I immediately ordered AB MacFarlane and AB Lacroix who were officially nominated as seaboat crew to man the port lifeboat. It has to be remembered that it was pitch dark and the only illumination was provided by the searchlight reflected back from the U-boat conning tower.

The *Petard* was now only about 100ft from the U-559 and the water in between was alive with swimming survivors. Sub Lt Connell was the officially nominated boarding officer and he clambered down from the gun director to the iron deck where the whaler was already being swung out for lowering. The seaboat was fully manned with Sub Connell as coxswain and AB Lacroix, AB Grazier and three other Able Seamen whose names I cannot recall.

The whaler was now manned and ready to go when First Lt Tony Fasson arrived on the iron deck having come down from the bridge. It had been a very hot day and everyone was wearing tropical gear but as the night grew colder most people on the upper deck had put on some form of warm coat. Now the coats were discarded as AB Grazier and the first lieutenant stepped into the boat, took up a place midships, and said, 'carry on Sub and leave the rest to me'. [Some reports suggest the men dived into the sea directly from the *Petard*.]

Meanwhile, totally unknown and unseen in the blackness of the night, the young slight figure of canteen assistant Tommy Brown had slid into the bow of the whaler and was crouching down out of sight.

Whilst all this was taking place Second Lt Spens-Black went to the captain and asked for permission to launch the starboard whaler and this was instantly given. So shortly after the port whaler had left the ship the starboard whaler was launched with a scratch crew, one of whom was AB MacFarlane. It was then rowed around the *Petard* also to reach the U-559.

As the port whaler approached the sub through a mass of U-boat survivors looking to be rescued, the first lieutenant sitting amidships in the whaler saw it would take some vital time to tie up alongside the U-boat, even though the sea was only moderate, and turning to the nearest rower, which happened to be AB Grazier, said 'come with me' and they both dived overboard when only a few yards from the sub.

Followed by AB Colin Grazier, First Lt Fasson climbed aboard the submarine and went straight down the conning tower and into the control room. Tommy Brown jumped out of the seaboat as soon as it went alongside and attempted to make fast, but did not succeed and, throwing the rope down in despair, he also ran across, climbing the conning tower and went below. The next man out of the whaler was AB Lacroix who climbed onto the upper deck, that is the outer deck of the conning tower.

They told Tommy to stand on the rungs of the ladder and pass out to AB Lacroix anything they gave him, which he did. The other members of the boat's crew had formed a chain back to the whaler and Sub Lt Gordon Connell who had stayed in charge took whatever came down to him and made sure they were placed in the safest and driest place possible.

Whilst this was happening the captain had placed the ship as near to the U-boat as possible, about 50ft away would be a rough guess. It would have been dangerous to go alongside and he never did – the seaboat would have been crushed to matchwood. In the meantime Lt Spens-Black in the starboard whaler had rowed around the ship and sizing up the situation organised a line from the bow of the ship and through the bullring of the U-boat to hold the two vessels steady.

Then the second seaboat was taken alongside the submarine where Lt Spens-Black and AB MacFarlane climbed aboard and went to the conning tower to see if they could give any assistance in getting the secret material down to the whaler. It was at this point a line was being used to hoist a square box about the size of a typewriter up to the top of the conning tower and no one at that time realised it was the four-rotor Enigma machine. It was safely brought up and was being lowered over the other side of the conning tower when Sub Lt Connell realised the sub was sinking and shouted at the top of his voice, 'abandon ship, abandon ship'.

In the panic that followed AB Lacroix and the other boat's crew members climbed back into the whaler and the important box fell into the sea. Sub Lt Gordon Connell spotted it still floating and managed to hold onto it and get it into the whaler. In the darkness and in the rush to get back aboard the whaler nobody noticed this. Tommy Brown who was still at the top of the conning tower ladder shouted down to tell the other two men to abandon ship as the sub was sinking and he said afterwards that he saw them make their way to the foot of the ladder. Too late – down went the sub and all three with it, but Tommy Brown who had managed to climb on to the submarine conning tower suddenly appeared above the surface. One of the crew grabbed him by the hair and held on until he could be pulled aboard. The members of the second sea boat also managed to get back aboard their whaler without any trouble.

Back aboard the ship Sub Lt de Pass had organised the upper deck crew to pass out the line which was secured to the sub, and let down the scramble nets and ladders over the side of the ship to pick up the survivors from the U-559 and put them down into the tiller flat, where Petty Officer Charlie Underwood was placed on guard. Lt Spens-Black and his boat's crew had successfully made their way back to the ship and on the way managed to rescue many survivors who were hoisted aboard.

The port seaboat was now preparing to leave the area of the sunken U-559 and return to the ship. On the bridge of the *Petard* stood the captain, Lt Cdr Mark Thornton, the Yeoman of the Signals, Yeoman Chapman, myself and four lookouts, one at each corner of the bridge.

The captain called out to me to go down to the iron deck and said that when the whaler comes alongside it is to be hoisted level with the iron deck and held there. No one in the boat is to be allowed to move or get out. He said you will personally take all items from the U-boat down to the wardroom as carefully as you can, however long it takes, and make sure nothing is dropped overboard or blown away in the wind. Only then when you are satisfied that all is well are the boat's crew allowed to disembark and stow the whaler.

There was an atmosphere of elation amongst those members of the crew who were on the upper deck as the seaboat came alongside, with everybody knowing the whole ship's company had done a really brilliant job with everyone pulling their weight. But the mood turned to disbelief as news of the loss of First Lt Tony Fasson and AB Grazier spread through the ship.

Most reports refer to documents only having been taken on the night of 30 October 1942, and some have suggested that a wooden box removed from the submarine could easily have been confused with the machine itself.

However, Eric is not alone in making the claim. In 1986, the first edition of West's *GCHQ* gives the first mention of an M4 Enigma machine being captured from U-559. Three years later an article in the *Observer*, dated 13 August 1989, stated that an Enigma machine as well as codebooks were recovered by Fasson, Grazier and Brown.

In the first edition of Gordon Connell's book *Fighting Destroyer*, which was published in 1976, material captured from the German submarine is described as 'papers'. Interestingly though, when the book was reprinted in 1994, the author added a note not included in the first edition stating, 'When this book was originally published I was not aware that the equipment recovered … was in fact an Enigma machine!'

However, in 1988 respected historian Ralph Erskine published 'Naval Enigma: The breaking of Heimisch and Triton – a paper in Intelligence and National Security' Vol 3 (1), pp 162-183. Erskine checked with the Public Records Office and the Naval Historical Branch to identify what had been taken from the U-559. He mentioned the *Wetterkurzschlüssel* and 'related documents' but did not refer to any equipment or an M4 being captured. He also stated that West was incorrect concerning the material taken from U-559.

The comments made to an inquiry shortly after the incident by Lacroix, McFarlane and Spens-Black leave the debate open. The measurements of the 'instrument' given by Lt

Spens-Black are not the same as an Enigma machine and he refers to it appearing to have glass on one side which is also not consistent with the genuine article. However, it could also be argued that it was a dark, action-packed evening and so the men's accounts could be expected to contain inaccuracies. Interestingly, they do refer to a box-like instrument (which Fasson had described as 'important') being brought to the top of the conning tower, then being lost amid the panic of the submarine suddenly sinking. Eric's report is consistent with this, but he says Connell then picked up the box which was floating in the sea. As mentioned earlier, Connell states in the later version of *Fighting Destroyer* that it turned out to have been an Enigma machine. At one point he also states that charts, documents 'and the Enigma machine' were handed over to naval intelligence officers flying into Palestine. Unfortunately Connell died in 1992 at the age of seventy-five and so can no longer shed any more light on the incident.

The statements from Lacroix, Spens-Black and MacFarlane, held by the Public Record Office, make fascinating reading. They are reproduced in full below:

KEN LACROIX, ABLE SEAMAN. P/SDX.1471:

QUESTION: When did you board the U-boat?
ANSWER: When it was alongside on the Port Quarter.
QUESTION: What did you do then?
ANSWER: I assisted to make fast a line onto the conning tower. This parted. A wire was passed out and was made fast on the Quarter Deck. A manila [thick rope] was passed out and was shackled into the Fairlead aft. I then pulled up some books from the control tower and waited for the whaler to come alongside, then passed over the books. No more books came up until nearer the end. The first lieutenant shouted up 'Go carefully with this instrument, it is very delicate.'

This was made fast to the end of a line for us to haul up. I went inside the control room [of the conning tower] and when the box came level with me, the first lieutenant shouted up again as we were hauling it up too fast and it was very delicate.

When the order came to abandon ship, water was pouring in the top and I did not see the box again. I later discovered from MacFarlane that the box was taken off the top of the conning tower. I was the last on the conning tower, water was pouring down and as I climbed the last two rungs of the ladder I had to pull against it to get out. There was still a suction as I swam away and was picked up by the whaler. There was a wounded man on top of the conning tower.

G.W MACFARLANE, ABLE SEAMAN. P/JX.222494:

QUESTION: When did you board the U-boat?
ANSWER: When she was alongside the Port side. I assisted in making fast. A wire which was already on the deck of the submarine, which we used, parted, also the grass. We then secured the manila aft. I then went onto the conning tower with the navigating office and helped with the confidential books. Later we hauled a box up to the top of the control tower. The

order came to abandon ship and I had to leave it as the water was rising above the conning tower. I gathered that it was a delicate instrument as the first lieutenant shouted up when we were hauling it up to go very carefully with it. I never realised that the ship was sinking, it happened very quickly.

LIEUTENANT SPENS-BLACK, R.N:

QUESTION: When did you board the U-boat?
ANSWER: As she came down the Port side just abreast the forward tubes.
QUESTION: What did you do then?
ANSWER: I first assisted with making fast with the grapnel and eventually got the manila secured through the bull ring aft. I then went up the conning tower where they were hauling up confidential books.
QUESTION: Did you see anything of a box being hauled up?
ANSWER: Yes! The first lieutenant shouted 'box coming up, be careful as it looks to me as if it's important.' As we were hauling it up the U-boat started to go down. I shouted 'abandon ship' and Lacroix and myself got onto the deck and had to leave the box. I had no time for a close inspection but judge it to have been about 2ft 6in x 18in square [Author's note: that equates to 76cm x 46 cm which is roughly twice the size of an Enigma machine which measures 34cm x 28 cm]. It appeared to have glass or some composition like glass on one side. Lacroix was standing at the top, not inside the conning tower. The instrument lights were on inside the conning tower when I first went in. The wireless aerials were completely shot away, also all of the rigging with the exception of a jumping wire aft.

The steel gratings of the flat surfaces of the U-boat were still intact. The whole of the top of the conning tower was a complete shambles. There were two holes which appeared to have been made by 4in shells, one right forward on the conning tower and the other further aft (also on the conning tower) and roughly two or three dozen smaller ones of about 1in in diameter.
QUESTION: How was the water getting into the U-boat?
ANSWER: I have no first hand information but the first lieutenant shouted up shortly after he had gone below that she was holed forward. I could see no water rushing in but the books were dry when they reached the top of the hatch.
SUGGESTION: Bags should be carried as part of the boarding parties' equipment for the handling of confidential books.

Given the comments by Eric Sellars and Gordon Connell, the references to the sensitive and important 'box' are certainly thought-provoking. I love the blindingly obvious official suggestion that boarding parties' equipment should contain bags to put confidential codebooks in – particularly useful, of course, as the books were printed in water-soluble ink.

The debate over whether or not an Enigma machine was captured from U-559, while intriguing, is not critical in terms of its impact on the war. As was the case with Balme's booty from the U-110, it was the codebooks that proved to be solid gold.

CHAPTER TWENTY-FOUR

A WINDOW OPENS

*It may have happened sixty years earlier, but the death of
her brother was clearly still hard to bear*

The Colin Grazier Hotel welcomed its first celebrity guest in February 2002. Sir Bob Geldof stayed at the hotel during his two-day appearance at Tamworth Assembly Rooms. *Herald* photographer Paul Barber photographed him in front of a portrait of Colin Grazier under the headline: 'Two world famous heroes!' Hotel manager Mike Roberts later revealed that Sir Bob had been fascinated with the *Herald* articles on the story which lined the walls. 'He appeared to know quite a bit about it,' said Mike.

A few weeks later, our attention turned to Tommy Brown, and the *Herald* was able to dedicate a full page to his superb tribute in the North East which our campaign had given rise to. *The Sun* newspaper produced a two-page preview of the unveiling of the colourful stained glass window in honour of Tommy Brown under the heading, 'Forgotten Hero of Enigma'.

The unveiling of Tommy Brown's window was attended by about 300 people and was also featured on television in the North East. I was a guest at the official unveiling ceremony which took place at the Saville Exchange in Tommy's home town of North Shields. The link between events in Tamworth and the tribute in North Shields was all down to one of our committee members, the late Bill Wilson. Bill, a Geordie by birth, lived in Tamworth for many years and was a friend of Gordon Hornsby, a North Shields man who worked tirelessly to make the Tommy Brown tribute a reality. Bill told Gordon all about our work in Tamworth and suggested that the North East should do something to honour its son. A committee was formed and the Tommy Brown window was commissioned.

I travelled up to the North East with Bill Wilson and his wife June. On the journey up Bill told me in graphic detail how he had been horrifically injured serving his country in 'the Forgotten War' in Korea in the 1950s. Bill's vehicle was ambushed by guerrilla fighters during the conflict in Malaysia. His friend died in the ambush and he was in hospital for months. He still had shrapnel in his body as a result of the surprise attack. I could see why Bill's heart was in our mission to honour the Enigma heroes. He knew first-hand what it takes to make personal sacrifices for your country.

Bill was a brave and lovely man but sadly died later of cancer. June asked me to say a few words about him at his funeral at St Editha's Church, a few yards from where the Colin Grazier Monument now stands. I was able to tell the congregation about his role in the campaign and I remember saying that the monument was a part of his legacy in the town that would last for centuries.

Right: Rock star and Band Aid organiser Bob Geldof was the first celebrity guest to check into the Colin Grazier Hotel.

Below left: The stained-glass window erected in the North East in memory of Tommy Brown, who narrowly escaped drowning in a German U-boat only to die in a house fire. Photo by John Millard of the *News Guardian*.

Below right: Tommy Brown's six remaining brothers and sisters pictured with Tony Fasson's great nephew Geordie (back row, third from left), Phil Shanahan and Grazier committee member Bill Wilson (far right), at the unveiling of the stained-glass window in memory of Tommy Brown. Photo by John Millard of the *News Guardian*.

During the ceremony in North Shields, I met another of the *Petard*'s survivors, Geoff Richards, who was the ship's sonar operator during the war. Like everybody else that day his thoughts were with Tommy Brown. 'Tommy was a really decent chap,' he said. 'We saw him all the time because we used to buy everything from fags to newspapers from his canteen on the ship.' Geoff was to feature in our own ceremony for the heroes a few months later.

It was great to be introduced to Tommy Brown's six remaining siblings and Tony Fasson's great-nephew Geordie d'Anyers-Willis. It was also nice to see Mick Powell carrying the standard of the Tamworth Royal Naval Association during the march which involved around forty other standards. As the band swept past the Brown family, I was very moved by the sight of one of Tommy's sisters with tears flowing freely down her cheeks. It might have happened sixty years earlier, but the death of her brother was clearly still hard to bear.

As a child I remember feeling quite detached during remembrance services. It all seemed ritualistic and I never fully appreciated the human tragedy that lay behind the ceremony. As I grew older I was able to sense how I would feel if I was paying tribute to my own friends or members of my family, and I began to understand deeply the significance and emotion attached to such occasions.

Every human feeling is present – pride, honour, glory, dignity, sadness and a strong sense of comradeship. Men paying tribute to friends they fought shoulder to shoulder with in the most desperate of situations; men who gave their lives for their country, while the lucky ones went home to have children and grandchildren. But you also get the feeling that the ones who survived would also have been prepared to give their lives for the men who they now ceremoniously remember. Bill and I felt all those emotions that day and we were also proud that our work more than 200 miles away had led to such an occasion in the North East.

I was also delighted to be in the area because of my own strong ties with the North East. My father, Jim, was a Sunderland man who had worked on the wiring of submarines during the Second World War. I can remember him saying that he used to go down in submarines for test runs. Perhaps that was another reason the story gave me such a strong sense of mission. I also had my own links with the area, having lived in Sunderland myself for three years while studying for a degree at what is now Sunderland University. I had a wonderful time up there.

Enigma expert Dr Mark Baldwin returned to Tamworth in February 2002 for his 'Code Breakers' evening and it turned out to be a 'cracking' night out for over 200 people who gathered at the town's Assembly Rooms. Because of Tamworth's strong connection with the story, Dr Baldwin brought along a rare four-rotor Enigma machine which he had recently acquired from Norway, as well as his three-rotor version which usually accompanies him on his travels. In one year alone, he took his Enigma roadshow to forty-three different venues throughout the UK. He even went to Northern Ireland and had to get special permission to take an Enigma machine onto the plane as hand luggage.

His talk included a detailed examination of the workings of Enigma machines and a gripping account of various captures of Enigma material which led to the enormously complex codes being broken. His lecture was illustrated by a fascinating collection of slides. For me, the most memorable part of the night was something which Dr Baldwin afterwards told us had never happened before. He is not used to being interrupted during his presentations, but was forced to pause for a considerable period of time when he began to graphically describe Colin Grazier's courage in boarding U-559. The audience suddenly burst into a spontaneous and prolonged round of applause as they were told of the heroism of their local hero. It was extremely heart-warming and made me think back to just a couple of years earlier when the name Grazier would have meant nothing in Tamworth.

The second half of the Enigma lecture focused more on the work of Bletchley Park and included mention of the brilliant but tragic life of mathematician Alan Turing who played such an influential part in breaking the Nazis' secret code. The British authorities never came to terms with Turing's homosexuality. When he was suspected of having a relationship with a young Manchester man, he was given the choice of going to prison or being 'treated' for homosexuality by being given hormone injections. Tragically, the man to whom we all owe so much took his own life by eating an apple dipped in cyanide at the age of forty-one.

Strangely, the genius who solved the Enigma code was destined to die in the same agonising way as the spy who handed over the first piece of the jigsaw. Hans-Thilo Schmidt was an executive in the German Defence Ministry Cipher Office in Berlin and in 1931 became as treacherous to his country as he had been to his wife, whom he cheated on with a string of other women. He abused his position to get his hands on Enigma secrets which he passed on to the French in return for large amounts of cash. Later he even set up a factory as a cover to explain his new-found income. Schmidt had been tempted into handing over Enigma manuals by a French secret agent who went under the name of Rodolphe Lemoine. A decade or so later he was arrested by the Germans and alerted them to Schmidt's activities. Schmidt's daughter, Gisela, helped to smuggle potassium pills to him while he was in captivity and he ended his life by poisoning himself just as Turing later did.

There the comparison ends for, unlike Schmidt, Turing's motivation was purely in the interests of his country. As with other players in the Enigma story, though, the world was slow to show its gratitude and for years after his death Turing never received anything like the recognition he deserved. I remember Reg Crang telling me that he once personally tried to get a small road named after the mathematician in Dorset, and was convinced that the reason it failed was because Turing was gay.

Fortunately, in more enlightened times, he has been celebrated in various ways. A plaque was put up at the Colonnade Hotel in London marking his birthplace and in 1994 part of Manchester's inner ring road was named after him. A lovely bronze sculpture of Turing sitting on a bench was unveiled in Central Park, Manchester, in 2001, on his birthday, 23 June. And in June 2007 I was invited to Bletchley Park for the unveiling of a wonderful slate sculpture of Alan Turing by the artist Stephen Kettle, made up of more than half a million pieces of Welsh slate. The day before, I got a call from the creator of the sculpture, asking if I would be there to see it unveiled.

'You won't believe this,' he said. 'I lived in Tamworth for ten years and my mother still lives there. And my wife worked for your newspaper for several years.'

Stephen told me that he had been commissioned by American billionaire Stanley Frank, a philantrophist, probably best known in the UK for his efforts to raise awareness of Reginald Mitchell, the legendary Spitfire designer. Stephen was previously commissioned by Mr Frank to create a sculpture of Mitchell which is now seen by thousands of people in London's Science Museum.

Stanley Frank, who died in 2006, was very interested in unsung military heroes and I would certainly have loved the chance to talk to him about our three men. At least Turing was benefiting – and from another Tamworth connection. It was amazing how many hands the town seemed to have on this story.

The tributes to Turing were mentioned by Dr Baldwin in a section of his talk dedicated to more recent developments in the Enigma saga, and it was good to see that

With his trademark cigar dangling from his mouth, sculptor Walenty Pytel puts the final touches to his impressive memorial.

his presentation now included several slides of landmarks in our own campaign. We had a fight on our hands to bring these developments to fruition, particularly the sculpture. Getting planning permission for a house extension can be a complicated enough affair, but for a new monument in a prominent and historic spot, slap bang in the middle of a town centre, it can be particularly challenging.

I have lost count of how many letters, meetings, and trips to the council I clocked up. That's not to say the council wasn't helpful. In fact, I have gone on record many times to thank the council for its valued support. It is just that the procedure can be laborious and the opinions of many have to be taken into account. Sometimes it seems that the head of the council is saying one thing and the tail something completely different.

I had two great allies at the local authority, though, who proved invaluable during this process. Peter Seekings, the leader of Tamworth Borough Council, was a big supporter of the Grazier campaign, and chief executive David Weatherley was always happy to give advice.

One time, during the early days of the campaign, I invited Peter Seekings to our boardroom to really impress on him the importance of Colin Grazier. Needless to say I had prepared him a special 'Grazier pack' and I had also set up a film show for him of the Enigma video I had seen for the first time at the RAFA Club.

Poor Peter was locked in the boardroom with John Harper and me for over two hours. He was given the full Grazier treatment – subjected to the full contents of a 'Grazier pack' and then shown the video. I really admired his stamina! Immediately after the meeting Peter showed his commitment by handing us a generous personal contribution to the appeal. Perhaps he thought it was the only way he was going to get out!

As leader of the council, I thought it was vital he should be given a comprehensive insight. It was the first time we had properly discussed the issue together. I needn't have worried really, because Peter had already been following our progress very closely and was extremely interested in it. I'll never forget his speech at the unveiling of the monument. He referred to the day we had dragged him into the boardroom. He pointed at me and said, 'They showed me a film and *he* was doing the commentary! Where does the *Tamworth Herald* get people like him and John Harper from?'

Peter played an invaluable part in the latter stages of the campaign, especially when we reached a point where we just seemed to be going round in circles. Our intention was always to consult with the council before we put in for formal planning permission. That way we thought we could overcome any potential stumbling blocks about the design of the sculpture or its precise location.

After handing in our ideas, I attended a meeting at the council and was told that many councillors liked the design but several had expressed concern about the sculpture being used as a 'climbing frame'. Apparently they were worried about people injuring themselves. I made Walenty Pytel aware of this objection and he went back to the drawing board and heightened the base. This way a drunk would have to bring a ladder with him to climb onto the monument, and if he then hurt himself, in my opinion anyway, he would deserve it.

I submitted the new drawings and months passed with no reaction forthcoming from the council. During that time we had collected enough money for the plans to start being put into action, so you can imagine how frustrated I was when I asked if any progress had been made and was told again that there were concerns over the monument being used as a climbing frame. Nobody, it seemed, had appreciated the fact that Walenty had submitted fresh drawings to overcome this objection. Talk about déjà vu! I wrote a long letter to Peter Seekings and organised a personal hearing with David Weatherley. After that things began to happen.

A working party was set up with a range of experts who could point out potential objections to any given place on St Editha's Square. I met a group of officers from several council departments at the proposed location for the monument to decide on the exact spot. Many factors had to be examined, including CCTV sight lines, underground pipes and cables, vehicular access to the square and even the position of market stalls. We moved slowly from one area to another with each one of us being asked to comment. Were there cables or pipes in the way? Could CCTV still cover the spot? Would it obstruct vehicles or market stalls, and did I think it was aesthetically acceptable?

Eventually the group shuffled to a place where we all gave the thumbs-up. I was delighted. It was one of the best positions on the square. The monument would be clearly seen from a distance away and yet it was within the eye range of the new Colin Grazier Hotel and the historic St Editha's Church made a fabulous backdrop. One of the members of the group got out a silver spray can and sprayed the initials C.G. on the paving stones.

Not the work of vandals as some people might have presumed. The initials CG mark the spot in St Editha's Square where a sculpture in Colin Grazier's honour is to be placed.

It was a beautiful sight to me, though I think many people walking across the square over the next few months would have dismissed it as the work of a graffiti artist.

On 21 March 2001, the *Herald* was able to announce that the sculpture was to be sited in St Editha's Square. Members of the borough council's cabinet unanimously agreed to approve the location and the design of the sculpture. Afterwards Peter Seekings said:

> I am very pleased that we have come to an arrangement with the Colin Grazier Committee to place the memorial in St Editha's Square. It is essential that none of us forget what Colin Grazier did for his country. His selfless actions ensured victory for the Allies. We must not forget the thousands like him who gave up their lives for this country, allowing us to live in freedom today. The memorial will act as a reminder to us all of the bravery of a man we can all be proud of.

Little did we know when we pencilled in the date for the unveiling of the memorial bench at the new National Memorial Arboretum in Alrewas, that months later it would clash exactly with the eagerly anticipated England *v.* Argentina match in the World Cup of 2002. Similarly, when we planned the date of the grand unveiling of the main memorial we could never have guessed that it would coincide with the worst weather on record for eleven years! Hindsight is a wonderful thing.

These unfortunate factors, however, failed to take the shine off either event. Around 1,000 people were to attend the opening of the three-anchors sculpture, and if anything the weather added a special and unforgettable atmosphere to the day.

Likewise, while England battled to send Argentina out of the World Cup, a packed congregation, including many with a keen interest in football, put their priorities in order and gathered at the Arboretum for the unveiling of the commemorative bench. There was no sign of any hidden radio sets.

I first visited the Arboretum on a bitterly cold January day in 2002 when I went to meet Jacqui Fisher, who was in day-to-day charge of the place. I took her a cheque for £500 for the memorial bench to our heroes, and I was delighted to learn that it was to be situated in the 'Y' group plot, an area dedicated to a group of people who did vital work for Bletchley Park during the war by intercepting coded German signals.

A few months later I returned to the Arboretum with Colin Grazier's relatives and representatives of ex-service organisations to attend a service in its tiny chapel conducted by Wilnecote vicar, the Revd Bob Neale. The Revd Neale had been invited along in his capacity as vicar of Colin's old church, and he became the latest campaign convert. In fact, from that day onwards, he was a familiar face at all our future committee meetings.

Standards from the Royal Naval Association, Merchant Navy Association, Staffordshire Old Comrades Association and Royal Army Service Corps Association were present along with Royal British Legion standards representing the branches of Tamworth, Baddesley, Baddesley Women's Section, Two Gates and Wilnecote and Warton. Representatives from the RAF and Fleet Air Arm Associations were also present. There could rarely have been such a service and ceremony surrounding the commemoration of a simple wooden bench. The *Last Post* was sounded and the standards lowered before the bench was formally unveiled by Colin Grazier's niece, Colleen Mason and sister-in-law Margaret Kirk.

'My sister, Olive, Colin's widow, would have loved the way this was all done,' Margaret commented afterwards. 'It has been a wonderful occasion.'

Colleen added: 'I'm glad that all three men are commemorated – they all played a significant role in recovering the Enigma codes.'

CHAPTER TWENTY-FIVE

A MONUMENTAL MOMENT

It's a wonderful design, extremely elegant and has an illusionary quality about it, in the sense that the steel anchors appear to be magically suspended in the air

On the front page of the *Herald* of 27 June 2002, we published for the first time details of the Colin Grazier Memorial. A front-page exclusive story carried a main headline stating, 'Monumental Moment for our War Hero', under a strap heading, 'How we plan to celebrate the man who helped shorten WWII'. I had been waiting for this day for two years.

I used a photograph of the model to illustrate the future focal point of St Editha's Square, which I also sent to *Navy News* in which it appeared prominently and also on the magazine's website. It was a highlight of the campaign, and we were confident that not just the Tamworth public, but all *Navy News* readers too would approve of the sculpture they had helped make possible. To this day we have received nothing but positive comments about its design.

The model of the Colin Grazier Memorial had sat next to my desk for the previous two years and I was delighted that at last we could show it off on the front page. I remembered how two years earlier a Carlton TV crew had been keen to film the model, but I had kept it hidden. The *Tamworth Herald* would be first to show it to the world. Now we could finally go public on it. We had the necessary funds in place, and formal approval from the council. It was a reality, no longer a pipe dream. I felt a sense of elation as the papers rolled off the press that week and my comments in the article summed up the mood of all the committee:

> It's a wonderful design, extremely elegant and has an illusionary quality about it, in the sense that the steel anchors appear to be almost magically suspended in the air. It will be a lasting tribute, made from the strongest metal available and will provide Tamworth with a major piece of art which should last centuries.
>
> It is important to remember that this monument not only recognises the courage of these men, but will also be a permanent celebration of the end of war. Tamworth should be so proud of its strong connections with that fact.

I had been waiting for this for a long time and was in no mood to underplay the moment. On page two, we used a picture of Walenty Pytel in Portsmouth, standing on the real anchor chain which had been donated by Harry Pounds shipyard in Portsmouth. The chain appeared rusty and neglected, but so too did the one used for the model before Walenty got his hands on it.

In July 2002, Tamworth borough councillors approved the planning application for the memorial. We also set the date for the opening ceremony, 27 October 2002. It was the nearest Sunday to the sixtieth anniversary of the day the men died. We also revealed the wording that would go on the £1,000 bronze plaque attached to the base of the monument:

Colin Grazier 1920-1942

This memorial is dedicated to Able Seaman Colin Grazier of Two Gates, Tamworth, who gave his life recovering vital Enigma codes from a German U-boat. His extraordinary bravery, together with that of Lt Tony Fasson and Tommy Brown (all of HMS *Petard*) changed the course of WWII, saving countless lives worldwide.

While undoubtedly one of the greatest war heroes, Grazier was also one of the least known. Details of his actions remained secret for decades, depriving him of the true recognition he so richly deserved. This tribute was erected in the year 2002, following a campaign in the *Tamworth Herald* which attracted worldwide interest. It was made possible with the support of local ex-service and civic organisations.

Erected in memory of all Tamworth people who died for their country.

As a child Maurice Lunn was one of Colin Grazier's best pals. The pair of them grew up together and remained friends as young men. In August 2002, Maurice got wind of what was happening in Tamworth and got in touch to talk about his friendship with Colin. He recounted stories of summer evenings swimming in the lake, cinema trips and chasing the girls with his old mate. Maurice, by now in his eighties, said he still greatly missed Colin. I'm so glad he got in touch with us because I was able to invite him to the Colin Grazier Memorial unveiling ceremony which turned out to be an exceptionally emotional day for him.

Maurice first met Colin at Two Gates Junior School. Maurice lived in Tamworth Road, Two Gates, just round the corner from Colin's home in Watling Street. 'Colin was in the class above me at school,' said Maurice:

But we knew each other in Two Gates and all the boys used to play out together. I can remember we used to play kiss and chase with the girls. Colin was a really good-looking lad and very popular with the girls. We used to walk to school together and we both learned to swim in the river over Black Woods and in the reservoir in Valley Lane, Wilnecote.

The pals teamed up again when they went on to study at Wilnecote High School and their friendship lasted into their teens. As they got older they also paired up to meet girls, go to the cinema, the pub and the working men's club. Maurice revealed that Colin did a stint on the railways around Tamworth, shovelling coal into the fireboxes of steam locomotives. They both joined the Royal Navy, but were parted for training. Two years later they bumped into each other on leave:

I met Colin and he told me he was getting married the following week and asked me if I would come. Obviously I accepted and it was a great wedding, which was held at Kingsbury church. There were a lot of people at the wedding, but Colin and I were the only sailors. It was a wonderful occasion and a good gathering despite the fact that it was wartime and stuff was rationed. I then had to walk back to Two Gates from Kingsbury, which is a hell of a walk in the Blackout!

Shortly afterwards Maurice was appalled to hear of Colin's premature death:

It was not long after the wedding that Colin was called back to his ship – and the next thing I heard via a letter was that he had died. It was a terrible shock. In wartime you never know who is going to be next, but you don't think it is going to be one of your closest friends.

After the war Maurice moved to London with his new wife, a Wren he had met during the conflict. Years later he learned about the details of Colin's death:

What he did was more than brave, and I'm delighted that he is now getting some recognition. I have such wonderful memories of our days together. Colin was such a nice chap. Who knows what he could have gone on to do? He was an adventurous type who loved life. I do miss him.

The period between August 2002, up until the monument was unveiled at the end of October, was incredibly stressful. The organisation required for the big day was immense. There was just so much to pull together.

We also had our work cut out co-ordinating the erection of the sculpture itself. It became very clear to me that one thing for certain was that we were going to be very close to the wire getting everything ready in time. In addition, there was all the other newspaper business to attend to. On top of all this, I was also preparing to move into a new house!

I took some time off in August to settle into my new home. I then received a bombshell of a telephone call from assistant editor John Harper. A letter had been sent to me at work from the borough council which John had opened in my absence and its contents had left him in a cold sweat. The council had decided that several safety issues had to be addressed to fully comply with health and safety regulations before the sculpture could be put in place. One of these was that the monument had to be 'pinned' to prevent it ever toppling over in the event of it being hit by a heavy vehicle. The estimated cost of this, together with other necessary work to the foundations, was between £7,000 and £10,000.

Throughout the campaign I had thought we should raise a good deal more than our early calculations indicated to cover us for any unexpected expenses. As it happened, I estimated we would have a generous surplus of £4,500, even after providing lighting to the monument. But to find an extra £10,000 with just three months to go was daunting. It ruined my holiday. The hassle of moving home was instantly replaced with the thought, 'what the hell are we going to do?' I was also frustrated that this matter had only just come to light. Surely it should have been flagged up during the planning procedure? We had been given planning permission weeks earlier and never once had it been said that it was subject to any additional health and safety work being carried out.

It wasn't as if we had not addressed the matter of the foundation work. In fact a few months earlier I had visited a structural engineer to ensure that the foundation work based on Walenty's propositions was adequate. The structural engineer instantly offered his services free of charge when he heard it was for the Colin Grazier Memorial and came back with a sheet of highly complicated looking figures. Apparently, they proved mathematically that the foundations for the sculpture were in order, taking into account various factors, such as weight, height of the sculpture and wind speed. This was submitted together with the formal planning application.

This new financial twist put me in a spin. After gathering my thoughts I told John that all we could do for now was to make it clear that we would be prepared to offer the council all the surplus in the fund – at least £4,000 towards the work – but the council itself would have to fund any extra costs on top of that. A meeting with the borough council's highways and transportation manager, Clive Thompson, was set up for the end of August. Until then, we would just have to sweat it out.

At the following meeting of the Colin Grazier Memorial Committee, Mr Thompson announced that the council would try to support us if the costs went beyond the amount the committee could afford. I gave him a cheque for £4,000 and impressed upon him the urgency to get the work started. We had just seven weeks before the historic unveiling day and so far not a single stone had been disturbed on the square.

The meeting was also attended by Richard Penn who would be supervising the work. At first it was just another job to Richard, but like so many of us before him, he soon became hooked on the subject. He did a marvellous job for us, and I remained in constant touch with him and sculptor Walenty Pytel.

During the next few weeks, I really don't know how I managed to attend to any other newspaper business. In between working on the bread and butter of the newspaper, I was sending out invitations, liaising with the sculptor and the council, as well as chairing regular committee meetings. My phone was constantly ringing with people wanting to know various details about the unveiling.

Dr Baldwin had kindly agreed to give a talk on the Enigma story during the service and to bring along one of his historic Enigma machines. We had also invited three representatives from Bletchley Park and they had offered to bring a replica model of HMS *Petard*. The managers of the Colin Grazier Hotel, where the reception was to be held, generously agreed to let us have exclusive use of the place for the entire weekend. Key guests, including relatives of the heroes who would be travelling from Scotland and the North East were offered free accommodation.

It was exciting to see workmen moving into St Editha's Square to begin the foundation work and create a raised circle of stone on which the monument would be sited. With just two weeks to go, the two-ton black base of the sculpture arrived and was planted firmly into the middle of the raised bed. Things were beginning to take shape.

Among the many VIPs the committee had invited to the commemoration of the monument was the Bishop of Wolverhampton, the Right Reverend Michael Bourke. He sent us a column for our church page with the Enigma story as its focus. In it, he touched on the 'true meaning' of the word Enigma:

> Prior to the unveiling we are giving thanks in a special service at St Editha's Church for the dedicated work which decoded the messages of the German U-boat Enigma machines.
>
> People are fascinated by puzzles and enigmas. Detective stories are bestsellers. But it is not only wickedness which tries to hide its traces and disguise its messages. Scientists can unravel the mysteries of creation by assuming that the truth is out there, hidden but waiting to be discovered if we can unravel the clues.
>
> The Greek word Enigma occurs in the New Testament in St Paul's famous passage about love in 1 Corinthians 13.12: 'Now we see through a mirror in a riddle (enigma)'. King James' version translates it: 'Now we see a puzzling reflection in a mirror'. The idea is that we glimpse God's presence and purpose in the world indirectly. In Jesus he has given us the clearest possible clue, but even here his love is like a secret treasure concealed in the darkness and suffering of the cross. One day we shall see God face to face.
>
> But for now we live by faith. God is the great Enigma, the chief suspect whose hidden but redeeming love is the clue to the meaning of the universe. Can we live by that faith of all discouragements, with the same perseverance as the brave men and women who decoded the Enigma messages?

Everyone it seemed was starting to talk about the Enigma story in some way – even the Bishop of Wolverhampton.

With just days to go, Walenty Pytel had the three enormous anchors moved from his home in Herefordshire to a specialist welding firm in Portsmouth where the ship's chain would be attached. Originally I had intended to go down with him for at least a day and maybe organise a press conference. In practice there was no way I could spare the time. Things were becoming frenetic back in Tamworth. The local paper in Ross-on-Wye sent us photographs of Walenty with the anchors at this home, and our old friends, the *Navy News*, sent a photographer to Portsmouth, so we were able to keep our readers up to date with the latest pictures.

I discovered that the size of the challenge was keeping Walenty awake at night. It's difficult enough wrapping a small chain around three tiny anchors for a working model but when it comes to the real thing, it is somewhat more difficult! Walenty and I both knew that it would be catastrophic if there was a last-minute hitch. I too was suffering from night sweats. All I could do was lose myself in the enormous body of work that needed to be done during the final few days.

I honestly don't know what I would have done without Christina Lunn, our editorial secretary, during that period. Christina typed letter after letter and was always up to date with all the details. Richard Penn was pulling out all the stops getting the foundation work completed in time and all the committee members were doing a fine job. Jim Welland was organising the parade. We had meetings with Tamworth vicar, the Revd

Alan Barrett, about the service, and with Alec Benwell, the mayor's officer, who gave us invaluable help with the civic arrangements. John Harper was also a tower of strength. Ian Gibson, from Tamworth Heritage Society, began to attend our regular committee meetings and offered his help in any way he could.

Things were chaotic but were at least progressing. I had even received confirmation that Tony Blair and the Duke of York would be sending personal messages for the day of the unveiling. This is something I had been working on for several weeks. The most important thing to me was that they should be personally signed. I have seen many messages from royals signed by ladies-in-waiting on their behalf, and frankly they don't carry much weight. In the past I have cringed to see newspapers proudly publishing messages from the Queen to mark certain milestones in their histories. They were probably signed by the same lady-in-waiting who replied to my five-year-old daughter on behalf of the Queen when she sent a Christmas card to Buckingham Palace.

These men deserved something much more important than that. Both the Duke of York and the Prime Minister had prior commitments on the unveiling day, but I hoped that they would acknowledge the significance of the occasion by personally signing their messages. I was not to be disappointed.

Replies began to flood in from people invited to the reception buffet at the Colin Grazier Hotel. Among them was one from Stephen Harper, author of *Capturing Enigma*. In a note accepting the invitation the former chief foreign correspondent of the *Daily Express* described the event we were commemorating as, 'the most important single action of the war'.

On Friday, 25 October (two days before the ceremony) all members of the Colin Grazier Memorial Committee gathered in St Editha's Square for the arrival of its new centrepiece. It arrived on a lorry from Portsmouth bang on time. Before the crane swung the anchors into position on the plinth, John Harper and I climbed onto the base to drop time capsules into a gap running right down its centre and immediately beneath where the anchors are now positioned.

We had collected a whole range of articles and pictures concerning the campaign and the Enigma story which may one day bring pleasure to future generations – maybe when the sculpture is given its 100-year spring clean!

Walenty Pytel had been in the square since dawn (we had even had reports of a mysterious stranger shaving in the middle of the square at daybreak!) and had managed to give the plinth a lick of black paint before the rain set in. Good job too, because boy did the heavens open. The rain could only be described as torrential as we stood and watched the huge sculpture swing high into the air and land perfectly on the plinth. As the safety chains came off, Walenty began to help bolt the monument into place. Although I knew that Walenty had intended to put the sculpture front-on to the church it somehow looked wrong. People arriving on the square from both sides would get a sideways view of it which did not show it off to its best effect when viewed from a distance. This would be particularly the case when the lights were on at night and it was to be the new focal point of the square.

Jim Welland and Mary Edwards urged us to say something to Walenty who was looking mightily relieved that the monument was safely in place. Great artists are known to have

The Colin Grazier Memorial Committee cordially invites

- -

to a buffet reception at the Colin Grazier Hotel, Church Street, Tamworth, following the

unveiling and dedication of the

COLIN GRAZIER MEMORIAL

on Sunday, October 27, 2002

*The monument, created by Walenty Pytel, will also be dedicated to the
memory of Tony Fasson and Tommy Brown*

*A parade starting from Ladybank at 1.30pm will arrive at St. Editha's Square
in time for a 2pm service at the site of the monument
(In case of inclement weather, the ceremony will be held inside the church)*

*Following the service, a brief talk by Enigma expert Mark Baldwin will be held in St Editha's Church
after which you are invited to attend a reception at the Colin Grazier Hotel*

Please bring this invitation with you (Remember this is the day the clocks go back)

RSVP: Phil Shanahan, Chairman of the Colin Grazier Memorial Committee, Tamworth Herald, Ventura Park Road, Bitterscote, Tamworth (Written confirmation of your attendance would be appreciated)

A *Herald* Campaign

An invitation to an historic occasion.

artistic temperaments but to give Walenty credit, he readily agreed to re-position the sculpture. The moment its position was altered it seemed just perfect.

The committee, together with a handful of onlookers, stood and admired the monument, almost oblivious to the fact that we were getting absolutely drenched by the rain which was by now bouncing high into the air off the paving stones. It seemed the weather always reacted to big landmarks in the campaign in dramatic fashion. Even in this downpour the memorial looked magnificent. It was as if it had always been there. Remove it now and there would be a strong sense of something missing, like Trafalgar Square without Nelson's Column. My favourite view of the monument had the historic St Editha's Church and the Colin Grazier Hotel as a backdrop. We had fought for years for this, but it had been worth every moment. The centre of Tamworth was changing dramatically in Grazier's honour. Suddenly aware of the rain, John Harper and I sprinted to the Colin Grazier Hotel car park where we were brought back down to earth with an unpleasant bump – my car had been mistakenly clamped!

Back at the office for a hectic day spent organising last-minute details, I received final confirmation that both Tony Blair and the Duke of York would be sending personal letters which could be read out in church. Everything was coming together for the historic day – but the weather was once again to show its hand. In fact this time it was saving its biggest fireworks in years for the very climax of the campaign.

At the eleventh hour I received some very bad news from Reg Crang, the man who is truly the 'glue' of the HMS *Petard* Association. Reg had been suffering from heart problems and, despite his great desire to attend the unveiling, he was far too ill to travel. I could not have felt sorrier for him. Reg has won great respect and affection from all the association members, and from my regular dealings with him I could see why. He had held the HMS *Petard* Association together for years, and had been my main point of contact. Reg had organised a suitable replacement to speak on behalf of the association at the reception. Stanley Rothwell, who served on the *Petard* after the capture of the codebooks, had been charged with the task.

Reg's absence was made all the more sad by the fact that he was also destined to miss a significant reunion of the *Petard* Association. Members had enjoyed reunion weekends annually for many years. The venues change but the get-togethers are nearly always held, aptly, on the coast. This year, though, it was to be held in Tamworth and would be particularly special. Not only would it fit in splendidly with the opening of the new monument but it was also on the eve of the sixtieth anniversary of the day the codebooks were seized.

CHAPTER TWENTY-SIX

A CORNER OF ENGLAND FOREVER GERMANY

A total of twenty-five German submariners are buried in my home county in the middle of England

Despite Staffordshire being inland, it was the perfect county for our sculpture to be situated because of its associations with Enigma and U-boats. These connections are somewhat bizarre and little known. Grazier's final resting place is in a German submarine, while a prominent U-boat commander is buried in one of the county's beauty spots a short distance away from Grazier's home town – and even closer to the village where I live. And not just him, but a total of twenty-five German submariners are buried in my home county, slap bang in the middle of England.

Covering twenty-six square miles, Cannock Chase is designated as an Area of Outstanding Natural Beauty. It's a wonderful mix of heathland, forest and bracken-covered hills containing some lovely natural water features and herds of wild deer. It is also the place where 5,000 German war dead spanning two world wars are buried in meticulously kept plots of heather. The cemetery, established after the war, was the result of cooperation between the Commonwealth War Graves Commission and the German War Graves Commission. Each year parties of young Germans arrive to tend the plots.

The name of Hans-Wilhelm von Dresky is included with several other men on a plain wooden cross above one of the shared graves. As I gazed at his grave, the ironic juxtaposition between his and Grazier's final resting places really struck me. In addition, Grazier died in an action against a submarine which handed the British the final pieces of the Enigma jigsaw. Dresky lost his life in a U-boat incident which gave away the first pieces of the puzzle at sea. Dresky was commander of the U-33 which had been picked to undertake a hugely important but risky raid on the Firth of Clyde in Scotland – a place where Grazier had sailed on the *Petard* during its test runs.

The young captain's dangerous mission in February 1940 was regarded so important that he was given a personal send-off by Doenitz at Wilhelmshaven. Five months earlier Adolf Hitler had travelled to the port to salute Dresky and his crew for a successful patrol as the U-33 lay in harbour. The thirty year old certainly had powerful connections.

Dresky's orders were to lay mines in the Firth of Clyde with the intention of destroying a number of British vessels in the estuary. Unfortunately for him and his shipmates, the U-33 was detected by HMS *Gleaner*, part of Britain's anti-submarine fleet. It was forced to the surface by a sequence of depth charge attacks. Dresky was last seen alive in the freezing waters and was said to have asked his men to give three cheers for the U-33 as it went down. Twenty-five of the U-33 crew died that day (12 February 1940) and only seven survived. Dresky's body was later recovered and buried with many of his crew in Colin Grazier's county.

The U-33 was the first German submarine to surrender Enigma secrets and seemingly because of a basic human weakness – panic. Enigma machine rotors were handed to the officers to throw into the sea as they jumped clear of the sinking submarine. In the heat of the moment one of the survivors forgot to do so and the two items resembling bicycle gears were subsequently discovered in his pockets. They were the first pieces of the Enigma hardware secured for Bletchley Park directly from a U-boat.

At this time the naval Enigma machine had eight rotors (three in the machine at any one time, plus five in a box). These were divided between several crew members. The ones captured from U-33 were rotors VI and VII. The last rotor (VIII), whose existence had not until then been suspected, was captured in a separate incident in August 1940.

There is a further link between Dresky, Staffordshire and the U-559. In 1939, Heidtmann (who went on to command U-559) was serving under Dresky on the U-33 when they became involved in a violent altercation. Dresky wanted to communicate with the British commander of a ship that had been attacked by the U-33. Heidtmann believed the British negotiation attempts were a trick and ordered the men to carry on firing at the crew, completely disobeying Dresky's orders. According to the author Hugh Sebag-Montefiore, this led to a blazing row culminating in Dresky producing his revolver and pointing it at Heidtmann's head.

◆ ✕ ◆

On the eve of the unveiling of the sculpture, I drove to Tamworth for a rendezvous with the *Petard* men at the Castle Hotel where they were all staying. En route I called in at the Colin Grazier Hotel to meet Tony Fasson's sister, Sheena, who was to be a guest of honour at the *Petard* dinner. I found Sheena amazing for her age and it was wonderful to meet her at last after years of exchanging letters and telephone calls.

Sheena had flown from Edinburgh to Birmingham Airport where she was met by a Tamworth taxi driver called Bob who gave her celebrity treatment. Bob had bumped into Sheena in a doctor's surgery north of the border a few weeks earlier. He had been in Scotland visiting relatives and needed a prescription. Sheena struck up a conversation with him after noticing a reference to Tamworth on his vehicle parked outside. Sheena thought it was an amazing coincidence and wondered if Bob could pick her up at the airport, and asked me to arrange it.

My problem was that I knew nothing about the man other than his occupation and first name. I managed to track him down after calling a number of local taxi firms and simply asking to speak to a driver called 'Bob' who had been visiting relatives in Scotland recently. I was also hoping to meet Tommy Brown's three brothers at the hotel but unfortunately they had left for a tour of the town and so that pleasure had to be postponed until the following day.

After visiting Sheena I called at the Castle Hotel and met the men from the *Petard* Association. They were a warm and friendly bunch and exceptionally enthusiastic about the

The crew of U-559 posing on deck. The emblem of the 23rd Flotilla is visible on the conning tower. Courtesy of the Deutsches U-Boot Museum.

U-559's commander, Hans Heidtmann (in the white cap) on the submarine's bridge. Courtesy of the Deutsches U-Boot Museum.

occasion. We had organised 1,000 high-quality colour programmes for the main event and I had taken a handful to give to the men. The programmes were sponsored by the *Herald*.

During the war, 211 men were on board HMS *Petard*, nine of whom were officers. About thirty men who served on the ship attended the reunion and unveiling ceremony, a dozen of whom were on duty on 30 October 1942.

The weekend will be remembered by the town for the unveiling itself, which may have overshadowed the significance of the reunion dinner that night. I think it ought to go down in Tamworth's records that on 26 October 2002, the crew of one of the most important ship's in British history held a reunion at the Castle Hotel. A special menu had been printed bearing the name of the association and Tony Fasson's sister was the guest of honour.

It was so special to be among those men. To me it was even more amazing than meeting the original members of the Dambusters. I was enjoying a drink with a handful of men who had taken part in a decisive moment of world history. Ginger Richards, Jack Hall, Stan Brown, Mervyn Romeril, Ted Saunders, Leslie Hemus, Eric Sellars, John Mackness and the rest were like household names to me. Their names were as familiar to me as the 1966 World Cup squad, but as a team they have been infinitely less celebrated for achieving so much more for their country. (I made this very point to them during an after-dinner speech in Bournemouth in 2007.) All of them expressed regret that Reg Crang could not be with them on such a meaningful day. Despite the youngest of them being in his eighties, all the men were determined to march to the monument. The committee had decided that they would join the parade at its latter stages, just before it reached the sculpture. I took some of the men to see where the parade would be halted the following day, to allow them to take their place in it.

As we walked through the town a group of yobs, who had been engaging in their Saturday night drinking ritual, paused for a moment to hurl some incoherent abuse in our direction. They did not realise they were not even fit enough to be standing in the same street as these men. Without such men they might not have even been in the street at all that night.

I also took the men to get their first glimpse of the new sculpture and they were in raptures over it. Before leaving them to enjoy their evening festivities, I left a handful of extra souvenir programmes and asked if they would all sign them. One of these now forms part of the Tamworth story exhibition in Bletchley Park's Hut 8.

CHAPTER TWENTY-SEVEN

ANCHORS AWEIGH

About 1,000 people braved what we later discovered to be the worst weather on record for eleven years to pay tribute to three men who had died sixty years earlier

To say the weather on the big day – Sunday, 27 October 2002 – was bad would be the understatement of the year. I woke up to repeated news broadcasts warning of structural damage to property. 'Don't venture out unless your journey is strictly necessary,' warned the radio presenter.

It had thrown it down when we had the first town tribute to Colin in the town's Assembly Rooms. The heavens opened when the monument was first swung into position and now the weather, like the campaign, was hell bent on a truly spectacular climax. It was like some sort of divine intervention.

The mayor's officer, Alec Benwell, had asked us to assemble in Tamworth Town Hall at 9 a.m. on the Sunday morning. As I drove the twenty-five miles or so from my home to Tamworth, I realised just how bad the weather was. My car was violently buffeted and I had to keep a firm grip on the steering wheel. The windscreen wipers were fighting a losing battle in keeping away ridiculous amounts of water being emptied from the sky. I drove a few miles out of my village then found that the road was blocked by a large tree that had surrendered to the wind. I managed to remove it with the help of another driver and carried on my journey. I was to drive past several more toppled trees before I reached Tamworth.

A small group of us sat clutching cups of tea in Tamworth's historic town hall discussing how we could salvage something from the day. We agreed that all the arrangements we had made for the ceremony on the square would have to be changed. We already had a Plan B in mind in case of inclement weather. But even that did not allow for the hurricane that was raging outside.

Between 9 a.m. and 11 a.m. hundreds of chairs, and a small stage complete with PA equipment were all to be assembled on the square. Alec had even produced nameplates for the VIPs. The entire ceremony was to have been carried out around the monument, with the assembly only moving into St Editha's Church for the Enigma talk and a selection of speeches. The formal opening was to take place part way through the service. Weeks of organisation bit the dust as we began to re-arrange the day's proceedings at the last moment. The formalities of unveiling the monument would now be carried out at the very beginning of the service, and then the entire congregation would move into St Editha's Church for the rest of the ceremony.

I drove home for a change of clothes, and returned with my wife Claire and daughter Bryony. My mum Thelma, sister Libby, brother-in-law Nev, niece Sally and nephew James were all on their way from Stoke-on-Trent to make the day even more special for me. I was so grateful that they had ignored the severe weather warnings to support me. I was able to show them the Enigma articles in the Grazier Hotel and the memorial itself before going back to the town hall for a sherry with the relatives of all three men and civic dignitaries.

Tony Fasson's sister was determined not to miss out on the early reception. Despite being confined to a wheelchair for much of the time, she climbed up the rickety steps inside the town hall to enjoy the sherry reception.

I chatted to Tommy Brown's brothers and to several of Colin Grazier's relatives. The atmosphere was already building up.

While we were sipping sherries, Jim Welland was outside in the storm assembling the parade. At that moment I heard some bad news. Julian Lewis MP was stranded at Oxford station after a tree had blocked railway lines. He had been trying to contact me on his mobile phone all morning. I was very sorry to hear the news because I knew this story was close to his heart and he had been following our progress for years. I made a mental note to one day present him with a precious memento of the day – one of the souvenir programmes signed by the *Petard* men.

We took up our positions next to the monument at around 1.45 p.m. The band struck up and the parade moved off. The wind howled and the rain resembled a high pressure hose as the parade wound its way into Church Street, a road which leads directly to the monument via the Colin Grazier Hotel. Despite this about 1,000 people braved what we later discovered was the worst weather on record for eleven years, to pay tribute to three heroes who died sixty years earlier. Many of them had travelled long distances to be present. It was incredibly emotional.

The expressions on the faces of relatives and colleagues showed just how much this all meant. Several people had tears streaming down their faces. The sound of the band grew louder as the parade neared us but was called to an abrupt halt by Jim Welland who invited members of the *Petard* Association to joins its ranks. The band struck up again and the men, all in their uniforms, began their march to the sculpture. This was such a poignant moment, heightened by the fact they were braving appalling weather conditions. Nothing could spoil the tribute they were making to their fallen colleagues – not even a howling gale.

Standard-bearers marching to St Editha's Square for the unveiling ceremony.

Tamworth Sea Cadets march in driving rain on the day of the unveiling of the memorial to pay their respects to three sailors who turned the tide of the war. It was the worst weather on record for eleven years.

The Lord Lieutenant of Staffordshire, Mr James Hawley, took the salute, shortly before the parade reached the Colin Grazier Hotel. The hairs on the back of my neck were tingling. Tears on people's faces mirrored the wet weather, but the atmosphere was not depressing. Pride and dignity were the dominant emotions.

I'm sure all members of the committee felt a sense of pride too. And we all felt especially proud of Colin Grazier, Tony Fasson and Tommy Brown. If only those three men could have witnessed what was happening in their honour that day. It wasn't just significant for Tamworth, it was an important day for the entire country.

Three clergymen were involved in the service – the vicar of Tamworth, the Revd Alan Barrett, the vicar of Colin Grazier's old parish, the Revd Bob Neale, and the Bishop of Wolverhampton, the Right Revd Michael Bourke. All three were standing next to the sculpture ready to welcome the parade, their robes billowing in the severe gales. The Revd Barrett was having to think on his feet and he did a sterling job considering the weather had tossed all our meticulous planning into the air.

As the crowd settled, the Bishop of Wolverhampton formally blessed the new monument and dedicated it to the three heroes. Hundreds of onlookers watched the short service as the wind and rain continued to throw everything at us. The Lord Lieutenant of Staffordshire then invited the most senior member of the HMS *Petard* Association, Commander Robert de Pass, to formally unveil the new monument. He approached elegantly, a folded umbrella in his hand (it was too windy to be opened), and pulled across the Union Jack to reveal the plaque. The thunderous applause that followed was a match for the weather.

Above: Poppy wreaths laid in memory of the three men remained in St Editha's Church months after the service to dedicate the sculpture.

Right: Phil Shanahan pauses to hold a wreath to the three men against the base of the sculpture. Wreaths could not be left at the monument because of the severe gales.

The Revd Barrett then invited several people to approach the sculpture to lay a wreath, but the wind was so severe that none could be left unattended – they would simply have been blown away. So people had to press their wreaths against the base of the sculpture for a few seconds before walking away still clutching their tributes.

Wreaths were presented by James Hawley, the Lord Lieutenant of Staffordshire; Colleen Mason, Colin Grazier's niece, on behalf of Two Gates and Wilnecote Royal British Legion; Joyce Radbourne (Colin Grazier's sister-in-law) for the Grazier family; Sheena d'Anyers-Willis, representing the Fasson family; Tommy Brown's brother Stanley on behalf of the Brown family; Ginger Richards for the HMS *Petard* Association; and myself on behalf of the Colin Grazier Memorial Committee.

Messages written on the flowers were no less personal than if they had been written at the time of the men's deaths. Sheena d'Anyers-Willis' words to her brother were straight from the heart and brought a lump to my throat. Her brother's body lay next to Colin's at the bottom of the Mediterranean. Tony had never had the kind of public send-off he deserved, until now.

Sheena insisted on walking alone to the sculpture with her wreath and her slow and determined approach with only the aid of a walking frame was extremely moving. She later told me she 'could now die happy'. It meant that much to her. A few weeks after the ceremony she wrote me a long letter thanking everyone who had helped with the campaign. It is a letter I will always treasure. She wrote:

When I think of the trouble, thought and understanding that has been put into the Grazier project it makes me feel humble and unbelievably grateful for what you have done to bring notice to my beloved Tony who must be quite swollen headed by your wonderful use of words to let the whole world know what he and Colin did.

A proud moment for Tony Fasson's sister, Sheena d'Anyers-Willis, as the sculpture is dedicated in memory of her brother and his two Royal Navy colleagues.

The occasion gave the men's families, colleagues and friends a chance to say farewell, satisfied that their actions had been fittingly commemorated.

Before the proceedings continued inside the church a minute's silence was observed. Then Ginger Richards said those beautifully conceived words: 'They shall not grow old as we that are left grow old. Age shall not weary them, nor the years condemn. At the going down of the sun and in the morning we will remember them.'

Ginger later told me how he first met Colin as the two of them made their way to Newcastle by train to join up with the *Petard* for its maiden voyage. Ginger, one of the four submarine detectors on board, was just eighteen years old at the time. 'Colin was only a few years older than me, but at that age it makes quite a difference,' he said. 'He was a thoroughly decent chap, the sort who would look out for you. I remember us joking on the train about the name *Petard*. Colin joked about it being an old French minesweeper.'

The *Last Post* and *Reveille* were sounded and the clear brass notes echoed across St Editha's Square. Jim Welland said the words of the Kohima Epitaph, 'When You Go Home, Tell Them Of Us And Say, For Their Tomorrow, We Gave Our Today'.

I had heard all these sentiments expressed at various memorial events in the past, but they had never affected me so deeply as on that afternoon. I looked across at Colin's best friend Maurice Lunn. He had stopped trying to hold back the tears and was openly weeping. At the reception afterwards, Maurice told me a story about Colin that I had never heard before.

As a boy Colin had witnessed a man drowning, which given the manner of his own death was quite a coincidence. Maurice remembered that it happened when they had gone swimming together in a local reservoir. 'We saw a chap dive in and we didn't see him come up,' he said. 'We told various people who were there, but nobody believed us. Four hours later, they dragged the reservoir and the poor devil was dead at the bottom.'

On a happier note he recalled how they once stocked a dormant pool with fish they had caught. Years later they drained it and it was teeming with thousands of fish. So maybe that's a sort of living legacy left by Colin in his home town. It's a nice thought.

Following the outdoor service in St Editha's Square, it was finally time for the gathering to move into the church for the remainder of the ceremony. During the service the Volunteer Band of the West Midlands Regiment struck up the well known hymns, *The Supreme Sacrifice* and *For Those in Peril on The Sea*. The National Anthem was also played. But this was no standard service. In between the hymns and the lowering of the standards, there were a number of unforgettable addresses. The Revd Bob Neale set the scene by telling the Grazier story to the hundreds of assembled guests. He referred to the courage of the three men as being 'hard to comprehend'.

The Revd Alan Barrett then invited the Lord Lieutenant of Staffordshire, to read the following personal message written for the day by HRH Prince Andrew, the Duke of York:

Buckingham Palace

On the 30th October 1942, three young British seamen recovered a vital Enigma code book and material from a sinking U-boat. The capture of the book allowed the code breakers at Bletchley Park to decipher U-boat movements in the Atlantic thereby making it possible to save over 500,000 tons of shipping in the first few months of 1943 alone. Historians acknowledge that this played a pivotal part in bringing the war in the Atlantic to an earlier close saving countless lives. Few acts of courage can ever have had such far-reaching consequences.

Able Seaman Colin Grazier, Lieutenant Tony Fasson and NAAFI Canteen Assistant Tommy Brown were serving in HMS *Petard* when it was involved in a ten-hour battle against the German submarine U-559 in the Mediterranean. They swam to the U-boat after it had been forced to the surface by their ship. Grazier and Fasson, who died when the U-boat sank with them on board, were posthumously awarded the George Cross. Brown, aged 16 years, survived but tragically died two years later in a house fire. He was awarded the George Medal.

Wartime heroics, carried out by young men, deserve to be recognised. It is right that we should now honour these unsung heroes by erecting a memorial to them in Tamworth, the home town of Colin Grazier, and by recognising the part they each played in the courageous event. Brown and Fasson have received recognition in their respective home towns - a stained glass window commemorating Tommy Brown has been installed in North Shields while a plaque honouring Tony Fasson has been erected in his local church near Jedburgh in Scotland.

The Colin Grazier Memorial will ensure that his country has a constant reminder of the heroic act performed by some of its sons which played a pivotal part in bringing the Battle of the Atlantic to an earlier close. The members of the crew of the HMS *Petard* and the Grazier, Brown and Fasson families should be justly proud.

Signed: Andrew.

The congregation must have sensed they were attending a service of national importance, and this feeling was increased when Tamworth MP Brian Jenkins approached the rostrum to read out a personal letter from the Prime Minister:

BUCKINGHAM PALACE

On the 30th October 1942, three young British Seamen recovered a vital Enigma code book and material from a sinking U-boat. The capture of the book allowed the code breakers at Bletchley Park to decipher U-boat movements in the Atlantic thereby making it possible to save over 500,000 tons of shipping in the first few months of 1943 alone. Historians acknowledge that this played a pivotal part in bringing the war in the Atlantic to an earlier close saving countless lives. Few acts of courage can ever have had such far-reaching consequences.

Able Seaman Colin Grazier, Lieutenant Tony Fasson and NAAFI Canteen Assistant Tommy Brown were serving in HMS PETARD when it was involved in a ten-hour battle against the German submarine U-559 in the Mediterranean. They swam to the U-boat after it had been forced to the surface by their ship. Grazier and Fasson, who died when the U-boat sank with them on board, were posthumously awarded the George Cross. Brown, aged 16 years, survived but tragically died two years later trying to save his sister from a house fire. He was awarded the George Medal.

Wartime heroics, carried out by young men, deserve to be recognised. It is right that we should now honour these unsung heroes by erecting a memorial to them in Tamworth, the home town of Colin Grazier and by recognising the part they each played in the courageous event. Brown and Fasson have received recognition in their respective home towns - a stained glass window commemorating Tommy Brown has been installed in North Shields while a plaque honouring Tony Fasson has been erected in his local church near Jedburgh in Scotland.

The Colin Grazier Memorial will ensure that this country has a constant reminder of the heroic act performed by some of its sons which played a pivotal part in bringing the Battle of the Atlantic to an earlier close. The members of the crew of HMS PETARD and the Grazier, Brown and Fasson families should be justly proud.

10 DOWNING STREET
LONDON SW1A 2AA

THE PRIME MINISTER

No greater honour can befall a man than to be recognised by his fellow citizens and this monument is a fine and fitting tribute to one of Tamworth's greatest citizens, a man whose bravery and self sacrifice are an example to us all.

On 30 October 1942 HMS PETARD, in company with other ships and aeroplanes, took part in a series of attacks on U559 in the eastern Mediterranean. After a long and ferocious battle, the submarine was forced to the surface and abandoned by her crew. Able Seaman Colin Grazier, accompanied by Lieutenant Tony Fasson and Tommy Brown, the Canteen Assistant, boarded the boat in an attempt to recover useful material and they were successful in obtaining the U-Boat's code books. Tragically, the crippled submarine sank and while Tommy Brown was able to escape, she took Colin Grazier and Tony Fasson to the bottom with her.

These men paid the ultimate price but their sacrifice was instrumental in allowing the code breakers at Bletchley Park to read the U-Boat signal traffic. This led in turn to countless lives being saved as convoys were routed around their opponents during Britain's darkest hour. Without a doubt Colin made a contribution to the winning of the War that few people could match.

This fitting memorial will serve as a constant reminder of the bravery and dedication that Colin and his two colleagues showed to their country.

Tony Blair

Above left: The message, signed by Prince Andrew, recognising the 'pivotal part' Grazier, Fasson and Brown played in bringing the Battle of the Atlantic to an earlier close. The tribute was read out at the memorial unveiling service at St Editha's Church, Tamworth, in October 2002.

Above right: Prime Minister Tony Blair said the monument to Colin Grazier was a 'fine and fitting tribute to one of Tamworth's greatest citizens, a man whose bravery and self sacrifice are an example to us all'. The tribute was also read out at the memorial unveiling service at St Editha's Church, Tamworth, in October 2002.

10 Downing Street

No greater honour can befall a man than to be recognised by his fellow citizens and this monument is a fine and fitting tribute to one of Tamworth's greatest citizens, a man whose bravery and self-sacrifice are an example to us all.

On 30 October 1942, HMS *Petard* in company with other ships and aeroplanes, took part in a series of attacks on U-559 in the eastern Mediterranean. After a long and ferocious battle, the submarine was forced to the surface and abandoned by her crew. Able Seaman Colin Grazier, accompanied by Lieutenant Tony Fasson, and Tommy Brown, the canteen assistant, boarded the boat in an attempt to recover useful material and they were successful in obtaining the U-boat's code books. Tragically, the crippled submarine sank and while Tommy Brown was able to escape, she took Colin Grazier and Tony Fasson to the bottom with her.

These men paid the ultimate price but their sacrifice was instrumental in allowing the code breakers at Bletchley Park to read the U-boat signal traffic. This led in turn to countless lives being saved as convoys were routed around their opponents during Britain's darkest hour. Without a doubt Colin made a contribution to the winning of the war that few people could match.

This fitting memorial will serve as a constant reminder of the bravery and dedication that Colin and his two colleagues showed to their country.

Signed: Tony Blair, October 27, 2002.

The group editor of *Central Independent Newspapers*, Sam Holliday, was next to speak. He gave a stirring speech delivered as a 'proud Tamworthian'. 'Today has got to be one of the proudest days in this town's, indeed this country's, history,' he said:

This is a story that has captured the attention of the world. We have heard today from Buckingham Palace and 10 Downing Street. It has attracted the national press. This is a truly remarkable story. Tamworth has had many proud days, but few, if any, have been as proud as today.

Sam then paid tribute to the 'remarkable passion and energy' of the Colin Grazier Memorial Committee who, he said, had been building up to this occasion for over four years. 'I am proud to call them fellow citizens,' he said before inviting the committee to stand up and receive a round of applause.

Resting on a table at the rear of St Editha's Church that day was a genuine German Enigma machine. It was an unusual sight, to say the least, in a church. Its owner, Dr Baldwin, advised the congregation to have a good look at it as they might never get another chance to look at one so closely.

I was really pleased that he had accepted my invitation to give a talk. I had set him the difficult task of putting the importance of the three men into a world context within a time limit of twenty minutes. He achieved that brilliantly and I only hope that the people who listened to him that afternoon appreciated they were being addressed by one of the finest speakers on the subject.

A rare sight in a church – an Enigma machine was on display in St Editha's Church, Tamworth, for the unveiling service.

Three of Tommy Brown's brothers represented his family at the service in St Editha's Church following the unveiling of the new memorial. To their right is committee member Ray Jennings.

Sitting in that church in Tamworth on that autumn day, I felt we were at the cutting edge of history. It was the climax of our work to highlight and celebrate one of the most important but least appreciated acts of heroism there has ever been. We had been charged with an incredibly important mission and on that day we were delivering. Dr Baldwin's eloquent words were bringing this home to me and I hope other members of the committee feel equally privileged to have worked on such a nationally important issue. He explained that following the recovery of documents from the U-559, Bletchley Park was never again completely at a loss to read the U-boat codes. There were some bad times, and some terrible losses, but from that point onwards the scales began to be tipped in favour of the Allies and the tide had turned in the Battle of the Atlantic. After being out of the picture for nearly a year, Bletchley was back in the thick of the action and influencing the outcome of the war.

'It is very doubtful that we would have otherwise won the war and certainly not in the timescale that it needed to be won,' Dr Baldwin told the riveted assembly:

All this must have been very much what Winston Churchill had in mind when he said that during the war there had been things that had worried him, but only one thing that had frightened him and that was the U-boat peril.

That capture from U-559 was the most important of the entire war. That is why it is fitting for us to be here sixty years later to salute the actions of these three young three men. Their action was not just heroic but also prompt and that was also vital. If they had hesitated the documents would never have been captured and it is right and proper that these young men are being honoured today.

Dr Baldwin took his seat to great applause and was thanked by John Harper. John then asked sculptor Walenty Pytel to stand up and take a bow for his breathtaking creation outside the church.

Guests were invited to make the short journey from St Editha's Church to the Colin Grazier Hotel for the reception. As we did so there was a brief but spectacular change in the weather. For no more than a few precious seconds the sky turned a deep blue and the silver steel sculpture was unexpectedly bathed in brilliant sunshine. Our photographer for the day, Marie Farrington, took advantage by taking a series of pictures of the monument.

Because of the significance of the event I had spent an hour with Marie at the site a few days earlier briefing her on the kind of photographs we would be looking for. I had long had the idea of a superb picture of the sculpture taking up the whole of our front page and had told Marie to look out for a good opportunity. The sky that day had been bleak for hours, but she suddenly got her chance and took it superbly.

The resulting photograph was exactly what I was hoping for and I used it as a poster front on that memorable edition of the *Herald*. Many people cannot believe the picture could possibly have been taken on that stormy day, but I can verify that the light was perfect for a few brief moments. Blink and you could have missed it. Thankfully Marie didn't. The photograph on the Lloyds TSB-sponsored display board, which now introduces The Tamworth Story Exhibition in Hut 8, was also captured in that short burst of sun.

The rain stops and the sun breaks through for a few precious seconds to allow *Herald* photographer Marie Farrington to capture the sculpture in all its glory on the day of the unveiling.

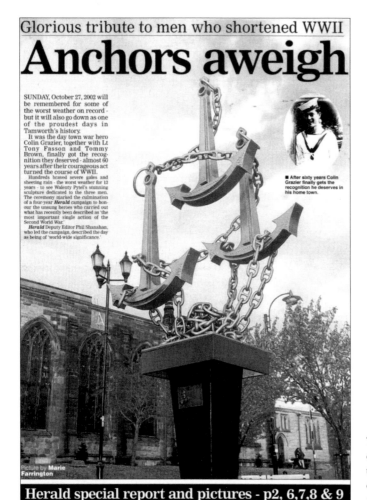

Glorious tribute to men who shortened WWII

Anchors aweigh

SUNDAY, October 27, 2002 will be remembered for some of the worst weather on record - but it will also go down as one of the proudest days in Tamworth's history.

It was the day town war hero Colin Grazier, together with Lt Tony Fasson and Tommy Brown, finally got the recognition they deserved - almost 60 years after their courageous act turned the course of WWII.

Hundreds braved severe gales and sheeting rain - the worst weather for 12 years - to see Walenty Pytel's stunning sculpture dedicated to the three men. The ceremony marked the culmination of a four-year *Herald* campaign to honour the unsung heroes who carried out what has recently been described as 'the most important single action of the Second World War'.

Herald Deputy Editor Phil Shanahan, who led the campaign, described the day as being of 'world-wide significance.'

■ After sixty years Colin Grazier finally gets the recognition he deserves in his home town.

Picture by Marie Farrington

Herald special report and pictures - p2, 6,7,8 & 9

The culmination of the campaign is reported on the front page of the *Herald* edition of 31 October 2002.

There was a tangible buzz in the air at the Colin Grazier Hotel that afternoon. It had the positive and warm atmosphere of a long-awaited wedding reception. The extensive buffet included a rice platter bearing the initials 'C.G.' A Central Television camera crew, who had been filming the whole event for the daytime and evening news bulletins, conducted several interviews at the reception and former *Herald* photographer John Walker captured part of the proceedings on video.

MP Brian Jenkins was full of enthusiasm and remarked that the statue was one of the first he had seen dedicated to an ordinary working serviceman:

> I've seen statues to admirals and generals, but never before to an able seaman. I am proud that has happened in my town. This has allowed the community to come together and has enhanced the depth of the community. Our community has recognised someone special. It is long overdue, but we have done it.

Walenty Pytel was the celebrity in demand at the reception and during a press interview he talked about how the sculpture was very different to the normal work he produced:

> I specialise in animals and birds, and in this project I was thinking about seahorses and very ornate ideas. But then I thought, should I try something really different? What could I do with anchors and chains?
>
>   I produced five drawings. Four were tremendously complex fine drawings. The fifth was a quick doodle and was the anchors and chain and, of course, the committee decided to choose this one. At the time I was delighted but was wrestling with the mechanics of it. The chain and anchors weigh something like four or five tons and involve the chain spiralling upwards. The mechanics of it were a challenge.

Walenty's Polish roots gave him a meaningful link with the story and he was proud that it was the Poles who had begun the process of cracking Enigma. Dr Baldwin had touched on the early Polish intelligence breakthroughs moments earlier during his talk. He had explained that the Polish contribution was crucial to subsequent codebreaking successes. Poland had realised it could not resist a German invasion and in July 1939 a decision was made to pass on all its knowledge of German Enigma codes to the British and the French. 'Had they not done so, the work at Bletchley Park would not have got off to such a flying start,' he said.

In 1999, Bletchley Park organised a Polish festival to acknowledge the Polish contribution to the cracking of the Enigma code. It was to mark the sixtieth anniversary of a dramatic and secretive meeting in the Kabackie Woods in Pyry, near Warsaw, where the Poles handed over their Enigma secrets to the British in a scene straight out of a spy movie. This is now an annual event at Bletchley and is attended by large numbers of Anglo-Polish people.

In the early 1930s, before Hitler came to power, Polish mathematicians Marian Rejewski, Jerzy Różycki and Henryk Zygalski had succeeded in unravelling the mystery of Enigma. They even went as far as reconstructing a machine. In 1939, after sharing the knowledge they had gained with their allies, the Poles passed on two replica Engima machines, one of which was destined for Bletchley Park. The first breakthrough came about in 1929 when a Polish customs officer became suspicious after receiving an urgent request to send back a parcel which had been misdirected. It was returned to Germany, but only after the Enigma machine inside the package had been painstakingly taken apart and every aspect of it thoroughly analysed. This enabled the Poles to gain basic knowledge about Enigma. They later bought a commercial model and this turned out to be very similar to the machine they had secretly examined. However, there were two fundamental differences between the commercial and military models. Firstly, the military machine had a steckerboard (plugboard) and secondly the wiring of its rotors was different to the commercial version. As each rotor could be wired in more than 400,000,000,000,000,000,000,000,000 different ways, the knowledge the Poles had of the commercial machine was not sufficient to enable them to crack the military codes. That took a great deal of imaginative and sophisticated mathematics developed by the Polish team. They also used information from Gustave Bertrand, the French intelligence officer, who had copied some Enigma manuals shown to him by the disloyal German, Hans-Thilo Schmidt.

Above left: Herald photographer Paul Barber captured the moment the lights of the memorial were switched on for the first time, exactly sixty years to the day that Grazier and Fasson lost their lives. Members of the Colin Grazier Memorial Committee gathered round the monument for the historic event.

Above right: Petard shipmates admire a model of the wartime destroyer they served on, during a reception at the Colin Grazier Hotel.

The Polish first broke the military codes in 1932, and then passed on the information about this to the British and French during the historic rendezvous in the Kabackie Woods in July, 1939. Polish Prime Minister Jerzy Buzek made a presentation to the families of the three mathematicians in 2000 and later that year the Duke of York travelled to Poland and presented Mr Buzek with an Enigma machine as a symbol of Britain's gratitude. The cloak of recognition for their role in the Enigma saga took a long time to land on Poland's shoulders. But as is the case with Grazier and his colleagues, it was a case of better late than never.

I began my speech at the reception by welcoming the families of Grazier, Fasson and Brown. 'I feel proud to come from the same country as them, so to come from the same family must be very special indeed,' I said. I then paid tribute to the party from HMS *Petard* Association and described their presence as 'an utter privilege'.

I had two significant announcements to make. We had held the ceremony on 27 October, because it was the nearest Sunday to 30 October. However, the sixtieth anniversary of the momentous day would be the following Wednesday. The council had worked wonders getting the foundations for the base ready in time, and the only aspect Richard Penn was dubious about was getting the lighting in place for the unveiling. I think he would have even pulled that off, because of his sheer dedication and that of his team.

But then it suddenly occurred to me that we should hold something back for the anniversary itself. It made sense that the lights should come on for the first time exactly sixty years to the day the codebooks were collected. I was able to announce our intentions on that Sunday afternoon.

On 30 October 2002, six members of the Colin Grazier Memorial Committee lined up for a private moment of reflection on a dark and cold night to see the sculpture illuminated by floodlights. It was subtle and very understated, in contrast with the pomp and ceremony of the public unveiling. Paul Barber took an atmospheric photograph of the committee members gazing at the lit sculpture exactly six decades after the event it was commemorating. It's one of my favourite images from the campaign and Bletchley Park now has a copy of it on display. Since then, the lights on the three anchors have been switched on every evening until midnight as a constant reminder of what three brave men achieved for the free world.

The second announcement I made was of equal importance and was something Reg Crang had been working hard to achieve. HMS *Argyll*, a Type 23 destroyer, was shortly to visit the spot in the Mediterranean where the two men lost their lives. A service would be held and floral tributes thrown into the sea. After sixty years, so many things were now happening in honour of these men.

Stanley Rothwell was next to speak on behalf of the *Petard* Association. He thanked the *Herald* for its excellent work and paid tribute to Reg Crang. 'Reg has put his heart and soul into all this,' he said. 'He has devoted all his time and efforts into this one story – the *Petard* story.'

In the next speech Tamworth Borough Council leader, Peter Seekings, reflected on the day, shortly after he had been appointed leader, that I invited him to the *Herald*'s offices for a film show and to be taken through the contents of a 'Grazier pack'. He also paid tribute to the people of Tamworth and beyond who had contributed to the cost of the memorial, as well as his own staff for meeting the tight deadline to complete all the work in St Editha's Square. Finally he thanked Walenty for a 'wonderful piece of art'. Tamworth mayor, Margaret Clarke, said she had been humbled by the day's proceedings and led three cheers to the three Enigma heroes.

Three people had travelled from Bletchley Park that day bringing with them a superb model of the *Petard* which provided a perfect prop for a photograph of the *Petard* veterans. One of the Bletchley representatives present was John Gallehawk whom I remembered seeing on television berating the controversial *U-571* movie. I remember an incident earlier in the evening involving John which again underlines just how emotional the day was.

I was showing John the material we had collected, when we paused to study a picture of Colin Grazier taken on his wedding day. We talked about how tragic it was that he was just twenty-two when he died, and how he had only been married for two days before setting off to join the *Petard*. I looked round and saw why John hadn't said anything for a while – he was wiping away tears with his handkerchief.

The following week's edition of the *Tamworth Herald* was, not surprisingly, dominated by coverage of the big day. The entire front page consisted of the eye-catching image that Marie had captured during that short but precious burst of sunshine. A short editorial described how the day would not only be remembered for some of the worst weather on record but would also go down as 'one of the proudest days in Tamworth's history'. I described the occasion in the piece as being 'of worldwide significance'.

Above: The crew of HMS *Argyll* pay their respects to Able Seaman Colin Grazier and Lieutenant Tony Fasson at the spot where they lost their lives in the Mediterranean. Picture courtesy of the Royal Navy.

Right: Grazier and Fasson's equivalent ranks on board HMS *Argyll*, seaman Matthew Bevan and first lieutenant Neil Ovenden, prepare to cast an anchor wreath overboard during a ceremony at sea to remember the men. They are pictured with Commander John Kingwell and chaplain David Thomas who conducted a service. Picture courtesy of the Royal Navy.

'It was a day town war hero Colin Grazier, together with Lt Tony Fasson and Tommy Brown, finally got the recognition they deserved – almost sixty years after their courageous act turned the course of WWII.'

Sam Holliday summed up the event when he wrote, 'Colin Grazier was a man who did what he did out of a sense of duty. Tamworth has now fulfilled its duty back and made sure that everyone now knows the full details of one of the greatest stories ever told. Look on your monument with sheer pride, Tamworth!'

It was an historic edition packed with unforgettable pictures and quotes. Joyce Radbourne, Colin's sister-in-law, said it would have meant so much to Olive. 'She would have been so pleased that Colin got this recognition,' she said.

Colin's niece Colleen Mason was equally enthusiastic. 'The memorial is beautiful. It will remind me of Colin every time I go into town. His memory will live on now.'

In my opinion piece I summed up my motivation for leading the campaign. 'The true focus was not to celebrate an act of war, but to recognise personal sacrifices made to bring about peace.'

A wreath was thrown into the sea on 9 November 2002, at the spot where Grazier and Fasson drowned. Men aboard HMS *Argyll* cast an anchor-shaped floral tribute into the waves. This was followed by a full service attended by the crew.

'It is absolutely very special because the Navy would only do this for something quite major,' said Reg Crang.

HMS *Argyll* was returning home to Plymouth after a successful six-month deployment to the Arabian Gulf and was glad to be able to delay her passage to pay her respects for the men of HMS *Petard*. Her captain, Commander John Kingwell, said:

> It is with great pride that we are able to remember the sailors of HMS *Petard* who lost their lives recovering the Enigma codes in those dark days of 1942. Although their actions have been kept top secret for so long, the bravery they showed in the selfless actions that day are an inspiration to us all.

We were wired three superb pictures of the event directly from the ship which we published along with an article in the *Herald*.

CHAPTER TWENTY-EIGHT

RAISE YOUR GLASSES

Sitting in the restaurant named after him that day, with his own image and paintings on the wall, Churchill did seem involved, albeit indirectly, in that exclusive but meaningful toast in the heart of the government

Shortly before Christmas 2002 I set off for the House of Commons for a day I will never forget, hosted by the newly announced Shadow Defence Minister, Julian Lewis. He had also invited Colin Grazier's second cousin Beryl Bauer, whom he had kept in touch with since appearing with her on the Gloria Hunniford programme. Beryl's partner John came along too.

Julian met us in the reception area of the House of Commons and I presented him with a framed programme of the unveiling ceremony signed by the *Petard* men involved in the U-559 drama. He seemed really pleased and surprised with his gift and promised it would occupy a prominent place in his home. I hope it made up for him being stranded by the gales when he had tried to reach Tamworth. He had followed the campaign for so long, and I was very sorry that he had missed out on the historic climax.

Julian reserved privileged seats for us to watch a Commons debate. We sat in an area normally occupied by specialist advisers and close relatives of leading politicians. Margaret Beckett's husband was sitting next to me. We had a grandstand view. The Prime Minister was not involved in the proceedings, but many political heavyweights were, including the late Robin Cook. It was a lively discussion which touched on the controversy surrounding allegations that Cherie Blair had asked a convicted fraudster to negotiate the purchase of two luxury flats in Bristol.

At one point Julian slid next to us to say he was about to put a question to Robin Cook about terrorist security. We were so close to the action, we could have been part of the debate.

Afterwards Julian took us on a tour of the Commons including a stroll on the MPs' terrace overlooking the Thames. We bumped into several prominent politicians, including Clare Short and Lord Fowler who was particularly interested to hear our reasons for being at the House. Julian then took us outside to see the magnificent Jubilee Fountain Sculpture in front of the Great Hall which is Walenty Pytel's most prestigious work of art. It was commissioned by Parliament for the Queen's Silver Jubilee year. The majestic landmark, now part of Britain's heritage, stands 26ft tall and features a selection of animals, birds and beasts representing Commonwealth countries. It took Walenty eighteen months to make and shows the standing of the man who fashioned the Colin Grazier Memorial in Tamworth.

The highlight of the day was having lunch in the Churchill Restaurant. It's a place the public rarely gets to see and its walls are adorned with original oil paintings produced by the great leader, who was a keen and talented artist. This link with Churchill seemed so fitting as Julian proposed a toast to Grazier, Fasson and Brown. We raised our glasses to the three men and in those surroundings the gesture took on magnified significance. The men's names were being celebrated in historic surroundings befitting what they had achieved for their country.

The three of us were thankful to Julian for that day and Beryl and I have reminisced about it several times since. Knowing the importance that Churchill attached to the Battle of the Atlantic, I felt sure Britain's greatest wartime leader would have been keen to pay his own tributes to the three heroes. Sitting in the restaurant named after him that day, with his own work on the walls, Churchill did at least seem involved, albeit indirectly, in that exclusive but meaningful toast in the heart of the government.

During one visit to Bletchley, he paid an unforgettable tribute to the 10,000 people or so who worked there, with another wonderfully crafted phrase. Churchill described the staff as 'the geese that laid the golden eggs – but never cackled'.

March 2003 was a highly successful month for the *Tamworth Herald*. The campaign had been shortlisted for two more national accolades. The first was a prestigious event organised by Northcliffe Newspapers. The Circulation, Editorial and Promotion Awards are held in a different part of the country each year, but I was pleased that in 2002 it was held at the Moat House Hotel in Stoke-on-Trent. It meant a return to my home city.

There was a bronze, silver and gold award up for grabs in each category. It was a lovely evening and I had the honour of accepting the gold award for Best Editorial Campaign of the year for all paid-for weekly titles.

A week later we won another national award. This time the setting was the plush Birmingham Metropole Hotel which hosted the Newspaper Society Awards. During the evening we were named the Newspaper Society's Weekly Campaigning Newspaper of the Year for Britain. It was one of the biggest awards ever won by the *Herald* and second only to the campaign's triumph in the Regional Press Awards in 2000 in which we were also pitted against every evening newspaper in the UK.

The Newspaper Society later described the campaign as 'outstanding' and a 'real labour of love'. Nothing like this had happened since the newspaper first rolled off the press in 1868. The newspaper had also been named BT Midlands Weekly Newspaper of the Year at a dinner held at the International Conference Centre in Birmingham.

I must emphasise, though, that we didn't start the campaign with awards in mind. We started out only to get glory for three unsung individuals, not ourselves. In the end we shared in their reflected glory, but I have always pointed out that every award we won was also an award for the three men. I can honestly say that I never lost sight of that. We all knew who the three real stars of this campaign were.

In August 2003, a striking memorial was unveiled at the new housing estate where the streets had been named on an Enigma theme. The developer, McLeans Homes, fulfilled its promise to build a simple brick plinth on which the replica of the plaque would be attached. Around 100 people, including the new mayor of Tamworth, Marion Couchman, relatives of Colin Grazier, and HMS *Petard* survivor Stan Brown attended the event.

Members of the Colin Grazier Memorial Committee were also present, as were many estate residents and members of Two Gates British Legion which hosted the day. Most of the spadework was carried out by committee and British Legion stalwart Jim Welland. It was Jim who had organised a raffle which had met the costs of the replica plaque.

I had been out of the country for two weeks and flew back the day before the do. Jim told me he had been unable to get a marching band, and I asked him if he had an alternative in mind. 'Just wait and see,' he said. He then disappeared with the standard-bearers and British Legion members, as the rest of us took our positions next to the new monument. From round the corner we heard the strains of muffled music as the parade began. I couldn't believe my eyes when it came into sight.

Jim was leading the parade in his car. He was driving exceptionally slowly, and had all his windows wound down so we could all hear the marching music blaring from his stereo. Jim's enterprise wasn't to end there either. As the Revd Bob Neale introduced the first hymn, I saw, in the corner of my eye, Jim's car move into position near the gathering. He had taped the relevant hymns from a church service that morning and, at the given moment, he kept driving into place to supply us with loud bursts of music.

It did go wrong for a few jolting moments right in the middle of the Lord's Prayer when we were treated to a deafening burst of Radio One. Jim fumbled furiously with the stereo controls, and after what I'm sure seemed like an agonisingly long time to him, eventually managed to regain control. The most solemn expressions cracked into broad smiles. John and I felt so guilty as we tried unsuccessfully to suppress our laughter during such a sensitive part of the service, but I'm sure Colin Grazier himself would have very much enjoyed the moment. Jim's a right character and did so much excellent work for the campaign. It really was a pleasure working with such people and I will always associate that monument on the Grazier estate with him, as well as the three men it commemorated.

I was really pleased that the plaque in the estate gave details about the Enigma story. Without it future residents may never get to know the meaning behind the names of the roads. I would hate there to be a possibility of people walking down Grazier Avenue, Brown Avenue, or Fasson Close, without them realising what these men had achieved. Thankfully that will not be the case here.

Left: The President of the Newspaper Society, Tim Bowdler, presents Phil Shanahan and Sam Holliday with the trophy for UK Campaigning Weekly Newspaper of the Year for 2002.

Below: Stan Brown, who manned the *Petard*'s oerlikon guns, visits the housing estate named after his former shipmates.

CHAPTER TWENTY-NINE

GRAZIER DAY

The unveiling of this spectacular sculpture should not mark the beginning of forgetting again

As we approached the first anniversary of the unveiling of the Colin Grazier Memorial, I felt we had an opportunity to introduce a new, quirky ceremony to Tamworth's folklore. It seemed vital to me that putting up the monument should not mark the beginning of forgetting again. Rather it should be the beginning of remembering. What I had in mind was 'Grazier Day' – a ceremony to be held each year in the town to raise a glass of rum to Colin's memory. I wanted it to be a positive, not sombre ceremony. It should be more of a celebration of Grazier's life – indeed of all three men's lives. The trouble was the first 'Grazier Day' would fall over the school holiday period and I had already booked a family break in Portugal. It was only three weeks away and a bit on the late side to organise anything elaborate, but I thought that if we could at least establish the tradition it could grow in future.

So I rallied the troops at the *Herald* offices and also invited Doug Heath from Tamworth Royal Naval Association. I had got to know Doug after he had brought me several excellent articles together with accompanying photographs of various RNA events. He is retired and had struck me as a highly motivated person.

At that meeting it was decided that 'Grazier Day' would be held on the nearest Sunday to 30 October each year. It was agreed that rum (it would always be the Navy's traditional Pusser's rum) would feature in the celebrations. However, I was a little worried about scores of people knocking back spirits in the centre of Tamworth, and so it was decided that that particular part of the proceedings would be for invited guests only and would take place at the Tamworth branch of the Royal Naval Association. We all thought it was absolutely essential that young people get involved. Therefore, Doug agreed to contact the Tamworth Sea Cadets and see if they could come along, even at such short notice.

Tamworth Sea Cadets are one of the most progressive branches in the country and I have had several dealings with them through the Grazier project. At one time I even saw them perform a brief play on the capture of the codebooks which was excellent. It is my hope that future generations of young people will ensure the continuation of this tradition in Tamworth.

My final involvement before the ceremony was to get the *Herald* to commit to sponsoring the Pusser's rum each year and also the buffet. I am confident that present and future owners of the newspaper will ensure that this is another tradition kept for posterity. I told the rest of the committee about my trip to Portugal at the last minute. It was a little embarrassing urging them all to get involved and then admitting that I would be unable to participate as I would be sunning myself on a foreign beach. Thankfully, I decided that my lack of attendance was far outweighed by the need to get something off the ground to mark the occasion.

I also agreed to take part in the Grazier rum toast from Portugal. Just before I left a curious gift was left for me in reception. Looking alarmingly like a urine sample in a small glass container, it took two attempts from Doug to get our receptionist to accept it. It turned out to be pure Pusser's rum to take with me on the trip. I decided not to attempt to smuggle it onto the plane due to the possibility of it being seized by customs officials, but all the family raised a glass to Grazier, Fasson and Brown in a small Portuguese restaurant. The gesture was repeated with a shot of 'the sample' on our return.

Considering it had been organised in such a short time, the first Grazier Day was a great success. There was a simple service at the monument, led by the Vicar of Tamworth, the Revd Alan Barrett. Representatives of Tamworth Sea Cadets were present, as well as a healthy sprinkling of people from local ex-servicemen's associations. A buffet was held at the Royal Naval Association's base in Victoria Road, where 'Up spirits' took place to toast Grazier and his fellow heroes with the rum.

John Harper put together a lovely verse which I have used for the main toast on all subsequent Grazier Days. It is now part of this new Tamworth tradition:

> This brave man of Tamworth who laid down his life,
> To capture the codes that helped end the strife,
> His sacrifice at sea we will never forget,
> So let's raise our glasses and honour the debt.

The toast that immediately follows is to all three men, and I want that to become another feature of Grazier Day.

CHAPTER THIRTY

HUT 8

Our exhibition was to be housed in the very hut where Alan Turing worked. Absolutely perfect

It was a shock to receive an apologetic letter from the management of the Colin Grazier Hotel in 2003 explaining that they were regrettably having to put the business up for sale. I immediately contacted the estate agents and impressed on them how important the hotel's links with the Enigma story had become and urged them to convey this to potential new owners. I repeated that plea in the *Herald* as I feared the hotel might become a bland office block, lacking any real identity. Several interested parties contacted me, promising to keep the name should their bid prove to be successful.

Thankfully, the new owner had no intention of changing the name. 'I don't think the people of Tamworth would forgive us if we did that,' Steve Cartmill told me. He did, however, have his own vision for the hotel which did not include it being a 'museum'. He wanted to make it a more accessible place for a drink or a meal and make it appeal to a younger clientele. From the moment the hotel was put on the market I had been worried about the future of the collection we had amassed for the hotel's previous management. My ultimate nightmare was that it might end up on a skip.

At the earliest opportunity I organised a meeting with the new owners to discuss the matter. They were frank and told me that the collection had no part to play in their plans. It was disappointing news, but I respected their decision which had been taken on purely commercial grounds. They did tell me, however, that in addition to keeping the hotel's name, they would be re-naming the lounge the U-bar to maintain the Enigma theme. Despite my early dealings with the Imperial War Museum, I had only one place in mind for the collection – Bletchley Park.

I immediately spoke to my contacts there and eventually received an email from the director of the trustees, Christine Large, who confirmed that she was very interested in looking at our material. This was great news, because I could see nowhere more fitting for it to be housed than in the very place where the codes were cracked.

My main worry was that Bletchley Park would not have the necessary space, but Christine indicated that she had big plans for it. She said: 'We are hopeful that we will locate the collection in Hut 8 (Turing's) which will of course be a true starring role for it.' It was becoming better by the minute. Our exhibition was to be housed in the very hut where Alan Turing worked. Absolutely perfect.

In December 2003, Christine Large drove to Tamworth with Bletchley Park guide Murlyn Hakon. At the *Herald*'s offices Christine presented me with the Freedom of Bletchley Park, an honour usually reserved for people who had directly contributed to the war effort at the codebreaking centre. It is something I will cherish for life and was presented in recognition of my work on the Enigma story over the previous five years.

The exhibition on the *Petard* men and the Tamworth story was opened in February 2008. It has taken a long time and a lot of hard work to secure the necessary funding. Asbestos was also discovered in the building and had to be removed.

One room is dedicated entirely to the story of the three men and the *Petard*. A smaller room leading off it consists of an exhibition called The Tamworth Story which is where our material is displayed. Lloyds TSB sponsored the main board introducing the story, which covers various milestones in the *Herald*'s campaign plus other material which we published. It's a perfect combination really, which mirrors the theme of this book. One section highlights the events of 1942, and then in the adjacent room visitors can see how the story continued sixty years later with the tributes to the men which we were responsible for.

During their visit to Tamworth I took Christine and Murlyn to see the sculpture and the Colin Grazier Hotel. They were very enthusiastic about our collection and took back with them well over fifty framed exhibits. I had also secured Colin Grazier's signed Royal Navy Bible and a piece of a lifejacket taken from a German U-559 prisoner. It is clearly marked with the number of the U-boat. Colin Grazier's niece Colleen agreed to loan the Bible to Bletchley Park indefinitely. Eric Ashley agreed to do the same with his souvenir from the German submarine. Robin Norris also allowed Bletchley Park to take the original painting of the U-559 incident he had paid £2,000 for. (The artist, Michael Roffe, later gave me permission to use his painting as the cover of this book.)

Some of the material cannot yet be displayed at Bletchley Park for various reasons. Our hope for the future is that as Bletchley gets more funding and progresses as a museum, it will find a way to display the rest of our collection to the public.

In addition to the large number of pictures and documents from the hotel, we handed over a framed copy of the messages from the Duke of York and Prime Minister, along with various other items. I was relieved to receive an email from Christine the next day saying that the collection was 'safely stowed'.

The following year I received an invitation from Christine to attend a private lunch with the Duke of Kent who, as chief patron of Bletchley Park, was to open 'The Bletchley Park Story' in phase one of the National Codes Centre's new exhibition complex – Block B.

I was lucky enough to be amongst the Duke's party for the entire day. An elderly couple from Sheffield who met at BP during the war were also among the group. Oliver and Sheila Lawn were conscripted to Bletchley from their respective universities where they were singled out as having brilliant intellects. They were fascinating to talk to. At one point during the day we were served coffee in the old mansion house and the memories came flooding back to them. They told me how they used to watch 'world class' chess matches between brilliant mathematicians in that very room during their leisure time. The head of Hut 8, Conel Hugh O'Donel Alexander, was the British national chess champion in 1938 and 1956.

Although Oliver and Sheila became romantically attached and eventually married, they did not discuss the nature of their codebreaking work with each other for more than three decades. They had signed the Official Secrets Act and did not take it lightly – but they

Above left: The author receives the Freedom of Bletchley Park from Christine Large, director of the trust which runs the former wartime codebreaking centre.

Above right: The architecture of the charming mansion house at Bletchley Park is as eccentric as some of its wartime inhabitants were.

knew that if they lived long enough they would one day be able to share their stories. Nearly forty years after first working together at Bletchley Park, the restrictions were lifted and the couple, by now middle-aged, stayed up all night amazing each other with their recollections of Bletchley's secrets. They had a lot to catch up on – and still have a lot to discuss. There is no way this couple are going to spend their dotage sitting in silence. Oliver Lawn gave the annual 'Turing lecture' at Bletchley Park in 2007.

I also met an official from GCHQ (Government Communications Headquarters) in Cheltenham who was a huge advocate of Bletchley Park as it was the forerunner of the secret organisation she now works for. She was obviously unable to reveal much about the nature of her own work, other than that it involved royal security, but she did say some of the people who worked at GCHQ had (in common with their past colleagues at Bletchley) brains 'the size of planets'.

People that intelligent, though, are often a little eccentric, and she told me a wonderful story about one particular modern-day genius. He apparently became extremely frustrated when he tried to make a telephone call only to find the person he needed to speak to was engaged. He very calmly removed all the telephone plugs and wires, opened the window which was several floors up, and then tossed the offending piece of equipment to the ground below. It certainly fuels the theory that there is a fine line between a genius and a madman!

Jean Valentine, who worked on the bombe machines during the war and is now a volunteer guide at the Park, says locals nicknamed the place the 'funny farm' during the war, because of the eccentricities and dishevelled appearance of many of its occupants. 'They saw Alan Turing riding his bicycle around the area with his gas mask on because he thought it would help his hay fever,' she said. 'Some of the locals thought he was completely mad.' Another codebreaker regularly ran around Bletchley Park's lake stark naked after dark, taking several people by surprise on moonlit nights.

Phil Shanahan has the honour of presenting the Duke of Kent with a Colin Grazier commemorative plate during a royal visit to Bletchley Park.

During the royal visit, I was also introduced to Sir Christopher Chattaway, then chairman of Bletchley Park Trust. He achieved fame for being Sir Roger Bannister's pacemaker when the great athlete became the first man in the world to run the four-minute mile. Sir Christopher was also in the same running club as Alan Turing at Cambridge University. Other VIPs present included the Polish ambassador.

I made a presentation to the Duke of Kent after lunch. I told him about the campaign in Tamworth and handed him one of the limited edition Colin Grazier commemorative plates that we commissioned. The Duke is very interested in the Enigma story and seemed pleased with his unexpected souvenir. Earlier in the day he had toured a new exhibition on the story of codebreaking at Bletchley and had also enjoyed a screening of the museum's new film, *Churchill's Secret Passion*. The film is introduced by the Duke and is narrated by actor Robert Hardy.

The royal visitor was also given a glimpse of the historic Hut 8 where our exhibition is now housed. For reasons I touched on earlier, the opening of that exhibition was put back by almost three years. During that time Christine Large left to take up the chief executive's position with the Ramblers' Assocation. Murlyn Hakon has also since left Bletchley Park. At first I was extremely worried about these two departures as both Christine and Murlyn had been very supportive and I wondered if Christine's successor would have the same enthusiasm for the exhibition. I need not have worried, however, as the new director, Simon Greenish, was just as keen to display the material. Indeed Simon has a lot of new plans for Bletchley and is working hard to attract major sponsorship.

CHAPTER THIRTY-ONE

A FULL HOUSE

It struck me that day just how much a new building had been given instant personality and character by being given Colin's name

After the monument was unveiled in 2002, I thought that the only remaining tribute to Colin Grazier and his *Petard* colleagues would be the annual Grazier Day (we have just celebrated the fifth event) and the ceremony in the Enigma housing estate. I was wrong.

In 2004, EDS, a leading IT services company, decided to name its new multi-million-pound offices in Tamworth after Colin Grazier. 'Grazier House' is now the 20,000sq.ft site of the branch of a global company which in 2003 was ranked eighty-seventh on the Fortune 500 list of the top 500 American public corporations, with an annual revenue of $21.5 billion. The name came about after an employee, Lindsay Corten, a business analyst at EDS, suggested 'Grazier House' in an internal competition to name the new offices. Bletchley Park was the home of the world's first computer and it is apt that a leading IT firm should be linked with the Enigma story in Grazier's home town.

The Colin Grazier Memorial Committee was invited to the opening of Grazier House and we were treated like VIPs. The event was organised by Rita Huland whose imagination had been fired by the antics of the Enigma heroes. She ordered a replica of the plaque which we commissioned for the main monument and this is now attached to the wall of the reception area. Next to it is a large framed photograph of Colin Grazier. Flowers are placed next to the picture as a mark of respect every 30 October. Similar tributes are made during the Remembrance Day period each year.

Sam Kingston, the managing director for EDS in the UK, invited Colin Grazier's second cousin, Beryl Bauer, to officially unveil the plaque. He said he was proud the new building had taken its name from such a noble man.

Rita Huland had made a display of our Enigma articles which generated a lot of interest among the employees. We fielded many questions about the Enigma story and the campaign. It struck me that day just how much a new building had been given instant personality and character by being given Colin's name. Planners take note! Names can add colour and interest to anything from buildings to streets. I still cringe to see names, which convey horrible images, being chosen for streets. Chemical Road, Power Station Road, Waterworks Road, Cemetery Lane and Pumping Station Lane are all examples I have groaned at in recent times. Whatever the location, there just has to be a meaningful or imaginative name that has relevance to the local community.

Such is the feeling for the Enigma heroes today that I am no longer surprised to hear of new tributes to them. I recently saw a local van drive past with a logo emblazoned

Above: Members of the Colin Grazier Committee join relatives of Colin Grazier and EDS employees at the opening of Grazier House.

Left: Hi-tech firm EDS has named its new, smart headquarters after Tamworth's Enigma hero.

across its side containing the word Enigma, and a football club has been set up under the name of Colin Grazier FC.

The fourth Grazier Day was particularly special, because I met another of Colin Grazier's relatives for the first time. It was a beautiful October day in 2006 and a good number of onlookers had gathered around the sculpture. I was introduced to a man in his eighties who was standing on the edge of the crowd. He was holding a photograph of Colin which I had never seen before. The man's name was Syd Lakin and he is Colin's first cousin.

Colin's mother Margaret was Syd's 'Aunty Mag'. It turned out that Syd had been watching our campaign unfold over the past few years from the shadows. He had seen everything, and attended various ceremonies, but had never made himself known. By his own admission, he is a man who shuns the limelight.

The photograph he was clutching showed Syd (then aged fourteen) with Colin (who was about eighteen at the time) and another cousin, Lillian Twyneham, who is the same age as Syd. Syd's mum, Colin's mum Margaret, and Lillian's father were brother and sisters. The cousins were known as the 'Three Musketeers'. He was also carrying an up-to-date photograph of just the remaining 'Two Musketeers', himself and Lillian.

I was amazed to discover that Syd was the eldest of twelve children, nine of whom were still alive and living in the Tamworth area. They too had been 'proudly' watching events from the sidelines. I later received a phone call from Syd's brother Arthur, who served in the Special Boat Service and in the Algerines (mine-sweepers). His hope is that Colin's nine cousins will get together to visit our exhibition at Bletchley.

I immediately invited Syd to the rum tot celebration. With a glass of Pusser's in his hand, Syd gave us more insights into the life of his legendary cousin. 'I used to visit his house every Saturday and Colin used to let me play with his beautiful Hornby train set,' he said. 'Colin was cheerful, kind and generous. He was a thinking sort of lad. He could swim like a fish. He was always out swimming in local canals and rivers.'

He also confirmed Colin's passion for neat vinegar:

When he went to the fish and chip shop he put absolutely loads of vinegar on his chips. They were wrapped in greaseproof paper in those days and when he had finished eating them he would roll up the paper into a funnel and pour the remaining vinegar down his throat.

Syd also revealed more about what Colin had done before joining the Navy:

When he first left school he worked for a local mill-owner called Mr Tolson. Afterwards he worked as a 'mate' on a coal lorry for a Kingsbury firm. Then he went to work at Mr Pemberton's fish and chip shop in Bolebridge Street. He used to bring us free bags of shrimps on Saturdays.

I later asked Syd what was going through his mind while he was standing in front of the monument that day listening to the service in honour of his cousin. He recalled what

A plaque telling the Enigma heroes' story appears on the base of the sculpture, in the reception area of Grazier House and on a plinth on Tamworth's 'Enigma' housing estate.

A new tradition for Tamworth – 'Grazier Day' now takes place on the Sunday nearest to 30 October each year. It begins with a service at the monument and is followed by rum tots at the Royal Naval Association. Phil Shanahan is pictured making the toast to the three Enigma heroes.

Colin's wife Olive had once told him, when she waved her husband goodbye for the last time at Tamworth railway station. We had already learned that Colin had had some sort of premonition as he told Olive not to turn round and watch him after they kissed goodbye that day. Thanks to Syd we now know what Olive's last words to him were – and they sent a shiver down my spine.

'Be careful on the Irish Sea because of all those U-boats.'

Colin replied, 'Don't worry Olive, they are our bread and butter. They won't get me on the Irish Sea.'

Seconds later he boarded the train.

I'm not sure why Olive referred to the Irish Sea, but she was clearly aware of the U-boat peril. Syd recalled the horror all the family experienced on learning of Colin's premature death:

When Colin died his mum and dad came to my home in Belgrave to tell my parents the news. I remember all the tears. I was so shocked. I was just a young teenager at the time.

Colin's big brother George was so terribly upset by Colin's death he decided to take his place in the Royal Navy. He had been working for Skeys the Potters at the time. He was devastated by the loss of his little brother – yet like most kid brothers they were always arguing. He also named his daughter Colleen [Mason] after him.

They were known as the Three Musketeers – cousins Syd Lakin, Lily Allsopp and Colin Grazier, photographed in 1938.

The two musketeers – Syd and Lily enjoying a cuppa together in 1999.

But Syd's thoughts were not just on Colin that day. He was also thinking about Olive whom he remembered singing in Kingsbury church choir. After the war Olive married Tom Dovey who was once her boss. Syd described him as a fine man who helped to organise the handing over of Colin's George Cross to the Navy.

Syd also donated one of Colin's medals to the Royal Navy. When Colin Grazier's father died, Colin's mother moved into a flat on her own. When she passed away, Syd's mum, Margaret, had the task of clearing the flat and found Colin's precious Atlantic Star. Syd handed it to the Royal Navy and it was put in the same frame as Colin's George Cross.

I have got the firm impression from talking to various people who knew Colin well that he was a brave but modest man with bags of integrity. And it has since become obvious to me that these qualities are very much in his family. His father was a miner, a man of honour, who could have received a large sum of money from selling Colin's George Cross, but that was forgone on principle. Through Syd I discovered that courage is a family trait.

I had great difficulty in persuading Syd to allow me to include the story of his own heroics in this book, after I managed to tease out of him the reason he was decorated for bravery during the Second World War. Syd is happy for Colin's courage to be known, but balks at any mention of his own heroism. During the Second World War, while serving with 143 Squadron Royal Engineers, Syd was awarded an Oak Leaf medal for rescuing two comrades from a minefield in Italy. His colleagues had strayed into the minefield and

Mementoes of a life cut short, Colin Grazier's Atlantic Star (left) and George Cross, awarded for his gallant action on the night of 30 October 1942.

set off one of the explosives, knocking one man unconscious and leaving the other in a semi-conscious state. Syd, who had been trained in the art of bomb disposal, crawled into the field and established a safe path for the men by rolling a white piece of sticky tape along the ground. The dazed man crawled out by following this white line to safety. The other man was lying injured on top of the mine. If he moved he would release the detonator mechanism, with fatal consequences.

Syd could see the telltale prongs of the mine sticking out from underneath the unconscious man's leg. He grabbed the soldier's metal helmet, and put it over the bomb so that the release was not activated. In doing so he had to lie on top of the mine and badly bruised his upper body. He then carried the man to safety.

Bravery, as I said, runs in the family.

Above and left: Phil Shanahan officially opens the newly restored Hut 8 which had been left in a state of disrepair since the end of the Second World War. Also pictured is Simon Greenish, the director of the trustees at Bletchley Park, who said it was a momentous occasion for the former codebreaking centre.

EPILOGUE

It's a spectacular sculpture memorialising an exceptional event
– Captain Richard J. Schlaff

As I write now, it is May 2010. Several key players in this story have sadly died since the first edition of this book was published. They include Eric Sellars, Beryl Bauer, Maurice Lunn and Stan Brown. I hope that this account helps to keep their memories alive and may they rest in peace. The exhibition in Hut 8 has already been seen by visitors from all over the world. In February 2008 I had the pleasure of officially opening Hut 8 to the public, following a £500,000 restoration project. It may be a humble wooden hut, but no building in the world could have been more relevant to the shortening of the Second World War, and I could not have been more proud if I had been asked to open a marbled palace. Simon Greenish, the director of the trustees at Bletchley Park, summed up the significance of that day when he told invited guests: 'Britain has got something to be proud of in the saving of this building.'

It has been an amazing journey for me. As a journalist you tend to flit from one story to another. News changes daily and there is always something new to attract the short-term attention. But this compelling story has been different. It's not just a phase I have gone through – I feel it is for life. I am involved in different stories every day. In the scheme of things they last for ten minutes. But I have never been able to completely walk away from this one and I have no desire to. Twelve years after first launching the campaign, I still find myself working on Enigma-related projects. I have also remained in touch with so many people I have met through my association with the subject – including some special men who served on the *Petard*.

My most memorable moment was being invited to Bletchley Park to present Prince Charles and the Duchess of Cornwall with a copy of *The Real Engima Heroes*. I was also able to show them around the exhibition in Hut 8, and tell them how important the action was. They were both fascinated and asked many questions. Camilla was amazed that Tommy Brown had been little more than a boy when he took part in the mission. Prince Charles described Bletchley as 'one of the greatest British success stories,' and said the visit was a 'treat' for him and Camilla.

Two men who served on HMS *Petard* were with me that day. First Lieutenant Robert de Pass and the ship's radar operator, Reg Crang, were able to give the royal couple first-hand accounts of the action. I was delighted for Reg as it helped to make up for his dissapointment in missing the unveiling of the monument through ill health. I was surprised to discover that Prince Charles had known Robert de Pass for most of his life, and instantly recognised him. How utterly extraordinary that he discovered a personal link with such a history-shaping event.

Prince Charles and the Duchess of Cornwall studying a model of the *Petard* and U-559.

The royal visit coincided with the day that 100 academics wrote to *The Times* demanding better financing for Bletchley Park. As Prince Charles unveiled a slate plaque commemorating the visit he joked, 'I woke up this morning and turned the radio on and heard something about Bletchley Park. I thought, "oh Lord, what have I done now?", but I was so pleased to hear that attention is being paid to the remarkable place'.

The Prince showed genuine passion for Bletchley and said the codebreakers had 'ensured this country finally emerged victorious'. Prince Charles's words were reported around the globe, and have certainly helped to put the place on the map.

Interest in Bletchley Park has rocketed and in the space of just three years annual visitor numbers have doubled to around 105,000. This, plus an injection of much-needed cash, has put Bletchley on a sound footing.

A combined total of £1.3 million has come in from English Heritage, local authority funding and from central Government. In addition, Bletchley has received a further £500,000 from lottery funds in the form of a design grant. But most significantly of all, if Bletchley can find another £1.5 million, it will qualify for an extra £4.1 million of lottery cash. Although £500,000 of that has already been found, there should be no room for complacency among potential sponsors. It would be tragedy of huge proportions if this money was not found, and I wish Trust Director Simon Greenish, and his team, the very best of luck in their continued efforts to transform Bletchley Park into a world class heritage site.

I continue to receive letters and emails from all over the world about the Enigma story. I was told by a fellow committee member that he had come across an elderly Australian man visiting Tamworth who could not believe the beauty of the sculpture or the events it commemorated. 'It is the most beautiful thing I have seen,' he told Jim Welland who happened to be admiring the sculpture at the same time. Jim was obviously able to give him more information. Several visitors to Tamworth, however, have since requested more details about the background to the memorial and I hope that this book will prove of use to people like them in the future.

Of all the communications I have received since the unveiling of the memorial, my favourite is one that suggests we were successful in providing a fitting tribute to three great men. Given the enormous consequences of what they achieved, that is a most rewarding thought. The email was sent by a retired US Navy intelligence officer who had previously written to me to tell me that the results of the campaign had left him 'in goose bumps'.

Left: The Colin Grazier Memorial sculpture glinting in the autumn sunlight. Picture by Doug Heath.

Below: The sculpture lit at night at Christmas time with St Editha's Church in the background. Picture by Paul Barber.

I have never met Captain Richard J. Schlaff of Michigan, but he went out of his way to visit the memorial and was obviously greatly moved by what he saw:

Ever since I read about the October 27, 2002 dedication of the Colin Grazier Memorial in Tamworth I had wanted to see it for myself. So, returning to London after a visit to Durham one day, I decided to get off the train and have a look. Yes, that was me wandering about your delightful town in early September. I was the one dragging those two suitcases and taking photos of just about everything. It was a beautiful Tuesday. St. Editha's Square was busy.

The memorial surpassed both my hope and expectation. It's a spectacular sculpture memorialising an exceptional event. As a retired US Navy intelligence officer, and as one quite familiar with Enigma and the work that went on at Bletchley Park, I believe the special tribute paid to Colin Grazier is much deserved. His name, I noted though, is but one of many on the wall in the parish church and I thought it fitting that Tamworth also chooses to remember them all on its other memorial: 'To Those Who Died That We Might Live'. Both, I think, are tributes to Tamworth and the delightful and friendly people I was able to talk with, albeit briefly, during my most rewarding visit. As I wandered the town I was struck by the thought that Tamworth is precisely the kind of place that wars have been fought to make possible.

Thanks and best wishes to you all!

Captain Richard J Schlaff, USN-RET

BIBLIOGRAPHY

This bibliography is designed for anyone wishing to follow up on any aspects of the story referred to in *The Real Enigma Heroes*.

GENERAL

BEESLY, P., *Very Special Intelligence: the story of the Admiralty's Operational Intelligence Centre 1939-1945*. (Greenhilll, 2000, revised edn).

CONNELL, G., *Fighting Destroyer: the story of HMS Petard*. (Kimber, 1976. 2nd edn: Crecy, 1994).

HARPER, S., *Capturing Enigma: How HMS Petard seized the German Naval Codes*. (Sutton, 1999).

HAUFLER, H., *Codebreakers' Victory*. (New American Lib, 2003).

HAWKINS, I., (ed.) *Destroyer: an anthology of first-hand accounts of the war at sea 1939-1945*. (Conway Maritime, 2003).

HINSLEY, F., *et al. British Intelligence in the Second World War*. 5 vols. (HMSO, 1979-1990). [There is also a one-volume abridged edition]

SINGH, S., *The Code Book: the science of secrecy from Ancient Egypt to quantum cryptography*. (Fourth Estate 1999).

WEST, N., *GCHQ: the secret wireless war, 1900-86*. (Weidenfeld & Nicolson, 1986).

BLETCHLEY PARK & ENIGMA

CALVOCORESSI, P., *Top Secret Ultra*. (Baldwin, 2001, revised edn).

ENEVER, T., *Britain's Best Kept Secret: Ultra's base at Bletchley Park*. (Sutton, 1999, 3rd edn).

HARRIS, R., *Enigma*. (Hutchinson, 1995). [A novel]

HINSLEY, H. & STRIPP, A., *Codebreakers: the inside story of Bletchley Park*. (OUP, 1993).

HODGES, A., *Alan Turing: the Enigma*. (Burnett, 1983).

KOZACZUK, W. & STRASZAK, J., *Enigma: how the Poles Broke the Nazi Code*. (Hippocrene, 2004).

SEBAG-MONTEFIORE, H., *Enigma: the Battle for the Code*. (Weidenfeld & Nicolson, 2000).

SMITH, M., *Station X: the Codebreakers of Bletchley Park*. (Channel 4, 1998).

SMITH, M. & ERSKINE, R., *Action This Day*. (Bantam, 2001).

WELCHMAN, G., *The Hut Six Story: Breaking the Enigma Codes*. (Baldwin, 1997, revised edn).

U-BOATS

COLLINS, M., *U-571*. (Macmillan, 2000). [novelization of US film].

DOENITZ, K., *Memoirs: ten years and twenty days*. (World Pubg, 1959. New edn: Naval Institute Press, Maryland, 1990).

DRUMMOND, J. H. M., *U-Boat*. (Allen, 1958). [U570, later HMS *Graph*]

GALLERY, D., *We Captured a U-Boat*. (Sidgwick & Jackson, 1957). [U505]

GOEBELER, H., *Steel Boats, Iron Hearts: a U-boat crewman's life aboard U-505*. (Beatie, 2005).

KAHN, D., *Seizing The Enigma: the race to break the German U-Boat codes*. (Houghton Mifflin, 1991).

ROHWER, J., *War at Sea: 1939-1945*. (Chatham, 1996).

ROSKILL, S., *The Secret Capture*. (Collins, 1959). [U110]

SHOWELL, J., *Enigma U-boats: breaking the code*. (Ian Allan, 2002, revised edn).

SHOWELL, J., *U-boats under the Swastika*. (Ian Allan, 1987, 2nd edn).

VAUSE, J., *Wolf: U-Boat Commanders in World War II*. (Airlife, 1997).

WERNER, H., *Iron Coffins: a U-Boat Commander's War 1939-1945*. (Da Capo, 1998).

WYNN, K., *U-Boat Operations of the Second World War*. 2 vols. (Chatham, 1997/8).

INDEX

If you are interested in purchasing other books published by The History Press, or in case you have difficulty finding any of our books in your local bookshop, you can also place orders directly through our website
www.thehistorypress.co.uk